Arts • Letters • Society

LIVERPOOL HISTORICAL STUDIES
published for the
Department of History, University of Liverpool

1. Patrick J. N. Tuck, *French Catholic Missionaries and the Politics of Imperialism in Vietnam, 1857-1914: A Documentary Survey*, 1987, 352pp. **(Out of print)**

2. Michael de Cossart, *Ida Rubinstein (1885-1960): A Theatrical Life*, 1987, 244pp.

3. P. E. H. Hair, ed., *Coals on Rails, Or the Reason of My Wrighting: The Autobiography of Anthony Errington, a Tyneside colliery waggon and waggonway wright, from his birth in 1778 to around 1825*, 1988, 288pp.

4. Peter Rowlands, *Oliver Lodge and the Liverpool Physical Society*, 1990, 336pp.

5. P. E. H. Hair, ed., *To Defend Your Empire and the Faith: Advice on a Global Strategy Offered c. 1590 to Philip, King of Spain and Portugal, by Manoel de Andrada Castel Blanco*, 1990, 304pp.

6. Christine Hillam, *Brass Plate and Brazen Impudence: Dental Practice in the Provinces 1755-1855*, 1991, 352pp.

7. John Shepherd, *The Crimean Doctors: A History of the British Medical Services in the Crimean War*, 1991, 2 vols, 704pp.

8. John Belchem, ed., *Popular Politics, Riot and Labour: Essays in Liverpool History 1790-1940*, 1992, 272pp.

9. Duncan Crewe, *Yellow Jack and the Worm: British Naval Administration in the West Indies, 1739-1748*, 1993, 352pp.

10. Stephen J. Braidwood, *Black Poor and White Philanthropists: London's Blacks and the Foundation of the Sierra Leone Settlement 1786-1791*, 1994, 336pp.

11. David Dutton, *'His Majesty's Loyal Opposition': The Unionist Party in Opposition 1905-1915*, 1992, 336pp.

12. Cecil H. Clough and P. E. H. Hair, eds., *The European Outthrust and Encounter: The First Phase c.1400-c.1700: Essays in Tribute to David Beers Quinn on His 85th Birthday*, 1994, 380pp.

13. David Dutton, ed., *Statecraft and Diplomacy in the Twentieth Century: Essays Presented to P. M. H. Bell*, 1995, 192pp.

14. Roger Swift, ed., *Victorian Chester: Essays in Social History 1830–1900*, 1996, 263pp.

15. P. E. H. Hair, ed., *Arts • Letters • Society: A Miscellany Commemorating the Centenary of the Faculty of Arts at the University of Liverpool*, 1996, 272pp.

Arts • Letters • Society

A Miscellany
Commemorating the Centenary of the Faculty of Arts at the University of Liverpool

edited by

P. E. H. HAIR

No Arts; No Letters; No Society; and which is worst of all,
... the life of man, solitary, poor, nasty, brutish, and short.
Thomas Hobbes (1588–1679)

LIVERPOOL UNIVERSITY PRESS
1996

Front cover illustration: John Donald Mackay, as a Highlander with upward gaze (from *The Sphinx* of 1901)

Liverpool Historical Studies, no. 15
General Editor: C. H. Clough

First published 1996
by Liverpool University Press
Senate House, Abercromby Square, Liverpool, L69 3BX

British Library Cataloguing in Publication Data
A British Library CIP record is available
ISBN 0-85323-502-3

Printed in the European Union by
Antony Rowe Limited, Chippenham, England

CONTENTS

INTRODUCTION

The studies of the Faculty, in our beginnings, were defined as Languages, Literature, History, Economics, Philosophy, Education, Art and Architecture. Of these Economics, Education, Art and Architecture now belong to our sister-faculty, the Faculty of Social and Environmental Studies. Archaeology and Music have joined us over the years, and different specific languages have come and gone - though there are still staff concerned with some of the lost fields. The division between Arts and Humanities on the one hand, and Social and Environmental Studies on the other, ensures that three Institutes (of Latin-American, Popular Music and Irish Studies) sit a little outside the formal Faculty structure, and that some Departments and some scholars feel a dual allegiance. Most outsiders - reasonably enough - assume that an Arts Faculty must have something to do with Art, but a more accurate list would now read 'Languages, Literature, History, Philosophy, Archaeology and Music' (variously contained in different Departments). In celebrating a hundred years of scholarship the present Faculty recalls a larger past, and conceives a future.

The centennial celebrations (no doubt to be repeated when some other Founding Moment is remembered) have coincided with the Government's decision to cut back, or privatise, the growth of Universities - restoring, some may think, the situation where we first began: reliant on the generosity of benefactors, and the enthusiasm of scholars. We aim not to lose any further areas of expertise, and even to retrieve some. Once upon a time (and not so long ago for those with long memories) we needed no more than time to think, read, write, talk and travel, and opportunity to open our own and other, mostly younger, minds to classic texts and unfamiliar customs. The cost even of 'pure Arts research' and teaching has risen with the expansion of technology. So has the number of students, absolutely and as a percentage of the population. In celebrating our successes we determine not to make past efforts vain.

Of the many celebratory events of Autumn 1996 it is well to record the Kenneth Allott Lecture (given this year by Blake Morrison), the Concert (including music composed and conducted by James Wishart) and the Centennial Lecture (given by Frank Walbank). Kenneth Muir, who was to have given that lecture, died just before the onset of this academic year: his text has been published as a separate pamphlet. In that same season the Arts Alumni Association was created, to provide occasions when old friends (and opponents) might meet again, and to support research and teaching at the University. What's past is prologue.

The Faculty is much indebted to Paul Hair, who took on, at fairly short notice, the considerable and expert task of editing the volume and preparing it for the press. In this he was assisted by Adrian Allan, the University Archivist, and clerical support was lent by Patricia Blythe and Susan Bradshaw. My thanks to them, to other officers of the Faculty, and to the Centennial Sub-Committee (including Adrian Allan, Doreen Bowsher, Reg Davies, Brian Nellist, Monica Nurnberg, Robert Orledge and Richard Wilde). The Friends of the University made money available for a Short Story Prize in honour of the events, and the Registrar gave financial backing to the Concert and the production of this volume. I commend it, and whatever we shall have made of the Faculty in the next hundred years, to the Bicentennial Sub-Committee of 2096.

Stephen R.L. Clark
Dean of the Faculty of Arts

PREFACE

It is difficult for a celebration volume not be pretentious. Of course we stand on the shoulders of those who went before us, so Let Us Praise Famous Men. But we need not be too solemn about it. Too much of a good thing can be not only unconvincing but unreadable. To commend the hundred years of the Faculty of Arts at Liverpool University - like the university's own centenary the exact date chosen for celebration is only one of several available, depending on the interpretation of the founding date - is very 'meet, right and our bounden duty', to quote the Prayer Book. Yet those touched by the claims of academia - and all the contributors to this volume are, or were, members of the university, staff or students - recognise other duties, including discrimination and truth. The volume therefore mixes a variety of testimonies, of varying solemnity and approach, and is organised to express this variety.

It begins with reminiscences, first those of former students, the contributors ranging in age from the early twenties to four score years and ten. The reminiscences are overwhelmingly upbeat, which appears to be not entirely due to nostalgia. In response to an invitation to all former Arts students still in contact with the university, some thirty sent in their reminiscences, and extracts from these have been edited, together with a few earlier reminiscences, to provide a panorama of student life over ten decades. Reminiscences of a smaller number of former staff follow.

The second part of the volume consists of essays by past and present staff of the Arts Faculty. A variety of approaches and interests is represented. Whereas former students describe simply being students *of* the Arts Faculty, staff can write about the design and working *within* the Faculty, as they witnessed it from various angles or were drawn into its thralls.

No apology is given for the patchwork nature of this commemorative volume. It is both the glory and the burden of the humanities that discrimination and truth are recognised as tricky beasts - like humanity itself. The necessary demands of institutional order only lightly enfold individual opiniation and the flux of time. Some enlightened souls see the history of the Arts Faculty as largely a clear, rational and linear process, other enlightened see it as (here and there) a mess. Admittedly, a highly productive and socially positive mess. So this volume lets a thousand blossoms bloom, in rich earth.

Nevertheless, the editor has exerted one positive control. An official - or at least semi-official - history of Liverpool University was published in 1981 and a shorter supplement covering the 1980s appeared in 1994. Both are essential reading, not only for factual detail but also for informed comments on the development of, *inter alia*, the Arts Faculty. In particular, they describe departments and staff. The editor of the present volume has attempted to limit overlap with KELLY and HARROP. This means that reminiscent details of more or less exclusively departmental interest, including brickbats and bouquets thrown at individual members of staff, particularly living ones, have been slimmed down or edited out, above all when repetititous. (But all contributions, in pure and unedited state, have been passed to the University Archives.) On the other hand, former students of certain disciplines and certain periods responded more enthusiastically, both in numbers and in length of contribution, than did others - and the editor therefore disclaims responsibility for uneven representation.

The summary biographical details appended to or introducing contributions are not always complete, because of lack of information; and the titles of departments, which often changed slightly over the decades, have been expressed in a standard summary form. In the contributions no consistent attempt has been made to correct misremembered details relating to distant times in the university.

It only remains to thank Richard Wilde (Arts Sub-Dean) and Robin Bloxsidge (Secretary, University Press) for help in the assembling of material and the preparation of the volume, and not least, Adrian Allan (University Archivist), without whose regular, expert and considerable assistance the work would not have been completed on time. And also, of course, to thank all the contributors, especially those who responded instantly to a late call. Finally, I thank the History Department for its facilities, the staff of the Faculty Office for all back-up, and the Dean and Centennial Committee for the honour of the invitation to contribute, in this modest way, to a notable occasion.

P.E.H.H.

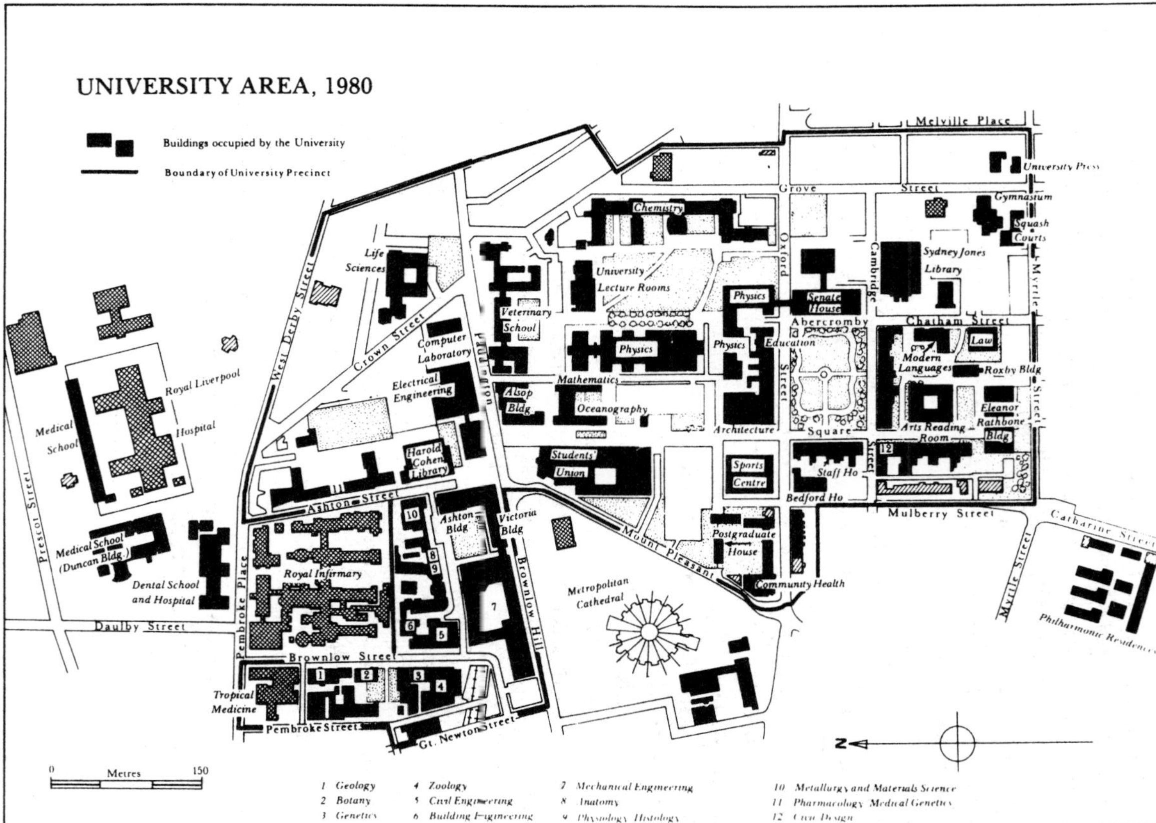
UNIVERSITY AREA, 1980
Buildings occupied by the University
Boundary of University Precinct
Melville Place
University Press
Grove Street
Gymnasium
Squash Courts
Myrtle Street
Chemistry
Sydney Jones Library
Cambridge Street
Oxford Street
University Lecture Rooms
Physics
Senate House
Abercromby Square
Chatham Street
Law
Modern Languages
Roxby Bldg
Education
Veterinary School
Life Sciences
West Derby Street
Crown Street
Computer Laboratory
Electrical Engineering
Mathematics
Alsop Bldg
Oceanography
Architecture
Arts Reading Room
Eleanor Rathbone Bldg
Staff Ho
Bedford Ho
Sports Centre
Students' Union
Harold Cohen Library
Ashton Street
Ashton Bldg
Victoria Bldg
Brownlow Hill
Mount Pleasant
Postgraduate House
Community Health
Mulberry Street
Catharine Street
Philharmonic Residences
Metropolitan Cathedral
Royal Infirmary
Brownlow Street
Pembroke Place
Pembroke Street
Gt. Newton Street
Tropical Medicine
Daulby Street
Prescot Street
Medical School
Royal Liverpool Hospital
Medical School (Duncan Bldg.)
Dental School and Hospital
N
0 Metres 150
1 Geology
2 Botany
3 Genetics
4 Zoology
5 Civil Engineering
6 Building Engineering
7 Mechanical Engineering
8 Anatomy
9 Physiology Histology
10 Metallurgy and Materials Science
11 Pharmacology Medical Genetics
12 Civic Design

PART ONE

I REMEMBER ..

'Studies serve for delight, for ornament, and for ability' (Bacon)

A few humanities subjects were studied at Liverpool for some years before there was an Arts Faculty, but thereafter the number of subjects increased. In 1971, the number was halved when the separate Faculty of Social and Environmental Studies was formed, but student reminiscences of the pre-1971 period relating to all pre-1971 Arts Faculty subjects are here included. Although its various institutional shapings had often semi-autonomous status, Education was notionally part of the Arts Faculty until it became part of a new faculty in 1983.

FORMER STUDENTS

Letters from former students invariably stated that they welcomed the opportunity to put down details of their student lives, and what was sent often included extensive details of life before and after studies at Liverpool. Such biographical details are only summarised below, and recollections relating to individual student friends have often been excluded, *pro bono publico*. Even so, there was far too much material to publish in full, and what follows is limited to extracts from reminiscences. Matters repeated in a number of accounts are included in only one, as far as possible. What the selection tries to express is the variety of student experience: study, leisure, practical survival, the city context. We move back by decades and years.

1980s

I remember when the professor was supposed to give a lecture and we all sat in the lecture theatre awaiting his arrival but he didn't turn up. Minutes passed, occupied by the usual student chat. Eventually, we began to pack up to leave when he dashed in and hurried to the lectern. 'Apparently I was supposed to give a lecture today but I forgot and I haven't any notes with me, so I'll just briefly outline what I was going to talk about.' He stepped away from the lectern, and hands clasped behind his back, he paced up and down and began to speak. And for a full hour, he spoke to us with fluency, enthusiasm and confidence. ... My last ever meeting with the professor occurred on my graduation day. After the ceremony, when we were all spilling out of the Philharmonic Hall, I spied him and went to bid my farewell. Dressed in all his academic finery he greeted my mother, shook hands with my father, and hugged me. My father was so proud. To his dying day he never forgot when - 'A professor hugged my daughter, the daughter of a working man, a labourer!' . . . .

Mrs Juliana Thompson [Reed], born Durham 1966, English 1985-1988, accountant and free-lance artist, writing from Gateshead

I came to Liverpool for the first time in September 1983 ... My first impression of the University staff was astonishing, as Professor Davies of the Department of Ancient History and Classical Archaeology welcomed me in perfect ancient Greek, and some days later he managed to find a room for me in the Philharmonic Hall of Residence. From then on, a year to remember began for me. As a postgraduate student of Classical Archaeology I attended various lectures and seminars which I shared with only few students, something strikingly different from my own educational background, as at the University of Athens numerous students were attending lectures in large halls. Besides, I appreciated the role of supervision, which, at that time, was only rare in my country, a great deal. ... In the Hall of Residence I made close friends and I had the opportunity to mingle with people from different countries and various cultural backgrounds. I really miss our cooking-exchange evenings! ... Having finished the first draft of my dissertation I handed it out to Professor Davies, saying I was rather disappointed because the result of my study couldn't positively support my first hypothesis. He answered: 'At least you have found out that you found nothing, and this takes a lot of effort'.

Panagiota Nikolaidou, postgraduate Classical Archaeology 1983-1984, writing from Athens

1970s

When I arrived at the Department of History in 1977, I must surely have been perceived as one of the least likely people to end up making their living as a historian. But in my current work, as a producer on BBC Woman's Hour, I have the joyful job of being the history editor. Very aptly, one of my most recent treats was to put together an entire programme celebrating the life of Eleanor Rathbone. And to think I used to have economic history lectures in the building named after her! I have to say that my earliest memories of the department are rather dismal. I had come up from London, having taken a year out when I'd lived with a boyfriend and worked at a number of jobs. By the time I moved to Liverpool (as a lodger in Lancaster Avenue - I was adamant about not going into a Hall), I felt very adult, very hip. I was not at all impressed by my fellow students, who doubtless didn't know what to make of me - a rather aloof young woman with hennaed hair, bright red boots and flowing second-hand floral print dresses. I couldn't get used to the Monday morning conversations at the start of lectures about which Mass everyone had gone to. Everyone seemed so sheltered. But, over the next three years I did make some very close friends. And I loved studying history.

I'll always remember my first tutorial groups with Dr Clough, in his crammed office, walls covered with learned tomes. The subjects we discussed seemed so highbrow - but it did introduce me to the wonders of the Venerable Bede. Probably my first love affair with a 'real' historical book. I have memories of medieval towns with Jenny Kermode, very relaxed; the seventeenth- and eighteenth-century Constitution with Mrs Collins, mesmerised by her voice and delivery; the occasional daunting lecture from Professor Myers, myself overwhelmed by his gravitas. My second year expanded into Irish history with Dr Buckland (where I rediscovered my roots); African history with Professor Hair (who inspired me to read Chinua Achebe); and late European history, up the winding stairs, in Dr Acton's office. The main course for my final year was with Professor Hennock studying 'Poverty as a social problem: 1870-1914'. Absolutely fascinating. We learned about so much, including the Victorian 'settlement' movement, and one of my first jobs after leaving university was in a settlement in London, where I ran the community café. (My ambition while I was at Liverpool was to be a cook - in fact, for the year after I graduated, I worked in the Everyman Bistro. That was before I got back into 'history'.)

One of my most proud boasts was that I had never visited the 'Cambridge' [pub]. Not until the day that I got my final results. Then I wondered why I had ever left it so long. I was slow to make friends at the university, as so much of my life went on outside. I think the turning point was the first residential course, at Gregynog, when at last I got to stay up late with others, talking into the night. By the time I went for our week at Rydal, in the final year, I was positively chummy with most people. Mind you, I was still out on a limb with my taste in music. Hardly anyone from the department turned out for the mind-blowing concerts that took place in the Students' Union - Siouxsie and the Banshees, the Jam, Steel Pulse,

Magazine (and of course, there was always Eric's, down the road in Mathew Street. Liverpool was the centre for Punk.)

I didn't go to my graduation. I liked the idea of being a rebel and decided it was all too twee - and I was making a stand against paying out the exorbitant £10 fee for the hire of the graduation gown. I think it's one of the few things in my life I do regret. I popped in for the afternoon tea on the day of the ceremony and saw all my friends dressed up to the nines, with their parents wearing hats and suits, and I wished mine were there too, to shake hands with my Prof. and look proud. They told me afterwards they would have liked to have gone. And it means there's no important looking photograph on the mantlepiece.

But my time in the Faculty of Arts did set me up for a highly fulfilling life. I've published four books - including one about women's history ... And Liverpool is such a brilliant place to have been. I certainly made the right move going there.

Kate (Catherine Elizabeth St John) Murphy, born London 1958, History 1977-1980, writing from London

I arrived in Liverpool in September 1972. My first experience of Liverpudlians as a breed of English came almost immediately. Stumbling off the station with my case I had got as far as the Yates' Wine Lodge (outside) and the case was impossible to carry. Suddenly a little old lady in a head scarf and Ena Sharples coat appeared before me and said 'd'yoo wanna 'and wi' tha', luv?' And so saying took a beautifully embroidered handkerchief from her purse and offered it to me. 'Ere 'yar, luv, take this for yer 'and.' And off she went. In the next three years this was fairly typical of the kindness and generosity of the people of the city. And I have never forgotten it. ...

As I have said, this was the early seventies. They were years which, certainly on the Arts campus, did not seem to realise that they were in the new decade. They continued to bask in the ever-dwindling afterglow of the swinging and hip sixties ... . Afghans, T-shirts and denims intermingled with duffel coats, 'tank tops' and cords. Individuals and groups trumpeting their 'Cause' lounged side by side (at least in tutorials and the Students' Union bar) with the outrageous swots. Culturally, the city was all abuzz. The Everyman Theatre was putting on fiercely avant garde plays in their new and exciting style - the bistro in its bowels was *the* place to eat, but more importantly to be *seen* eating at. The Students' Union often staged artists who later achieved cult status. ... Roger McGough, Adrian Henri and other Scouser poets were young and at their witty first and best. The Liver Building was Lowry black. There were scaffold poles up one side of the Anglican cathedral in Hope Street - as there had been in one form or another since 1906. The Catholic cathedral still looked brand spanking new, and showed no signs of graffiti of any sort. And Abercromby Square was a quiet island of tranquillity amid the History, Sociology and Senate buildings.

It was always a picture, that square, whether in autumn with its patina of gold and copper leaves or in spring with its daffodils and tulips laid out in formal array - a fine place in which to meet. It was usually across this square that I would make my way to the Library or the Faculty buildings. The innards of the Department of History itself, I recall, had that learned scent of bees-wax, wood polish and mouldy books. The students' rest rooms in the basement, on the other hand, had their own heady odours. Its walls were generally dotted with the odd ragged poster of Che Guevara and Jimmy Hendrix and although I cannot place the exact colours my impression is one of ghastly two-tone yellow and brown. The furnishings were basic. There was a selection of armchairs, all of them having seen better days in the tutorial rooms elsewhere. There was a settee covered with Corfam (like the shoes, remember?) - all matt black and shiny with yellow foam stuffing bursting out at the arms. Most of all, I remember the table football machine in one of the basement's dim cubby holes. I regret now to relate that I spent enough time on that contraption to become an ace. I'm sure that the touch of rheumatism I suffer in my wrists now is a legacy from the many hours spent bending over the 'footie table' between tutorials. ...

I had a grant of about £1,700 for the three terms which came in term instalments. It was more money than I had ever had before. Even so, I do not know how I managed to survive ... I had to get all my books and stationery out of this grant, plus, of course, rent and all living costs. I soon settled into a dietary regime which all students will recognise. The Chinese seemed to have cornered the fish and chip business, and they offered a very filling, if not altogether nutritious supper of curried chips for just 10 new pence ... In the first two terms I stayed in McNair Hall of Residence, but soon moved into a three-roomed garret atop an ancient mid-Victorian town house in Upper Parliament Street. The building was one of the few in the vicinity surviving the war. The week's rent of £10 was quite reasonable, once shared between myself, two others, and the rats. And with so much of this part of the city still laid waste from the attentions of the Luftwaffe some thirty years before, the views were spectacular. ... Although I eventually moved on to Anfield and within earshot of the Kop, the time in the inner city was a rich, wild, cosmopolitan experience that still brings back fond moments.

Mark Sims, born Enfield 1954, Modern History 1972-1975

I turned up on registration day, enrolled for classes, grew my hair a little longer and went on my way, singing a gypsy song. People sometimes used to ask me, how do you get on with the other students, you being a writer and so much older than the rest of them? It was a fair question. All I could say in reply was that it never bothered me and it never seemed to bother anybody else. I was just a student, older and more battered-looking than the rest. To begin with, one or two of the staff called me (perhaps ironically) 'Commander'. I protested that all that was in another country. And that was the end of that. Occasionally one was reminded of the passage of time. To my slight surprise, when I mentioned it in a seminar none of the other students had heard of Anzio. To my much greater surprise the lecturer, a man not all that much younger than myself, had never heard of it either. All that blood and agony at Anzio was, to him, no more than if it had been written in one of the books the Sybil destroyed. That did, suddenly, make me feel ancient.

The course required tremendous mental adjustment - although much more was required of some other mature students. One married woman on our course had four children, all under the age of ten. I always used to think that the way she ran her family household and did her studies was a miracle of application, organisation and timing. Many a first lieutenant could learn something from her. In the end, she took a very good degree, too. For me, the main requirement was, simply, to relearn how to learn. I had to find out again how to study a text closely; how to get full value from a lecture; how to present a difficult theme for discussion. There is an art in being talked at, just as there is in talking. The chief reward, I found, was the sheer intellectual pleasure of rubbing one's mind against others. To prepare a subject and then to defend and dispute it against others who have also prepared it is so unusual an activity for me these days as to be a rare luxury. I have found it very pleasing to have tutors ready, waiting, and willing, in their seminar discussions, to take us on in intellectual combat. ...

Students have had a bad press in recent years. Perhaps some of it was justified, but it is still sad to see excellent newspapers encouraging their readers' prejudices by what amounts to an anti-student campaign, not so much by misrepresentation as by distorted emphasis. The longer I was at university the harder it became for me to reconcile the popular image of students with the forty or fifty young people whose company I shared during our studies. They seemed to me much less aggressive and much more civilised than our generation at their age. Of a class of fifty, only one dropped out in the three years. No doubt there was some drug-taking - for experiment. I refuse to believe that any drug-taker could have borne the pressure of the three years' work needed to get a degree. No doubt some of them drank a bit, but much less than I do myself, because they could not afford it. Some of them shared 'mixed' flats and one occasionally heard lurid tales of sexual adventures, but in general their personal relationships always appeared to me almost alarmingly innocent and well-balanced. ...

Would a university education, earlier in life, have made me a better naval officer? I honestly do think, yes, it would. Apart from intangible benefits, such as flexibility and breadth of mind, which are impossible to quantify, there is at least one important part of the university teaching technique which is directly applicable to the Services. This is the seminar, which very closely resembles a working situation which occurs again and again in a naval career. Seminars encourage the ability to make, and take, a point; to put up an argument and follow it through, against intense opposing pressure; and to criticise another's argument and subject that to intense pressure. This is a situation which constantly occurs in the Navy, all the way from ship's Heads of Department's meetings right up to the Admiralty Board. The seminar technique may be taught at staff colleges. I hope it is. I cannot remember it ever coming up in the normal training of an ordinary hewer of wood and drawer of water such as I was.

My family were present on the day to see me get my B.A. ... My daughter remarked how pleasant it was for them all to go to *my* prize-giving for a change. Finally I must admit to one very small disappointment. I got an upper second - not a first. This confounded a secret and never confessed conceit of mine. I got a first in Engineering subjects at Manadon. Another first in an Arts honours degree would have made a marvellous 'Renaissance double'. However, at least my Shakespeare course was not wasted. At Cheltenham in March I backed Comedy of Errors in the Champion Hurdle. And of course it won, like a gentleman.

John Pratt, retired Lieutenant-Commander R.N., novelist and naval historian, mature student, English Language and Literature 1970-1973, extracts from an article published in The Naval Review *in 1974, now writing from Llandyrnog*

1960s

The years I spent at Liverpool were among the happiest I remember. I entered as a mature student (ten years older than the other undergraduates), a rarity in 1959, to study Spanish. My first year in Liverpool was difficult in many ways; I was not accustomed to an academic life; I was a Southerner and older than the other students. I also had less background preparation as my Spanish had been taken by correspondence and private lessons, reinforced by the practical experience of two years in Barcelona, but not geared to a degree programme.

I was fortunate in having a Major County Award from East Sussex County Council and an additional amount for bus fares to and from Dale Hall where I was one of the first students, and where I spent two happy years. Dale Hall for me was a model hall of residence, and under Miss Leese's expert direction, was an ideal environment for study. Despite the fact that I was older than the other students I made friends in my year both in Hispanic Studies and in Dale Hall, but I never really enjoyed the social life most people associate with University. This changed somewhat during my Education year when as President of the Education Students' Society and a member of the University second tennis team I had a different relationship with my fellow students; furthermore, the pressure to keep up and do well was no longer so important or, for that matter, so difficult. ...

During my time at Liverpool I particularly appreciated the small classes, the tutorials and the individual attention of the staff. I kept up with some of the people who taught me: the late Derek Lomax who gave me my lifelong interest in Spanish history, Firmino Crespo, the Portuguese lecturer, whom I frequently visited in Lisbon in later years and with whom I discussed my Portuguese classes in Toronto, and to a lesser degree Victoria de Lara, the late Harold Hall and the Hispanic Studies Departmental Secretary, the late Miss White. ...

Of course, at the time I was in Hispanic Studies the Department was in the Victoria Building and we had to climb to the top floor to attend lectures; as I remember, even the washrooms were attached to the cloakroom on the main floor. We used the Cohen Library although some students made use of the Liverpool Public Library. We also had a small class library attached to Hispanic Studies; Pat O'Riordan and I shared the duties of class librarian during one session. This was considered strange as previously those holding the position did not share it and were honoured to have it!

In those days one of the highlights of Hispanic Studies was the time spent abroad; one summer divided between Portugal for Portuguese at Coimbra, and Spain for either Catalan or Castilian. It was there (in Barcelona where I had worked some years before) that I first had my real academic contact with Catalan; in fact I had chosen Liverpool specifically because Catalan was taught there and I had become interested in it when I was a secretary in Barcelona. I am still in touch with the people I met during the Catalan course in 1961!

I remember my undergraduate general curriculum as well-balanced, interesting and useful in my later studies; the insistence on excellence, accuracy and fluency in Spanish, Portuguese and in my case, Catalan, stood me in good stead during my years in Toronto. The only lack for me was in Latin American Studies which I did not take because of my deep interest in Catalan. Later in Toronto I was to pay for that omission but I never acquired the interest in it; it is now an important part of the Toronto programme. I believe that any success I have enjoyed in later years was largely due to the excellent basis for research I received during my undergraduate years in the Arts Faculty at Liverpool, and then my postgraduate years at Nottingham.

Jill R. Webster, born London 1931, Spanish 1959-1962, Education 1964-1965, research Nottingham and Toronto universities, lecturer, etc, Professor of Spanish and Portuguese, University of Toronto 1965-1995, writing from Toronto, Canada

1950s

Throughout my schooling my mother was a constant source of encouragement but it was my own choice to aim for university. My soul had been stirred by Browning's Grammarian who sought knowledge even while 'Calculus racked him'. At the other extreme I had observed students capering through the streets on Rag Days and I had seen the film *Doctor in the House*. It would be good, I believed, to be a student. And better still, to be a student well away from my home town of Leeds. Liverpool fitted the bill because I also wanted to read geography. Another reason was that Alan Griffiths, my friendly and knowledgeable geography teacher, was a Liverpool graduate. ...

My scholarship, in my first year, was valued at a handsome £232, so I could readily afford books, beer and baccy, and I could eat well too. As well as an 'English' breakfast and a three-course dinner I invariably had a three-course lunch. Before our third year this was often taken in the Union. As we moved to and from the Union, those who lived in somewhat dilapidated properties close to the Union might well have perceived us as an élite. Virtually every student flaunted one of the several University scarves. Blazers were a commonplace. Otherwise boys wore sports jackets and girls looked particularly pretty in dresses and short skirts. Jeans were scarcely ever worn. ...

The Open Air Club, like other Union societies, brought contact with students from a wide range of courses. But interests also overlapped, as in some complex Venn diagram. So the society included John Harvey and Glyn Morris, both of whom were geographers in my year. John was a keen rock-climber and, somewhat unusually, sported a beard. Glyn was tall and thin and attended the same chapel as myself. Once or twice we had swum in Lodge Lane Baths but had found the place too uninviting to go often. Glyn hailed from Portsmouth but we northerners forgave him the lapse. We wandered the by-ways of the Wirral; we conquered Billinge Hill; we explored the fastnesses of West Wales. And it was at King's Youth Hostel, Dolgellau, at that period when 'lights out' was no later than 10.30 p.m., that we daringly held a midnight feast. A trifle, but it does, I think, say something about ourselves.

The focus of my university life was the Department of Geography, housed in 12 Abercromby Square. Marginal to that focus were the Union and my subsidiary subject, geology. The palatial geology building resembled a provincial museum on a hot summer's day. Though it was much better appointed than our own no. 12, our building seemed more alive, more welcoming. The silence in the geology building must have owed something to the paucity of students; in my class there were only six of us. On Friday afternoons the silence must have deepened, for, tired of trilobites, we adjourned to a Pembroke Street café for a well-earned break that was never less than an hour long. Over cups of tea and tobacco smoke we engaged in convivial conversation which rarely, if at all, touched on matters geological. It pleases me to record that we also wasted time in geography. Immediately on entering no. 12 there lay, on the left, the library. This included, in the rear, a periodicals room. The idea was that one sat there demurely taking notes from some recommended article. And indeed one started with good intentions. More often than not these went unrealised as conversation developed, occasionally to the consternation of the more studious. Visible from the periodicals room was a long low annexe that housed the first year cartography studio, nothing more really than a set of tables and stools. But these formed the setting, one Saturday, for an impromptu skiffle session which nicely delayed our cartography.

Opposite the library was the Exhibition Room, used more, in our first two years, as an unofficial common room than for any other purpose. In our third year we were very pleased to obtain a cellar common room.

Our acquisition owed much to the then Geographical Society President, David Jenkinson and the Lady President, Mary Mason. It was also through their efforts that the society obtained its own scarf and tie. David was a pipe-smoker and prone to wearing waistcoats that suggested that he, too, had watched *Doctor in the House*. We were both keen on jazz and gave record recitals in the common room. Belatedly I must thank David for widening my knowledge of jazz.

Field trips were a compulsory part of our course but, in truth, their value lay at least as much in promoting our sense of community as in advancing our knowledge. Each trip brought shared experiences and a greater understanding of each other. Three examples must suffice: tramping the Brendon Hills on a day of ceaseless rain; snow-balling on a lower Alpine slope in France; visiting a jazz club in Avignon - which proved a fitting end to our final field trip. Even then one of our number managed to surprise the rest by displaying an unexpected talent for jiving.

Our relatively small numbers, scarcely 30 in our final year, and our self-contained department also strengthened our communal identity but the staff probably played the greatest role. Sometimes they joined us in our evening relaxation on field trips. Sometimes they would chat informally in no. 12. All third years, in small groups, enjoyed a meal with Professor and Eileen Steel at their home. Other members of staff invited us to their homes too. So some friends and I had a most pleasant evening's meal and conversation with Stanley and Marjorie Gregory. Such kindness and concern were the hallmark of our lecturers.

Lectures were the main method of teaching and most were held in a large room on the first floor of no. 12. The room was rather spartan, with wooden chairs and benches. The teaching aids were a blackboard and projector. If equipment was minimal there was compensation in the clarity of the lectures. No doubt we all had our own favourite lecturers; mine included Stanley Gregory, Richard Lawton and Andrew Learmonth. Seminars, with their opportunity for debate with four or five captive students, well suited me. If time and resources had allowed I would have been happy to have had more frequent seminars, provided the number of essays to be handed to our tutor did not also increase! Quite often I would be told that my essays were marred by poor English. Plus ça change! ...

Just before formal graduation, Mary Mason and Rosemary Lamb

threw a party to mark the end of our undergraduate lives. As on some other occasions an inordinate amount of alcohol seemed to be consumed; tobacco was smoked; but nothing worse. My fellow students were nice people to know.

On graduating in 1959 I gratefully seized the opportunity to begin two years of research. Thanks to a studentship and a teaching fee from the University I had an income of approximately £350 a year, ample for my needs. We research students were privileged to join the staff at break times. The civilised and stimulating discussions that then took place almost tempted me to seek a university career. However, I had come to realise that research mattered less to me than teaching. Consequently, in my final year at Liverpool, I became a student teacher based in Abercromby House. This building was more impressive than no. 12, but the camaraderie of the Geography Department was largely lacking in the Education Department. This different ethos arose from contrasting courses. The Education course was short, and much of the available time was spent on teaching practice. There were no field trips and, in most lectures, student numbers were far larger than for any given year in geography. Lectures taken by the whole student body were held in a large room below pavement level so there were no outside distractions. But, in sometimes chatting or reading newspapers in lectures, our behaviour left something to be desired of budding teachers. Nevertheless, the course was valuable and not merely, as some have at times asserted, for teaching practice. Courses on the History of Education, the Philosophy of Education and not least our specialist subjects brought home that there was more to education than instruction. Even the compulsory P.T. class had the advantage of reminding me how it felt to endure a disliked school subject.

Anthony Silson, born Wharfedale 1938, Geography 1956-1959, Education 1959-1960, M.Sc. 1961, school-teacher 1960-1993, writing from Leeds

'You will remember Vienna'. The Geography class of 1957 certainly will, for reasons which will emerge. Departments based in Abercromby Square tended to be self-sufficient. Social life was provided by their own A [subject-based] societies, they were not members of A.S.A. [Arts

Students' Association] and the physical distance to the Union often encouraged them to spend their spare time in one of the many spare rooms in the department. Geographers, lawyers, economists, social scientists and postgraduate education students did become isolated from other students, but formed themselves into very close-knit communities. The Geographical Society organised a very full programme of social and cultural activities, including theatre visits, lectures by eminent academics - one particularly memorable one from Professor Simey on Hawaii, where he and his family were stranded through much of the war - and socials in the fairly small lecture room cleared of its tables. ... Strictly speaking, I was not a pure geographer as I was reading for an Honours degree in General Studies - a most worthwhile course which gave a broader background than a narrowly specialised Honours degree and was particularly useful for prospective teachers. Over three years it involved, for me, reading six courses in the main subject (Geography), two in a second subject (Economic History) and one each in two other subjects (Naval and Maritime History and Prehistoric Archaeology). ...

Until 1953 Abercromby Square had been a wilderness overlooked by the west front of the bombed-out St Catherine's Church (on the site of the present Senate House). In that year it was tidied up, and the words HAEC OTIA STUDIA FOVENT inscribed in large silver letters on the facade of the church, in anticipation of a visit by the Queen Mother. In the event she did not come. But at least Abercromby Square benefitted.

For many years the most important member of Geog. Soc. was Panto Pete, a rag doll awarded annually to the A society which collected most per capita in Panto week. A fairly small society which made a particular effort had a great advantage and so Panto week was a major event for Geog. Soc. This was especially so in 1956 when the Suez Crisis was looming, a popular local MP, Bessie Braddock, had exposed the illegal sale of arms to Egypt, and Geog. Soc.'s float was a superbly made tank populated by traditionally dressed Egyptians. In one Panto week a Geography student acquired a little more than his due fifteen minutes of fame by accepting a challenge to take a lifebelt and jump off a ferry boat. The outgoing tide took him two miles downstream before he was picked up. The feeling of bonding in the Geography department extended to the staff who took part in all Geog. Soc.'s activities. ...

The highlight of the whole course was the final fieldwork course in Vienna. Nights were spent exploring Vienna and its many attractions. On the last night a large group of men returned late and a card school began. A young lady invited herself to the group and immediately strip poker was suggested. She agreed, claiming later that she had never previously heard of the game but having agreed to play felt that she could not withdraw. She put down the fact that she lost every hand to her inexperience at the game. Before finally retiring we swore each other to silence - not so much to protect her reputation as to protect our own careers. The permissive Sixties were still three years away and we were uncertain how the staff might view the incident.

The following year, spent in the Department of Education, was something of an anti-climax, though teaching practice reminded us that there was a life after university and provided a valuable transition into the real world. Many students were Geography graduates, including several who had said they would do anything rather than teach but now found the prospect at least preferable to two years in the army. Despite the varied academic disciplines from which they were drawn, old loyalties were soon forgotten and Ed. Soc. quickly unified this very amorphous group by a full programme of social events. Students spent even more of their spare time in the department than other inhabitants of the Square. This was possibly because many weeks spent away from the university on teaching practice made it difficult to play an active part in Guild affairs and possibly because we were an older age group than most undergraduates. Nevertheless we were determined to enjoy our last Panto Day. Teaching Practice left us little time for artistic effort to prepare an elaborate float and so we loaded a lorry with much of the department's furniture to represent a schoolroom. A few 'masters' wore academic dress - the rest of us found our old school uniforms. An essential item of schoolboy equipment, of course, is a water pistol which was a good excuse for firing on the crowd. In the event, buckets (even bins) full of water loaded on to the float as ammunition were unnecessary as the crowds (and students) were thoroughly soaked by one of the wettest Panto Days ever known.

Samuel Alastair Munro, born Liverpool 1934, Geography 1954-1957, Education 1957-1958, school-teacher 1958-1989, writing from Liverpool

We were both undergraduates in the Department of Economics. Neither of us had gone to Liverpool with the intention of taking Economics, a subject then seldom taught in schools. ... But the Faculty was anxious to ensure that students had a broad coverage of subjects in their first year so both of us tried Economics as part of this broadening process. And, at the end of that year, both of us were kidnapped (only a minor exaggeration) by Professor Hyde who was desperately building up what was then a very small department. For one of us, Economics had the virtue - alone in the Faculty of Arts - of making a Single Honours degree available to those who lacked a qualification in Latin. ...

Within Economics, Professor Hyde's attempts to build up the Department were not unsuccessful. The numbers graduating reached nine in Margaret's year, having risen from six in David's and three in the year before that. (There was also a considerable number of students taking the B.Comm., but this degree - perhaps because it was practical and useful - had a tendency to attract the kind of jokes now levied at, for much the same reason, Ladas and Skodas.) Professor Hyde himself, despite his invariable kindness, seemed to students a remote and forbidding figure walking round the department clad (like all staff at the time) in a gown over a waistcoated suit and tie. Both of us, like most other students, were 'first generation graduates' - no one else in our families or acquaintance had ever been to university - and, looking back, it now seems that it was this, rather than his own personality, that made our Head of Department seem so distant. To give some bounds to our awe of him, we used to laugh about the occasional consequences of his extreme short-sightedness - like the occasion when he mistook David (notoriously thin) for a rather well-built female student. It is said that he once gave a lecture to a room occupied only by two decorators, but this is hearsay!

Economics was very unusual at the time in being a two-professor department. Professor Shackle (a Shackle-and-Hyde department, we used to say, not entirely inappropriately we thought) corresponded in our innocent eyes to everything that our limited reading had suggested an academic should be - diffident, precise, meticulous, frighteningly learned and apparently quite unworldly. The first year class was a fairly large one and often a little rowdy, but Professor Shackle invariably began his lectures by addressing us as 'Ladies and Gentlemen', never betraying a hint that even he can hardly have supposed that such an appellation had the slightest justification. Most memorably, he held the belief that it was impossible for students to listen to a lecture and to make notes at the same time. In consequence, he wrote our notes for us. In the days before xeroxing this was done on blackboards, as many as four for a lecture, which Professor Shackle - quite a small man, and not a young one - could sometimes be seen carrying round Abercromby Square in the Liverpool gales. The availability of the blackboard notes meant that we would spend the whole lecture copying them down instead of listening to what were (if you did listen for an instant) the most beautifully constructed and polished lectures ever likely to fall from the lips of an economist.

Compared with the current situation in universities, a distinguishing feature of the non-professorial staff of the department was their youthfulness. Another difference from current practice was their mode of arrival. Some came on foot, some by bus, and others by bicycle (the bikes were wheeled through the front door and kept in the department). None, as far as we can recollect, came by car, though Professor Hyde used a taxi, a mode of transport which mirrored his dignity in our minds since both his status and his taxi were equally remote from our own experience.

After graduation, jobs were not an immediate problem, at least for men - there was National Service to be done first. Taking a post-graduate degree offered an incentive unknown to modern students, the deferment of military service, with the hope that in the meantime it would be abolished. ... We have both worked as economists in the business community, although David returned to academia. We discovered in the 'real world' both the need for quantification and the importance of institutional constraints, two elements largely lacking from our academic training in economics.

A final comment. Liverpool had just about 3,000 students in our time. We thought it was huge and a little frightening. What must they think now? Or don't they notice?

David Bateman, born Stony Stratfield 1935, Economics 1953-1956, postgraduate 1956-1958, M.A. 1958, Professor of Agricultural Economics, University of Wales at Aberystwyth 1977-date; Margaret Bateman [Yearsley], Economics 1954-1957, Education 1957-1958

My mother was a hoarder and so am I. As a result I have a pile of letters from my university days, 1951-1956, spent in the Classics and Education Departments. It seems a pity not to use them. Dickens preferred letters to diary entries for recording events, but his were not full of - 'Would you renew my Library books?', 'Would you pay the fines on my books?' (3d a week), 'Please, would you collect my nylons from the repairers?'. My first letter, written just before the Freshers' dance in Freshers' week, began - 'I have arrived and it's wonderful'. The arrival from Carlisle was by train to Lime Street and taxi to the University to register (I hadn't been to Liverpool before). The Dean was annoyed that I had forgotten my School Certificate to prove that I had Latin. Had he noticed that Latin was one of my main subjects?

I registered in one of the lecture rooms in the Victoria Building - not beautiful, but it had atmosphere. At seminars in Professor Armstrong's room (for Greek), you could dream away looking down on a wide expanse of quad. The Classics Library was a meeting place. There was studious quiet in the Cohen Library, but I find that Jackie Kewley and I were singing excerpts from *The Yeomen of the Guard* one day in the Classics Library. The house on the corner of Abercromby Square to which we moved in 1953 had no such atmosphere. I felt isolated from the rest of the University. Perhaps it was something to do with being next to the Yellow Fever Clinic - or was it that it had once been the Yellow Fever Clinic?

Those of us doing a full Classics degree were few in number: five in my year, two in the year above and one in the third year, six boys, two girls. Students and lecturers were sociable. We went to the theatre together as a group, we saw the London production of *Carousel* at the Royal Court, also *A Day by the Sea* with Sir John Gielgud, Ralph Richardson and Dame Sybil Thorndike (she forgot her words), and *Caesar and Cleopatra* with Laurence Olivier and Vivienne Leigh. The Professors, Armstrong, Brink (Latin), and Walbank (Ancient History), invited us to parties. I was introduced to deck tennis on Professor Brink's lawn by Mr Townsend, the handsome Latin lecturer who was always very smartly dressed, though his bow ties were inclined to be showy. We sang songs round the piano, did treasure hunts, and ate quantities of food (I wasted pages and pages describing meals in minute detail).

'On Wednesday (May 1953) one of lecturers, John Pinsent - the young, mad one - invited us for tea.' This was a regular occurrence. All eight of us went to read Homer and drink tea at his various flats, the first round the corner from Ullet Road, the next may have been in Abercromby Square, and at some time the locality was Upper Parliament Street. He was a kind man and a great help to me, but if the booming voice of the Public Orator-to-be hailed you on a bus in Liverpool 8, you were embarrassed.

Taking a job during term time was frowned upon. I did do it in 1951, but only after exams and lectures were over and before end of term celebrations - the films and dances in the Union, and a Garden Party. I earned £6 2s 0d at C. & A.s for two weeks' work. I had a full grant from Carlisle Education Authority of £143 for that year, whereas State Scholarships were £250. I paid Rankin Hall fees of £90-99 for the year, and after other expenses I had only £11 a term to live on. Bus fares from Rankin Hall were 4d, or 2½d if you got off the stop before. I spent a 1s a day on lunches (Ryvita, cheese and milk). My friends on State Scholarships offered to send me a food parcel! I assured my parents that I could manage and that entertainment in the Union was either free or very cheap - 4d for lunchtime hops on Tuesdays and Thursday, free debates in the Gilmour Hall, free political speakers, and I was 'taken out' to dances, balls and theatres.

Mrs Marjorie Dunham [Perriam], born South Shields 1933, Classics 1951-1955, Education 1955-1956, schoolteacher 1957-1963, writing from Shrewsbury

1940s

I came to Liverpool, a Manchester man elevated to the status of a Liverpool gentleman, to study 'social science'. The department occupied what had once been the Bishop's Palace at the east end of the northern side of Abercromby Square. To the west were the departments of Education and Architecture; opposite the departments of Economics and Geography. The square itself was sadly dilapidated since the iron railings which had surrounded it had been taken down and the grass and flower-beds had been totally neglected during the war and for some years afterwards. Though the building in which the department was located was, to my mind, rather severe, it had style and dignity. An elegant staircase lit by a lantern gave access to the upper floors and the dignity of the building seemed to endorse the University's motto *Haec otia studia fovent* - In this leisure studies flourish. Among some of the staff there was a feeling that the university, with about 3,000 students, had already become far too big and they looked to a time when the numbers might go down, not perhaps to the ideal of about 1,500 of before the war, but to, say, a tolerable 2,000.

As for the departmental accommodation, the room on the left of the entrance-hall served as the departmental library, running from the front of the building to the back, presided over by Miss Lythgoe. The room to the right, which ran to the end of the building, was the main lecture room. At the back, a small room, grandly designated as 'The Board Room', was used as a staff room, where the staff met for coffee and tea in the afternoon, and to gossip and conduct their business. The professor's room was a large room at the back of the building on the first floor, with an ante-room or office occupied by the professor's secretary, a formidable Miss Eaves who, severely dressed in black, guarded her professor with the ferocity of a bulldog. Above the lecture room on the first floor was a room in which lived some of the research workers in the department, who also occupied the rooms in the attic from which came down the (to us students) rather mysterious research workers - whom we would also occasionally see clustering at a table in the little Chinese café that was run, if I remember correctly, by a Mrs Lee, just along Bedford Street. Presiding over this empire was Professor Simey, a tall man and a striking sight with his long craggy face and a mouth which always seemed to me like a trumpet. In 1948, he was just into his forties. ...

To a student, even a rather mature one of 22, the University was an august institution to which one went to be inducted into a body of knowledge which, as I look back, seemed to me at that time to be something that was a given and was certainly *static*. I do not recall having any idea that knowledge was changing or that it was through research that that change took place. But this ignorance was soon to change. For the department had a strong tradition of empirical research, established largely by the work of Caradog Jones, under Alexander Carr-Saunders, notably in the several volumes of the *Social Survey of Merseyside* which had been published in the 1930s. Tom Simey carried on this empirical tradition, and by the late 1940s he had already begun to win the grants from the likes of the Nuffield Foundation which soon made the Liverpool School the leading research department in the country. Thus, arguing that our empirical knowledge of contemporary Britain was at best sketchy, and that before sociology could be taught it was essential to discover what society was like, Simey appointed young academics to research posts. While, as an undergraduate, one would be taught by the regular staff - Penelope Hall, Dennis Chapman, Madelaine Kerr and the Prof. himself - one increasingly became aware that there were also all these other rather mysterious people who were 'doing research', whatever that might be, in the distant attics of the building. Some of these research workers would be given the opportunity to teach sociology, so that in due course I was taught by people like Duncan Mitchell and Tony Richmond who subsequently occupied chairs in the subject in universities in this country and abroad. In this way, Tom Simey contributed to the development of sociology by offering a much needed foot-hold in academia to young and aspiring sociologists when academic appointments in the field were relatively scarce. This practice also brought the small number of us - four in my year - who were studying sociology at that time into direct and beneficial contact with active research.

For me, however, it was certainly Simey who had the most influence upon my academic development. He was an academic *provocateur* with a vengeance. He once said that his aim was to grab his undergraduates by the scruffs of their necks, drag them to the edge of the pit of knowledge, force them to look over and then to train them to do so without fainting. His rambling lectures were often difficult to follow; but I remember that the four of us who were studying sociology at the turn of the fifties would go out of his lectures to try to unravel what he had been saying to us over a cup of tea in the Students' Union, so that they teased us, so to speak, into thinking. In a similar vein, I recall with particular pleasure the first year seminar in which, with just one direct comment on an essay that I had read, Simey changed my whole conception of what academic activity was all about. I had read this paper in which, as I recall, I had simply recited the various views that sociologists had taken of the concept 'social class'. Simey had sat behind his desk giving the impression of interest, only to burst upon my unsuspecting self with the cry - 'Well, Broady, that's competent, that's all very well; but what do YOU think about it all?' So competence was not the great virtue that I had thought it to be, but merely the start of academic activity; and that activity was concerned not just with learning what all the great books had to say but with what I thought about them. What a challenge and how I responded to it! ...

Two incidents will show how personal was a student's relationship with his mentors in those days. Both of them took place shortly after I had returned from a postgraduate year in the USA. I had to make some arrangements about my salary as a junior research worker and went to the *guichet* on the first floor of the Victoria Building at which, as a student, I had drawn my grant, as an ex-serviceman, of £212 a year. The clerk who came to the *guichet* saw me and, registering that I was now on the staff of the university, said that I should now come in by the main door of the finance office to which he directed me and which he opened with a flourish to allow me to enter. A week or two later it must have been, when I was crossing the hall in the Victoria Building, I happened to see the rather small figure of Dr Wiener coming down the stairs. A refugee from Nazism, Dr Wiener had taught both my wife and myself German. We greeted each other and, after a brief chat, Dr Wiener, with a little embarrassment, tentatively inquired whether I was now married. With even greater embarrassment, he asked 'To Miss Love?'. Yes, I admitted; to which he replied with genuine pleasure, 'Aaach, I am veeeeery haaaapy'. At which point it dawned on me that our romance must have been, totally unknown or suspected by us two, a topic of conversation among our teachers for most of our time as undergraduates in the Faculty!

Maurice Broady, Social Science 1948-1951, postgraduate 1951-1952, researcher, lecturer, etc 1953-1970, Professor of Social Policy, University of Wales (Aberystwyth) 1970-1982

In 1947 Liverpool was still a humming commercial hub, still a great international seaport. The docks, from Princes to Gladstone, and from Albert south towards the inner reaches of the river, still received shipping from across the world. The warehouses were busy, the Mersey a vital waterway. Looking up from the river, the solid outline of the Anglican Cathedral loomed, its sandstone shrapnel-pitted from earlier bombing raids. But the modern grey concrete crown of the new Catholic Cathedral had not yet been built. The most imposing structure in that area remained the Victoria Arts Building of the University of Liverpool, which had stood at the top of Brownlow Hill for just over fifty years. The Beatles were still in their Primary schools, and 'pop' was a fizzy drink bought in the Students' Union for 6d a bottle. Wartime Britain was still surfacing.

The zenith of my ambition at that time was to get myself behind the red-brick facade of the Victoria Building, and start to widen my learning horizons. For too long they had been confined. The war years meant restriction on travel, on book publication, on language interchange, on employment opportunities. Schools remained strictly sex-segregated, frequently staffed by teachers too old to have fought, or so recently returned from war zones that their outlook was still coloured by a disrupted past, incapable of much forward-looking towards an organised future. What would today's students think of a first-year undergraduate who had never crossed the Channel, had never heard fluent French spoken by a true Frenchman, and yet hoped to enter the Language and Geography Departments ?

In 1947 there were more women 'freshers', as first-year students were usually called, in the Arts Faculty than in any other faculty. Yet there was a noticeable dearth of women students overall. University places, quite rightly, went first to those ex-servicemen - and ex-service-women too, but there were fewer of these - returning from the war, their studies disrupted by their call-up four or five years previously. To such as myself, straight from a local school, this was a major advantage. Older students brought their wealth of experience, their already expanded outlook, their informed opinion to every aspect of our studying, and we were the better for it. Apart from 'evacuation', away from the Liverpool blitzes, many of us had never been any distance out of our own local area. Rationing was still in place. Living at home had to be encouraged amongst the large majority of students, and Hall places were difficult to come by. Trams ran regularly past the Victoria Building, and for a 3d fare, the Pier Head and the ferries to the Wirral were in easy reach, as well as, of course, the suburbs of the city in the opposite direction. Trams rarely needed to stop to pick up students. It was a point of honour to catch one on the run, blue scarf flying, bag under one arm, the other outstretched to grasp the bar. ...

In those early post-war years, students in the Arts Faculty were divided into those wanting to obtain an 'ordinary B.A.', and those 'intending Honours', that is, students whose ambition it was to enter the subject department of their choice to sit for a B.A. Hons., once they had achieved a good enough result in their first-year examinations, in all the three subjects they were required to take. My own subject combination was English, French and Geography, and as a 'fresher', my ambition was to read English Literature as my Honours subject. It was not to be. My English was up to the required standard, and after some initial struggle, so was my French. But the required Latin element in my Higher School Certificate was insufficient. To my great disappointment, it looked as if I was destined for an 'ordinary degree'. I was at home in Wallasey when the telephone rang. I was requested to present myself in the Geography Department, then in Abercromby Square, that afternoon, where Professor Darby wished to discuss my first-year examination results with me. Filled with apprehension I arrived at his office door, in no way prepared for an interview that would change the whole course of my career. I had never been all that interested in Geography, taking it as a third first-year subject merely because I had a good grade in my HSC. However, I had certainly enjoyed the scope of the subject, the books I had started to read, and the sheer enthusiasm with which it was taught in Abercromby Square. I was shown in to meet the Professor, by a younger lecturer, Frank Monkhouse, whose talks on the regional divisions of Europe, on the underlying geology and the consequent human activities, had been rivetting me for a year. I remember so well my amazement at being offered a place in the Honours School of Geography. ...

Prof. Darby's dry sense of humour remains with me, his enthusiasm for all aspects of Historical Geography, his amazing knowledge, his belief that what all geographers needed most of all was a pair of 'stouter boots', his professed dislike of any women in his Department, and yet his very beautiful fair-haired Scandinavian wife. When he interviewed me on that memorable day in 1948, he said, 'I shall have to have you, of course, with these results, but women have no place in stouter boots, and if you ever get a degree out of it, I'll take my hat off to you.' At the Jubilee celebrations in the September of 1967, he did just that, doffing a hastily-obtained mortar board with real aplomb and great good humour.

The quiet of the Cohen Library, row upon row of secluded desk areas, each one discreetly lit, the even more erudite and hardly won carrels: in these places we studied, immersed in our books, until time for that last tram home ....

The focus of our social life was the Students' Union, across the road from the Victoria Building, and en route to Geography, Education, Social Sciences, Architecture and Psychology, all housed in converted residences around the railed centre of Abercromby Square. The Tuesday and Thursday 'hops' in the Stanley Hall saw the start of many a life-time friendship. Here Arts and Sciences met on common ground, and found relaxation away from study. The smaller Gilmour Hall was used for debating and various Society meetings. Here those destined for Government office could sharpen their political teeth. On most Saturday nights there was an informal dance in the Stanley, usually organised by one of the multitude of societies which every student joined, and where like minds met. The annual Commem. Ball meant ball-gowns varying from frothy snowballs of white tulle, layer upon layer of underskirt, to slinky satin sheathes often re-made from our mother's pre-war finery, because there was still little in the shops, we didn't have all that much money, and the war had taught us to be enterprising with our needles. Our escorts were resplendent in unaccustomed black tie and dinner jacket, in many cases borrowed from Dad. Few women, if any, wore trousers. War-time austerity and clothing coupons had given way to Dior's 'New Look'. Our cinched waists and full long skirts announced a new and almost assertive femininity. As women we were beginning to arrive,

Petrol was scarce, so hardly any students had cars. Drugs had not reached our scene, although a blue haze of cheap Woodbines coupled with those green packets of 'roll-your-own' was commonplace in the Canteen, and in the 'Round Lounges' of the S.U.

Graduation at the Philharmonic Hall was an occasion. Wonderful to have that authorization to enter the carpeted dignity of Ravenscroft and Willis to be fitted with a gown. Women graduates wore their mortar boards. The men tucked theirs under the left arm. Consequently there was always the chance of an exchange with a male colleague if one's cap wouldn't balance or seemed to come down over one's ears. Afterwards there were the usual photo sessions, before repairing to the Kardomah in Bold Street with family and friends. For the vast majority of us it was over. ... But in 1953 I married Robert Foulds, a contemporary in the Science Faculty.

Liverpool is a very changed place from the city I knew. In my final year, in 1950, I wrote my geography thesis on the Liverpool Docks, mainly a commercial treatise about shipping and busy warehouses. In 1967, I was back in the Department for the Jubilee celebrations, and met a young man also interested in the Docks who asked me about my contribution to 'historical geography'. It took me some time to realise that my thesis was now history.

Elizabeth Jean Foulds [MacFarlane], born in Ireland 1929, Geography 1947-1950, Education 1950-1951, school-teacher, then in Further Education 1979-1993, writing from Maidstone

When I had taken my degree in History at Oxford and was looking for a career, I came across an advertisement in the *Times Educational Supplement* for a new postgraduate Diploma in the Study of Records and the Administration of Archives offered by the Faculty of Arts in the University of Liverpool. I sent off an application which was accepted and so, early in October 1947, I arrived at the Victoria Building to enrol on the Diploma course. I had never been in an industrial city before, and I found Liverpool, with its blackened buildings, its considerable areas of war damage and its trams, most intimidating. The red brick building of the University with its tall tower standing on an almost derelict Brownlow Hill was scarcely less so. But these were just first impressions, and although I never learned to like Liverpool as a city, I have very warm memories of the Diploma course and my year at Liverpool University.

On that first afternoon I found my way to the Department of History and met Professor Geoffrey Barraclough [Medieval History 1945-1956] and Dr Oschinsky, and also my fellow student. There were only two of us who took the course that year. It was clearly built on two existing assets within the Faculty of Arts. One was the long-established Lectureship in

Palaeography, and the other was Professor Barraclough's interest and expertise in medieval palaeography and diplomatic. ... It was a well-planned course. We spent a lot of time on Palaeography with Dr Oschinsky who was a kind and encouraging teacher with very high standards which she was determined to pass on to us. She taught us in seminar fashion, sometimes in conjunction with a small group of History undergraduates who were also studying Palaeography, and the teaching was practically based. Her aim, she told us many times, was to make us palaeographers good enough to date a document from its handwriting alone. I have rarely been required to attempt this, perhaps once or twice in my career, and I doubt if it is possible, but I am sure that the excellent training I received from Dr Oschinsky has stood me in good stead. ...

Professor Barraclough was very clear that the course was vocational and its students were to be equipped to go out and do a job of work at the end of the year. To this end he arranged that our lectures on Archive Administration were given by Mr Sharpe France, the County Archivist for Lancashire. These lectures took place in the evening so that Mr Sharpe France could come over to Liverpool from Preston after his day's work, and this had the additional advantage that the Diploma course could be taken on a part-time basis over two years by people who were working during the day. ...

The year went by quickly because there was so much to be learnt and so much work to do. One of the problems was getting the books we needed. My memory of the University Library is not a happy one. The card index catalogue was arranged on a different system from the one I was used to, and because the Library had an open stack the staff were unwilling to help the confused student find the required book. In any case, quite a number of books we needed were not available in the Library but some of these were provided for us within the Department of History. ...

In 1979 I was elected Honorary Secretary of the Society of Archivists and it was as a result of my term in this office that I was appointed in 1989 by the Society to be a member of a small team of archivists to assess the five postgraduate archive training courses. And so, in March 1990, I returned, with two colleagues in the Society, to the Faculty of Arts in Liverpool. The Diploma course of 1947 had become a course leading to the degree of Master in Archive Administration ... It was a great pleasure to find the course flourishing and developing in all sorts of ways to meet the changing needs of the archive profession.

Cynthia Short [Hill], post-graduate Archives Administration 1947-1948, archivist, county archivist 1948-1986

October 1945. Bedford Street lined with surface shelters, the road strewn with bricks. Abercromby Square a sea of mud with a forlorn little wreck of a shelter in the middle. 'Fog everywhere. Fog up the river where it flowed among green aits and meadows; fog down the river where it rolled defiled among tiers of shipping, and the waterside pollution of a great (and dirty) city'. Fog in the eyes and nose of the muffled-up tram driver as he peered through the yellow gloom that enveloped his No. 8 in Oxford Street. Fog truncating the great tower of the Victoria Building and obliterating its clockface. Fog 'pinching the toes and fingers' of a straggling line of young people as they were swallowed up by the entrance below. Fog without and fog within: this was registration day.

The Dean's office was at the end of a long corridor on the ground floor of the New Arts Building opposite the Cohen library. Outside it the straggling line transformed itself into a seething sea of confused humanity which increased as time rolled by. Nobody knew what was happening; nobody knew what to expect. From time to time three or four were drained off into the Dean's ante-room, and one was admitted to the hallowed presence. ... However, as the hours went by the mood of those left milling around outside was becoming rebellious. The new Dean was Professor Ormerod, a kindly old gentleman, but some of the crueller elements in the crowd, having consulted the lucky few who had already been admitted, voiced the opinion that the Dean was obviously not fully conversant with the courses which his Faculty was offering. The mood of some, who had travelled considerable distances, reached boiling point when it was announced that they would have to come back the following day. Thus the pantomime was extended to at least forty-eight hours, and no-one was ecstatic over their first introduction to the Faculty.

The Faculty of Arts in 1945 was situated between a gigantic coke stack which covered the Quadrangle, and the Cohen Library across Ashton Street. However, down the middle of Ashton Street lay the gleaming rails of the Liverpool Corporation Passenger Transport System, and down those rails at regular intervals passed those ancient boneshakers which led to the letters L.C.P.T. being interpreted as 'Last City to Preserve Trams'. As they shook, rattled and rolled, lectures came to a halt, competition being both fruitless and pointless. No human voice could compete with an antediluvian Liverpool tram.

Lectures in 1945 were meant to be taken seriously despite some of the arrangements made by the Faculty itself. In all due fairness it must be remembered that the Faculty was jammed to the gunnels with returning ex-servicemen, American and Canadian soldiers on short courses, and a sprinkling of jolly nuns, as well as the new intake straight from school. The result was that the principal lecture hall was often filled to capacity and, as lectures were compulsory, some record of attendance had to be made. The infallible solution to the problem was to have every student sign on a piece of paper, which was passed round at the beginning of the lecture. Needless to say, after signing for themselves the less desirable elements would then sign for absent friends. As the paper ended up at the back of the lecture theatre in close proximity to an unlocked door, unscrupulous types were seen to crawl in on their hands and knees and crawl out again having given the Faculty evidence of their fleeting presence. ...

For some reason, best known to itself, the Faculty had decided that all students should study phonetics. Whether this was an exercise in standardisation intended to eradicate all accents whether American, Canadian, Polish or Scouse will never be known, but when the news was received an air of gloom descended upon the multi-ethnic contents of the first year. However, all was not lost for the air of gloom was soon to be dispelled by the lecturer assigned to the course, one Simeon Potter, a distinguished philologist. Professor Potter [English Language and Philology 1945-1965] was a very serious gentleman. However, he didn't so much as lecture as play to packed houses. This was the result of his vocal demonstrations of all the idiosyncratic sounds that could emanate through the human mouth. The problem was that some of these strange sounds were almost identifiable as sounds which usually emanated from a totally different orifice. His pièce de resistance was his bi-labial fricative which literally brought the house down. Professor Potter was not amused!

Another gentleman whose lectures were remembered for their delivery rather than their content was the kind and ever helpful Dr Hans Liebeschütz. He lectured in Medieval History, or so we were told, but the problem in his case was a lack of fluency in the English language. To overcome this difficulty he recruited two other European languages, and the combination of these three in any one sentence, allied to the periodical perambulations of the trams down Ashton Street, caused more than one student to ask 'What the Hell was all that about?' at the end of a lecture. ... From time to time the sad figure of an elderly bearded gentleman would be seen on the staircase, always alone and always hugging the wall. This was Jean Eggli, Professor of French [1920-1946], whose retirement home in France had been wrecked by the Germans. Two ladies on the staff of the Faculty, Dr Dorothy Knowles and Dr Miriam Farris, certainly did their best to brighten up the cavernous corridors of the New Arts Building. The former lectured in French, the latter in English, but with their magnificent costumes and their exotic hats they looked as if they were about to enter Ascot's Royal Enclosure on Ladies' Day rather than the cool confines of the Victoria Building. ...

1949 registration day: chaos resolved: a new Dean, Professor Hyde. Professor Ormerod, now full of confidence, acting in the advisory capacity to the new incumbent. ... Having been tranquillised by the British Army, I entered into the spirit of academic things for the first time. Accommodation being a priority, I sought advice. Apparently the University provided a list of approved accommodation which everyone with spirit avoided like poison. Now I had a father who, apart from an outward appearance of utter respectability, was an avid reader of *The News of the World*, and who was very much displeased when he discovered that I was residing in digs in Grove Street, a street whose residents featured regularly in the centre page. ...

By 1949 Abercromby Square had been rescued and its surface shelters had gone. The backlog of students who had returned from the war had worked its way through the system. However, austerity was still the order of the day. Everything was rationed from clothes to sweets. What was most remarkable in an age of clothing coupons was the smartness of the attire of the average undergraduate. When rumour had it that a roll of University blazer cloth had arrived at the premises of Ravenscroft and

Willis the place was besieged.

For an intending schoolmaster the next logical step after graduation was the Department of Education in Abercromby Square. ... Professor Porteous was a very amiable little man. The staff in his department were all very amiable ladies and gentlemen. Having said that, it was perfectly obvious that they loved teaching so much that they'd go to Hell out of a classroom at the earliest opportunity. Being a philosopher, Professor Porteous exposed us to the infection of Plato and Aristotle in the hope that the disease might catch on: it didn't. ... When you were trying to hold down a class in the Scotland Road area in a school that had been built on the lines of Walton Prison, Plato and Aristotle didn't help much. ...

My greatest regret is that I abandoned a course of English Literature presided over by a brilliant and most enthusiastic young lecturer and tutor after just half of one term. Having worked my way merrily through 'The Wife of Bath', I discovered that the next Chaucerian offering was 'Troilus and Cressida'. Wearily I turned over page after tissue thin page in Skeat's edition. Finally my nerve broke and I hurled myself down the corridor to Professor Mark Thomson's room and pleaded sanctuary. Mercifully it was granted and a Modern History course replaced Chaucer. I have always regretted having to desert that young lecturer. Happily he is still with us: his name is Reg Davies.

Norman Charles Bernsen, born Lytham St Annes 1928, English/History 1945-1947, 1949-1951, Education 1951-1952, school-teacher 1952-1982, writing from Lytham St Annes

As I read the invitation to the Arts Faculty Centenary celebrations, I recalled how few we were in my student days in the last three years of the Second World War. In the years 1942-1945 the Geography Department was an important part of the Arts Faculty. ... I emerged in 1945 much to my surprise with a first class honours in Geography. We had been a very small year group with just one man in it! He also got a first which made us quite an exceptional year. We were housed in Abercromby Square 'on the far side', already outcast from the Arts Building, I suppose. We occupied a three-storey terrace house; the university was spilling over into several of the houses on both sides of the Square, both Education and

Social Science being on the 'near side'. However, first-years were compelled to study a great variety of other disciplines and so spent more time than most of them wished 'down the road', on Brownlow Hill, in the main building that I remember most for its 'lavatorial' tiling! I remember a course on Medieval History taught by Professor Roxby's fairly new wife - after a lifetime of bachelorhood the romance had blossomed during the university evacuation at the beginning of the war. Then there was a compulsory (compulsory that is for all first-year Arts students) Phonetics course, an extraordinary affair. We, geographers, also had to take a foreign language and I well remember struggling with my very weak German in a small group, all the others being budding Hons. German students. ...

The Geography Department was a very happy family, the envy of many for our social activities and our student-staff relations. No doubt all that went on would be considered very dull by today's students but my recollections of 'Professor's Birthday Party' still give me pleasure. Social life was restricted, of course, by such things as the blackout. By the time I arrived in Liverpool the worst of its blitz was over, but there was considerable devastation around. However, the repertory theatre flourished and I remember concerts in the Philharmonic Hall. There was even an occasional 'hop' in the Union. We had a formal dance once a year in no. 44 Ullet Road and there was a reciprocal one in Derby Hall, the men's hall. The cheap Mersey ferry often carried us across to the comparatively undisturbed peace of the Wirral. Trams took us from Ullet Road to the University if we were not intrepid cyclists, prepared to negotiate the hazard of tram lines.

In my year the majority were 'local' in the sense that they lived at home. With the minority, I spent my three years in the houses on Ullet Road, the only women's accommodation during the war. The women's hall had been commandeered by His Majesty's Government. For two years I shared a room with three others and in the third year was privileged to be in a room for two. Not the easiest way to study but, without doubt, a splendid way to learn a lot of other social skills. Memories are of extreme cold - we had a tiny fireplace in each room and an even tinier ration of coal each day. There was no other heating. Most work was done swathed in blankets and often in bed. There must have been warm summer days but I cannot remember them. The coal ration did not increase at the weekend and, of course, no one went home!

Food, or more accurately the lack of it, also figures much in my memory. Rabbit for dinner in Hall was very popular amongst the few of us who could bring themselves to eat it. There was considerably more to go round than usual. Then there was a friend from Cumbria whose mother sent her roast pigeons. In my third year, assisted by a slightly more affluent friend, I found a Chinese restaurant on Mount Pleasant that served steaks at a remarkably reasonable price, obviously horse-meat but nutritious. I sometimes reflect that I owe my degree to that enterprising Chinese family.

Money equivalents are difficult. Certainly most of us had very little. The only way I had got myself to university was by agreeing to teach. My parents provided me with 5s a week. I did go home for one special occasion but had to cycle to Rochdale using the then main road, the East Lancs, and on a bike with no gears. My father took pity on me and paid my rail fare back.

Irene Whittaker, born Rochdale 1924, Geography 1942-1945, school-teacher, school head 1945-1985, writing from York

The holder of a Miners' Welfare National scholarship that gave entry to any university in Britain, I came to Liverpool as a 17 year-old from Houghton-le-Spring Grammar School in October 1942. It was to prove a happy choice that established a lifetime association. Several reasons drew me to Liverpool: first, the academic reputation of its Geography Department; secondly, the enthusiasm of my junior geography teacher, Doris Parkinson (herself a Liverpool graduate), whose energy and enthusiasm made the subject live; thirdly, the advice of Herbert Brittain (B.A. 1949), a year ahead of me in the sixth form, who had come up in 1941 and strongly commended the Department and Derby Hall; and, finally, the strong conviction that I would benefit by studying away from home. Those expectations were not disappointed. Most of my closest friends at that time were in Hall, where my House Tutor was, by happy chance, Kenneth Baker, a Lecturer in Geography and later the founder of one of the first Geography Departments in anglophone tropical Africa, at

Makerere College, Uganda ... In a relatively small university it was also possible to meet people from other Faculties and, in the Union and through sport (I played both soccer and cricket for University teams), I made many friendships and reaped the wider educational benefit of discussions on all manner of subjects with fellow-students of very different academic and social backgrounds.

The Faculty of Arts that I entered still had considerable cohesion and identity. It was, by present standards, small and it had a coherent academic structure. Although I had come to Liverpool primarily for its reputation in Geography, the first year of studies was a general Arts year in which the notional 'Prospective Honours' provided only an additional seminar class in geography. All students were required to study three subjects, one of which was a language (for me, French), and with a fourth 'non-examination' subject to add breadth (Economics in my case). All subjects had to be passed before proceeding to Part I of the B.A., and most students still went on to study for the General degree in which Honours (first or second class) was rarely conferred. Those who went on to read Special Honours had to pass a translation test in their foreign language and take a subsidiary subject: any who failed the language test were denied a classified degree, regardless of their performance in their Special Honours course. There were advantages, both academic and social, in this spread of interest. The relatively narrow range of subjects offered in the small sixth forms of the grammar schools of that era focused undergraduate choice on a relatively few subsidiary subjects: English, History and, among the languages, French, were major beneficiaries. Studying a subsidiary subject, one was likely to encounter students from across the whole of the Faculty (Architecture, with its own degree structure, apart). Even then, however, departments were physically separated, with the later Social and Environmental Studies departments concentrated in the Abercromby Square-Bedford Street area and the humanities departments mainly in the Victoria and New Arts buildings. One very large class was in General Phonetics which was compulsory for all modern languages and included a large proportion of the first year students. It was taught by Professor J.H.G. Grattan, one of a number of retired staff who had extended their teaching to help remedy the wartime staff shortage, but whose largely inaudible delivery lost much of his humour and superb dialect impressions to those who chose to sit at the back of the New Arts lecture room and to slip out of the rear door as soon as they had signed the attendance register. Another Emeritus Professor, George Coopland, gave the Medieval History course and was an inspiring teacher whose lectures on monasticism fired my imagination (and who had a book in the press when he died in his 99th year).

In the wartime university, all, staff and students alike, were expected - or, in the case of those like myself still too young for military service, were required - to join either emergency services, such as fire-watching or Air Raid Precautions, or one of the University military training divisions. I joined the newly-formed Naval Division, the first in the country, which by recruiting to a 'Y Scheme' for the training of naval officers took in both existing undergraduates and those who wished to come to the university after the war. With a minimal input from Royal Navy Petty Officer instructors, the Division was commanded by Dr R.T. Daniel (Lt. Cdr., Special RNVR), the oceanographer, while a number of academics assisted in the training courses: Sub-Lt. (Special) Frank Fletcher flagged his semaphore signals from a 'bridge' on top of the air-raid shelters in Abercromby Square (F.T.H. Fletcher, Professor of French, 1946-1965); and Sub-Lt. Wilfred Smith (John Rankin Professor of Geography, 1950-1955) taught elements of meteorology. We were a motley crew!

The city also fascinated me, as it has continued to do. It had, for me strange contradictions: a northern city that was cosmopolitan and quite different from those of the industrial north, whether Lancashire or, especially, my native North East England; a city with widespread poverty but, still, substantial if declining commercial wealth; of deep class and sectarian divisions; of working-class dockside residential areas with extensive slums and, in many parts, considerable squalor, and vast Corporation housing estates on its eastern periphery, both of these in stark contrast to the substantial merchant, middle-class mansions and suburbs of leafy south Liverpool. Equally puzzling was its sectarian politics - never, up to that time, a Labour Council and not a single Labour MP (until 1945). However, I relished its cultural life, not least the Philharmonic Hall and orchestra.

The war-time Faculty of Arts, not long returned from evacuation to Coleg Harlech (with Professor Roxby in charge), was small. Geography had only three full-time members of staff (the fourth was on war service) and an 'intending Geography Honours' group of around a dozen who met weekly in Professor Roxby's seminar (the 1942 entry graduated only eight in the 1945 Honours School). In all there were, I suppose, around 25 Geography Honours students and perhaps around the same number studying geography in the B.A. General Degree. It was a remarkably cohesive department with a strong sense of identity. Much of the credit for that ethos, as well as for its high academic reputation, went to Roxby - an imposing man, a superb and inspirational lecturer, and a charismatic individual who dominated his department and whose students were important to him, an attitude that extended to his staff. Not only was the department a centre of academic excellence, the graduates from which taught in schools, colleges and universities throughout Britain and overseas, but it was also an academic community with a strong social life and a genuine concern for the individual. The course was dominated by regional and human geography, with a strong historical and cultural approach (very much influenced by the French 'School' of Geography), and a deep involvement with the Merseyside Region, both in, and with, its economic, social and planning problems. Moreover, Roxby was a strong supporter of, and frequent lecturer for, the Workers' Educational Association and university extension classes: among Roxbiana deposited with the University Archives are hand-written lectures for such classes on a variety of world issues of the pre-war and wartime period. Such personal and departmental involvements recall the need in the minds of those in the early days of the Arts Faculty who set up courses in commerce and economics, courses designed to promote subjects seen of particular relevance to a city dependent on world-wide trade and commerce and reflected in geography's contribution to the Faculty's Bachelor of Commerce degree. With my, then common, Higher School Certificate qualifications in Geography, History and English, plus subsidiary Latin, this was an ideal framework of study. Moreover, it led me to a conviction, still firmly held, that a university should have strong roots in its region and a positive commitment to enhancing the quality of life of its local communities rather than just to teach its students.

Returning to my studies in the Autumn of 1946 after service in the Royal Navy I found much change. Roxby had resigned his Chair in 1944 to lead the British Council's activities in China. The new John Rankin Professor, Clifford Darby, a Cambridge historical geographer with a very different approach from Roxby, re-shaped the syllabus with a stronger emphasis on systematic, analytical approaches to geography. He appointed keen young staff and greatly strengthened the research drive of the department. The beneficiaries included a considerable influx of ex-servicemen, some like myself, completing studies begun before or during the war, others new to higher education and eager to take advantage of ex-servicement's grants and an opportunity to develop the basis for new careers. It was a challenging but exciting time for both staff and students. Mature students, many with pre-war work experience and considerable wartime responsibility, were demanding as well as rewarding to teach. They had no time to waste and worked hard and purposefully. Graduating classes doubled, though resources did not match the pace of growth. Since student numbers were expected to return to pre-war participation levels, few additional teaching appointments were made. Yet despite heavy pressure on the academic and support staff, a wide range of research was developed: Darby's own studies of the geography of Domesday England; Wilfred Smith's work on the economic geography of Britain, as well as work on Scandinavia and Yugoslavia. In addition physical geography began to assume more importance.

I have no doubt that this enhanced research commitment brushed off on undergraduates like myself, not least through the immediacy and freshness of the content of the honours courses. There was a deepening of the learning experience which matched the increased expectations of a changing student body. A high-quality teaching department that produced generations of good teachers also produced academics (ten of the fifty graduates in the years 1948-1950 became College or University teachers, four of whom later held chairs in the UK or abroad) while a number - increasing over the years - went into careers where their geography was applied, notably in regional and town planning. One additional benefit of this research emphasis was in postgraduate research. The department had always had relatively substantial numbers of Master's Degrees by thesis, mainly through part-time study and often of people in the teaching profession. But a number of Chinese and Egyptian postgraduates, including one or two pre-war Ph.D.s, reflected Roxby's contacts with individuals of high standing in those countries. The last of the pre-Communist-era Chinese were to graduate in 1948 and 1949 respectively: Wu Chang Jun was later to become head of the Geography section of the Academica Sinica and Hou Ren Chi the doyen of Chinese historical geographers. I shared a room with Hou in my year of postgraduate study in 1948-1949 and, to my delight, hosted the departmental dinner in his honour when the University conferred on him an Honorary D.Sc. in 1984.

Despite changes in curriculum and academic emphasis the departmental ethos of close staff-student relations was maintained. Students were known, individually, to staff; there was close contact between tutees and personal and academic tutors; small-group and practical classes and departmental field classes (in which, up to the early 1950s, all years participated together to the benefit of both inter-year and staff-student links); an active student Geographical Society greatly helped to maintain a strong sense of departmental identity. Such events as the 'official' Professor's Birthday Party - in those less sophisticated times a real party with games, charades and the like - were enjoyed by all and certainly removed the mystique from 'The Professor' and his colleagues, even for freshman. There is no doubt that a separate 'home', at that time in the pleasant surroundings of 12 Abercromby Square, did much to foster that 'family atmosphere'. It was easy to encounter staff on the staircases or in the corridors, or over cups of tea (dispensed for staff, postgrads and final honours year students on Thursday afternoons in Darby's time). I recall, too, the pleasure of being able to gaze out of the first-floor lecture room (no doubt the drawing room of the merchant families who lived there in the years from 1834 until after the First World War) across the 'Abercromby Steppelands', as we called the devastated gardens. This was especially delightful during an 11.30 a.m. lecture, when tantalizing lunchtime smells floated up from the student boarding-house in no. 13. By 1953 that house had become incorporated into the Department as a further phase of its development got under way.

Richard Lawton, born 1925 Newbottle, Geography 1942-1943, 1946-1948, postgraduate 1948-1949, lecturer, etc 1949-1970, Professor of Geography 1970-1983, Dean of the Social and Environmental Studies Faculty 1977-1980, writing from Yorkshire

I went up to Liverpool University in October 1942. My brother, then a law student, had persuaded me that I should read economics which he thought would suit me better than social science to which I was attracted. ... Aged seventeen and armed with a Higher School Certificate, I reported to the Dean of the Arts Faculty, then Professor Mountford. He tried to dissuade me from reading economics, which only served to make me more determined. I later discovered that he had no staff, the Economics Professor being away on war-time government service and the acting head of department having died during the vacation. After some discussion on the reasons for my choice, I was registered to read for an honours degree in economics.

The Economics school, along with Social Science and Commerce, was located at 19 Abercromby Square, the Bishop's Palace, as it was known. It was a very elegant house and we were fortunate to have such pleasant surroundings. The departmental library was a very good place to work in and had a good stock of material. This was felicitous because the supply of new books was limited during the war, and second-hand ones were scarce. I remember that the librarian was particularly helpful when I was writing my dissertation in my third year. At that time, reading for an honours degree did not exempt the students from taking three other subjects in their first year and I found myself doing courses in French, medieval history and social administration, each of which seemed to absorb more of my time than economics. It seemed a waste of time to have to do this sort of foundation course when it was clear to me that French and medieval history were completely outside my study plan; and the lectures in the latter were extremely poor. Social administration was much more acceptable because it had a relationship to economics and because we had an exceptionally good teacher in Dr Wilson who made us see the relevance of the subject. However it was the economics course that I naturally remember best. Arrangements had been made for Mrs Ursula Hicks to come from Manchester twice a week to give the first-year economics course. This was attended by geography, commerce and social science students as well as those reading economics. ...

In my second year trade cycle theory and Keynesian economics were the keystones of the course; and in small classes Mrs Hicks helped us to make better progress. Two or three junior lecturers were appointed and I remember especially D.J. Morgan on the international trade theory and Ken Connell's economic history courses which included United States and Russian economic history as well as Britain's. Ken was a very tall and rather gangling man and he was then courting his future wife, Hannah Schümer, who was a lecturer in German. They used to meet up in the Cohen Library staff room, access to which was through the main reading room. When one of them walked through, we knew the other would shortly follow - and that they would leave together. There was also an interesting course of a descriptive kind on economic structure and policy; another on modern political institutions; and courses in statistics with Mr Caradog Jones. These were very enjoyable. I had wanted to include mathematics in my curriculum, but I was not allowed to. At that time one could not easily mix Arts and Science subjects and mathematics was definitely a Science subject. The statistics that I learnt from Mr Caradog Jones were very useful in my subsequent career, but it would have been more helpful if I had been allowed to carry on with mathematics.

In my third year Professor G.C. Allen returned from the Board of Trade, and Dr Hyde also returned from some temporary war-time employment, so that the department was considerably stronger. It was only in the third year that there was a tutorial system, which of course enhanced the quality of the teaching. Professor Allen had spent some time organising the war-time price control system and he clearly enjoyed telling us about that. He was also an expert on Japan and gave us an interesting course on pre-war developments there. I had to write a dissertation for my degree and chose the subject 'Government intervention in the coal, cotton and iron and steel industries in the 1930's'. ...

Social life in the University was limited by the war and there was only the occasional evening activity in the Students' Union. Extra-mural activities revolved round the various societies. My main interest was the Music Society, membership of which entitled one to attend rehearsals at the Philharmonic Hall. It was there that I heard performances by many eminent musicians. We also attended some performances free, by becoming programme sellers. In my second year we put on a nativity play in Hall. I sang in the choir and we were trained to a high standard by David Webster, then at the Liverpool Philharmonic and later at Covent Garden. ... One condition of our exemption from national service was that we did voluntary work one day a week. I worked in the children's hospital. Physical training was also compulsory and we had to do first aid and home nursing courses. In the long vacation we were given one month's academic work in the form of essays and we had to do a month's holiday job to assist the war effort. In my case this took the form of working on a fruit farm in Cheshire.

I was awarded my degree in 1945 (call-up of women had ceased in 1944 so that I was able to complete my course). Degree day was July 7. The Chancellor was Lord Derby. He seemed very old and was in a wheel chair so that we did not actually receive our degree from him. We had to bow to him as we passed his wheel chair and then receive the document and handshake from the Vice-Chancellor, Sir Arnold McNair. The cost of all this fell on my father who was an accountant in Birkenhead. The tuition fees were around £20 a term and there was also an annual fee of £5 for the compulsory membership of the Student's Union. The cost of residence at Rankin Hall was about £75 a year. Spending money for books, writing material, fares, lunches, and other expenses, including the very occasional visit to the Playhouse (I saw Laurence Olivier and Vivienne Leigh in *The School for Scandal* amongst other Old Vic productions) was also provided by my father, around £200 a year. This would have been a significant sum for him, and I was always aware that I must be restrained in my spending.

Katherine Jones [Howell], born Birkenhead, Economics 1942-1945, government economist, Secretary of the National Institute of Economic and Social Research 1968-1990, writing from London

My earliest memories of Rankin Hall, of which I believe I am the oldest continuous inhabitant, actually go back further than 1950, when I first became a resident tutor, to the year 1941 and the 'Blitz'. On the night that Lewis's store was burnt out, a landmine fell opposite the front door of Notre Dame Training College, where I lived as an undergraduate, shattering six hundred windows. As a result of this the college was closed and the students despatched to their home towns. I and four other second-year students decided to throw ourselves on the mercy of Miss Amy Buller, the formidable warden of University Hall, then housed in Rankin

Hall, explaining that, as the University had not closed, we had a duty to continue our studies, and that not being sick, infants or aged, we had neither the right nor the desire to leave the stricken city. Miss Buller came to our assistance with great kindness and promptitude by making over to us the then Common Room in House 46, and we gratefully became members of the Hall for the rest of the session.

Although there was a war on, to 'carry on as usual' was the order of the day, and indeed the framework of our daily existence retained much of a pre-war flavour. Members of High Table still changed into long dresses for dinner (Miss Buller devised a very clever divided skirt which enabled her to leap into a siren suit without delay if the air-raid warning should sound), and student guests changed into their best frocks; a Latin grace was sung before and after the meal, as it continued to be until 1970. Conversation could be daunting but was usually interesting, as Miss Buller had an endless fund of anecdotes about the high and mighty who were her personal friends or acquaintances and there was always the chance of encountering some eminent guest. Miss Buller's book *Darkness over Germany* was recounted to colleagues and students long before it saw print after the war, and as we read it we could catch her vibrant tones on every page.

Most of the household chores such as table-laying and washing up were done by students on a rota system. Fire-watching was duty carried out with suitable solemnity, though what would have happened had we ever been put to the test I do not know. The cellars in House 44 had been turned into an air-raid shelter organised with military precision. Rankin students were encouraged to take part in all kinds of assistance, e.g. making sandwiches all night in the kitchens of a hospital, for use the following day in rest centres for air-raid victims. Miss Buller was, of course, the founder and driving force behind the Liverpool University Women's Training Corps. Not all of us appreciated the physical fitness classes at 9.30 a.m. in the gym! Patriotism could be pushed too far.

Lucrezia Alexandra Zaina, born London 1921, French 1939-1943, M.A. 1947, lecturer in French, then lecturer, etc in Italian 1948-1988, extracts from the account in A.R. Allan, ed., Rankin Hall 1922-1972, *Liverpool, 1972*

1930s

We were a small, carefree group of first-year students who entered the Faculty of Arts in October, 1938. We would foregather before and after lectures near the War Memorial in the Victoria Building and talk about the erudition and the idiosyncrasies of our lecturers. On a Saturday evening at hops in Derby Hall we would admire Dr Dorothy Knowles, Lecturer in French, as she executed with her partner complicated steps on the dance floor. Our student group comprised Priscilla Roaf (granddaughter of Sir William Herdman, Professor of successively Natural History, Zoology and Oceanography 1881-1920, daughter of Herbert Eldon Roaf, Professor of Physiology 1932-1944 and sister of Robert Roaf, Professor of Orthopaedic Surgery 1964-1976), Marjorie Ashton, Alice Jones, Henry Burrows, Stewart Sutcliffe (a relative of the cricketer Herbert Sutcliffe who played for Lancashire), Dermot D'Arcy and myself. Marjorie and Alice both played for the University Women's hockey team, and no keener sportswomen were to be found in the Faculty. As might be expected, Stewart played cricket for the University.

We could no longer be called carefree when we all met for the last time in the autumn of 1939, for war had been declared. The men had been interviewed by the Joint Recruiting Council in the University and awaited call-up instructions. Priscilla had volunteered for the W.A.A.F. and was soon scrubbing floors at R.A.F. (Liverpool Airport). Later she became a plotter. Finally, because of her knowledge of German, she was posted with the rank of Flight-Sergeant to the R.A.F.'s new and secret Y Section. She left the W.A.A.F. in 1944 and returned to the Faculty of Arts, to be awarded two years later a Certificate in Social Science. Priscilla and I were married in 1945 and she worked for some time as an assistant to Dr Dennis Chapman, Senior Lecturer in Social Science. ... Stewart was killed during the war; like ourselves, the others resumed their lives and in most cases their studies.

In 1938 the University Officers' Training Corps was affiliated to the Depot of the King's Regiment at Seaforth Barracks, so, as I had been a member of the O.T.C., it was perhaps not surprising that I should join that regiment when I was commissioned in the 13th Battalion in 1940. When the Congress Party grew restless in 1941, Winston Churchill sent the 13th King's and other units to reinforce our troops in India. Shortly after I arrived in India I learned with great sorrow that my brother, Roy Penrose Cottrell, a fourth-year student in the School of Architecture before joining the Royal Naval Volunteer Reserve, had been killed in the Mediterranean, as his ship gave close escort to a convoy proceeding to theo relief of Malta. In May 1942, Brigadier Orde Charles Wingate selected the 13th King's as the British element in the brigade which was to face the Japanese in Northern Burma, and which was later to become known as 'The Chindits'. When ordered to withdraw from Burma in late March 1943, 7 Column, of which I was adjutant, found its withdrawal westward blocked by the enemy at the Irrawaddy River, so turned about and withdrew eastward. After covering 1,500 miles in 110 days, 7 Column reached Paoshan in the Chinese province of Yunnan. The 13th King's lost nearly half their men on this expedition and of those captured fewer than eighty survived.

When I returned to the University in the summer of 1946 to arrange to be re-admitted, I had the good fortune to meet Professor Eggli [French 1920-1946], who welcomed me back most courteously. He was packing his books in tea chests as he was about to retire. I graduated in French Language and Literature in 1949. Has any other student, I wonder, taken as long as eleven years to gain a first degree?

Lesley Rundle Cottrell, French 1938-1939, 1946-1949, Education 1949-1950, M.A. 1959, school-teacher, headmaster 1950-1977, writing from Sheffield

From 1936 I resided in Rankin Hall in Houses 42 and 44. My Professor, Percy Maude Roxby, and another Geography Department Lecturer, S.J. Kenneth Baker, also lived in Rankin Hall. In the Autumn of 1936 several Fresher events were held. At Hostel, the 'Trial' involved (if I recall rightly) running through the grounds, avoiding water and soot, and climbing through a window, all in the dark. Afterwards we were refreshed with hot drinks. The 'Trial' of the Arts Faculty involved, on this occasion, pulling a car round the Victoria Building Quadrangle while being pelted or showered with water and bags of flour from the surrounding buildings, particularly by the Engineers! At the conclusion the car was pulled on to Brownlow Hill. I cannot recall what really happened then, but I do remember that somehow the car caught alight and petrol was running down the tram-lines and burning!

During my first year I roomed with two second-year Medical students. In the second year I was with a Geography Department student and one from the Chemistry Department, both of whom became lifelong friends. In 1938 and 1939 we cycled in France, Germany and Switzerland and walked - and worked in a youth hostel camp - in Norway. At that time I and many of my friends hiked and cycled, hardly any had cars or motor-cycles. ... Huge pots of tea to have with sandwiches were obtainable in pubs and farms. We did little rambling while in Liverpool apart from during vacations, but we had an Open Air Club at Harlech, to which about 30-35 Education-year students were evacuated in September 1939, together with 90 second- and third-year students from the Geography and English departments. Professor Roxby was College Principal, being helped by Miss Marjorie Howden from History - in late 1940 or early 1941 they married, much to the delight of everyone.

From 1936 we undertook most of our private study in our hostel rooms. We each had a desk, a single bed and space for books - the rooms were not particularly spacious but we certainly learned to live together and generally to accept or to put up with any differences. Washing and other facilities were along the corridor or off the landing. I recall with pleasure the deep flat-bottomed bath with an enclosed shower with spray jets from the sides. Breakfast and dinner were served in the panelled dining room in the main house, on long tables. The lecturers and invited guests or senior students sat at High Table; they had their own hot-plate. I found the meals very good and varied though we had numerous comments to make! We spoke of 'granite chips' but the egg-sauce with them and the fish were tasty. We often missed dinner in order to have a full evening's study in the Picton Library in town. Ordered cold suppers were laid out in the dining room; they often included sliced pork-roll of a pink colour vulgarly called 'elephant's tool'! Meals were regaled now and then by the Medics recounting their lurid stories from the anatomy and dissection labs. ...

I recall that on reaching University it was really necessary to be able to dance. I was not very good at this so I and another student (with whom I'm still happily in touch) enrolled in a dancing school near the top of Bold Street - years later I found it still there. The classes cost about 2s 6d, including tea and biscuits! We learned sufficient to enjoy the many dances held over the years in the University. We invited two girls we met there to a University dance. Afterwards we took the girls to their homes at the far end of Scotland Road. By that time we had missed the last tram so we had a long walk back to Hostel, reaching there at about 4 a.m. On one occasion there was a shortage of partners so two or three of us went along to the nearby nurses' home and appealed to the Matron who managed to rouse several girls. I remember one was from Peru and one from Cumbria. Dances were held in the Students' Union, one in Rankin Hall and another in the Women's Hall. For these dances it was necessary to have a dress-suit. Mine was purchased from a family firm in Stoke and it served my purpose until the 1970's; it is now in the City Museum in Hanley!

I was the wrong shape for many sports. However I had been Rugger Captain at school; I continued with rugger at University but never progressed beyond the third team. In 1938 and 1939 I took up rowing. Being fourteen stone, I was number 4 in the eight. Practice was in a tank somewhere in the Docks and by rowing on the Dee at Chester.

Memories of hostel life include a vain attempt one dark night to move the Sefton Park Lake Pirate Ship from its moorings, and going out to sing carols. I recall the practices in no. 46, in the main Common Room, particularly those for the Coventry Carol. I also recall late discussions in our room with young political groups from the City (on one occasion they left after 10 p.m. and as they included a young lady, we received a reproachful comment from Kenneth Baker, our House warden).

Student Societies were many: there were innumerable lectures and many films and events to attend. A glance through my diaries reveals how busy life was. The week beginning 20 November 1938 lists a talk by Professor Allen on Japan, Hostel mass meeting and choir practice, a P.P.U. [Peace Pledge Union] meeting, two Keep Fit classes, a meeting with the Lord Mayor at the Social Service Club, a Peace Council Sub-Committee, a film and talk on China, three thesis discussion sessions, a Birthday Party, rowing at Chester, and the Hostel dance. ... I was on the committee of several societies and was particularly active in those concerned with peace and international relations, as well as being in the Geography Society. The 1938-1939 Geog. Soc. programme included two excursions, Prof.'s Birthday Party, Prof.'s Presidential Address, a Panto Party, a Freshers' Social, Panto Day Display and Procession, collections and sale of the Rag magazine. That year the display included a huge globe and the Society retained the Panto Trophy for the largest per capita collection at £3 1s 7d. I collected £14 12s 4d. I sold *The Rag Mag* in pubs and on the streets, including Lime Street, where I also sold *Peace News*. ... Prof.'s parties always had games and songs, e.g. 'The Last Ichthyosaurus', and others from the Students' Song Book. Prof. enjoyed parties - he was a boy at heart. I recall his entering fully into the spirit when at my 21st in Hostel. ...

September 1939 saw 22 men and about 90 women students evacuated to Coleg Harlech on the Cambrian coast. The scenery across to the Lleyn Peninsula and to Snowdon entranced us at all seasons. Not all were happy, several missing the larger university surroundings and contacts. We who had been in the homely no. 12 Abercromby Square enjoyed the even closer contacts with staff. Besides Prof. and Marjorie Howden, there were Richard Palmer (his wife made tasty jam tarts), Bill Varley between his mysterious disappearances [Editor: later said to be on Secret Service in Occupied Europe], Professor Porteous who dealt with the Principles, History and Philosophy of Education (he tended to talk with his eyes on his notes and failed for a time to spot the exit of certain students through the windows of the Library), Professor Martin of the English Department, who helped me to soften my rather strong Potteries accent, Grace Trenery (one of her asides was 'there are streaks in Bacon'), Florence Laverock who took us for Arts and Crafts (I still have drawings, lino-cuts and a woven scarf), and another member of staff whose name eludes me and who dealt with teaching methods ...

To write about our stay in Harlech really calls for several more pages. Briefly we worked hard; we walked and cycled widely; we enjoyed the late Saturday breakfast of hot buttered toast, honey and tea in the Plas Café; there were eminent visiting lecturers; we attempted Welsh and learned First Aid; we had dances; we helped with evacuated children in the village; we learned and performed an Oratorio; we performed plays; we had our own Students' Union; we men 'enjoyed' wooden-hutted quarters below the college and near the kitchen and dining room; some took a preliminary diploma exam at Easter in case call-up took place before June; four or five of the 22 men registered as CO's [Conscientious Objectors] and appeared before North Wales Tribunal; each was granted exemption. As one of them, I received a packet of white feathers anonymously from North Staffs - these were shared between all the men!

Gilbert L. Marson, born Hanley 1917, Geography 1936-1939, Education 1939-1940, M.A. 1949, school-teacher, then Education officer 1940-1979, writing from Hornchurch

I belong to the select group who failed the 11+ and yet took a first-class Honours degree ... The German Department before the war was in the New Arts Building in Ashton Street, a handsome classical building with good lighting, cork linoleum flooring, central heating and good solid furniture. The German Department looked inward on to the 'quad', and consisted of Professor Collinson's room, a lecture room, and the Class Library, which we shared with the English Language Department. I was Honorary Class Librarian for a year, for which I was paid £5. Also on this floor were the French Department and the Department of Pure Mathematics. Professor Collinson was almost idolised by his students because of his vast knowledge and his great personal kindness. He was a brilliant lecturer, combining weighty erudition with clarity. He was so outstanding as a scholar within his field that the School of German was inevitably rather one-sided, and modern studies were less well served. ...

Among the students were Hannah Schümer, daughter of an anti-Nazi industrialist, later Mrs Connell, who collaborated with Collinson on the Penguin German Dictionary; and Charles Luther D'Aubigny Patterson, from St Lucia, a delightful man and a great personal friend. I asked him, when he took his degree, whether he would return to St Lucia to teach, or stay in this country. He said, 'I am going to the Gambia; I want to help my people'.

I had very little social life at the University; apart from the fact that we were kept *very* busy, I had no money. How I survived financially, in retrospect I do not know. I had a Ministry of Education studentship, which paid my tuition fees and gave me £26 per annum - ten old shillings per week, to cover all other expenses. Living was cheap, but this was very frugal. I often dispensed with lunch, and walked instead of taking the tram. When I had to spend a year in Germany for my Honours degree, the £26 was cut off - it was not intended to be spent outside the U.K. I borrowed £26 from the Vice-Chancellor's Fund, used the savings certificates my mother had bought in my name when I was an infant; and in Leipzig I got work teaching English in the Berlitz School; somehow I got through, but I don't know how. I regret that there was not greater provision for advice and consultation, especially in deciding the direction of further studies. I was awarded a Higher Research Scholarship, which I never took up; in 1939 I could not settle on the right course to follow, while in 1945 I had at last to earn some money, and simply could not afford to accept it. ...

An interesting episode was a piece of work I did for the Department of Physics in 1939. This was the translation of a series of papers which had appeared in *Die Naturwissenschaften* for that year on 'The fragments produced by the splitting of the uranium atom'. Although I translated the papers to the satisfaction of Professor Chadwick and his staff, I had no real idea what they were about until 1945, when, serving in North Germany, I heard the BBC news discussing the Hiroshima bomb, and learned that earlier a device had been exploded in the Californian desert which had vaporised the steel tower which supported it, that the fundamental energy of the universe had been tapped, and that the British research contribution had been centred in Liverpool.

If these were not exactly 'golden years', my time in the Arts Faculty determined the rest of my life, and I remain deeply grateful for all I gained there.

William Alexander Iland, born Liverpool 1914, German 1935-1938, Education 1938-1939, school-teacher 1946-1977, writing from London

When I arrived at University I found that the majority of students in the Arts Faculty appeared to be drawn from the same nearby localities as those of most of the seven taking Honours History - only one of whom lived in Hall. I failed to obtain a scholarship but had a tax free loan, covered by Life Assurance, which met my fees. My parents supported me and gave me an allowance of 10s per week for fares, meals out, etc.

Professor G.S. Veitch was head of the Department of Modern

History. His lectures were often the first in the day at 9.30 a.m. I remember well the occasion when he ceased his lecture in mid-sentence and said, 'I came here to speak to a class not a procession. Good morning.' With those words he picked up his papers and strode out of the room. Professor Coopland was head of the School of Medieval History. His writings tended to be dull if erudite, but I became so absorbed in his lectures that I frequently forgot to make any notes. Mr Routledge was a well-liked and respected lecturer, a specialist in seventeenth-century history if I recollect correctly. The fourth member of staff was a lady, a tutor, whose name escapes me. In the first year I had to follow a course in French to ordinary degree standard. It served me well since the subject of my thesis in Part II was 'The University of Paris in the fifteenth century'. Professor Twemlow instructed us in the mysteries of palaeography. He was the archetype of an absent-minded professor. After replacing a dozen board dusters 'stolen' from the Professor's room, the porter suggested that the room should be searched. The stolen dusters were found locked in the safe where the Professor had put them for safety. The majority of lectures took place in the New Arts Building. There was a History Library in that area but it was little larger than the average classroom and was used more as a common room than as a source of information. Most serious work was done in the Tate or in the Picton Reference Library.

After graduation I moved to the Department of Education, presided over by Professor Campagnac, reputed to choose his students on the advice of his parrot, which was never far away. In the early days we were summoned to have a voice test. I managed to be in pain and was informed that I need not put in another appearance. I learned little of the art of teaching inside Abercromby House but I did learn to appreciate Plato.

I took no active part in Students' Union politics but enjoyed the student life associated with it. In 1933 I joined the Arts group who fought with the Engineers and others over possession of the Doll (the name of which I cannot recall). This was the official (?) commencement of Panto Week. Arts won with a tactic which must be regarded as doubtful. When we got the doll, we passed it into the keeping of the Librarian at the Tate. Even the Engineers did not dare to invade those hallowed precincts! In 1933 and 1934 I took part in the collections for the hospitals, and in the following year I was Business Manager for PANTOSFINX. I sang in the

'Choir' in 1933 when we vacated the Union and moved into Reilly's Cowshed for a year, during which the Union was extended. The 'Cowshed' - formally part of the School of Architecture - was a single-storey building situated roughly where the Cohen Library stands today. I was present when the union debated the motion going around the universities at that time, 'that this House would not fight for King and Country'. I think that the motion lost by a small margin, and I know that two of its supporters were in the Auxiliary Forces before September 1939. Apart from the walking and cycling made essential by a chronic shortage of funds, mixed (very) hockey in winter, tennis in summer, and early morning training with the swimming team in Cornwallis Street Baths provided the bulk of my exercise.

Ernest Smith, born Liverpool 1914, History 1932-1935, Education 1935-1936, M.A. 1939, school-teacher, headmaster 1936-1940, 1946-1978, writing from Liverpool

In 1929-1933 the School of Geography was in Abercromby Square, next to the School of Archaeology, which at that time was in a much larger building. I was told by a student that in Archaeology there were six professors and about three students altogether - most being concerned with excavation in Jericho. Next door, in the School of Geography we had less palatial surroundings. It was typical of a town house, with rooms on one side and a staircase on the other. The front room held some bookcases and was used as a library. Behind that was a small room, and then behind that an annexe which was the Map Room, with high wooden desks, about four in number, each able to take one person with large maps. Finally there was a small garden beyond, in which was installed the rain-gauge and other weather recording instruments. On the first floor was the main lecture room and a smaller lecture room, with rooms for individual lecturers. I think Professor Roxby's study must have been on the second floor above the lecture room. One room up there had sloping attic roofs and was used by students and lecturers, especially when it came to thesis time.

In my period the whole School consisted of 36 students, including some postgraduates. Our own year started with 32 applicants for places, out of which seven were chosen in the first term and two, myself and one other, in the second term. The entry was by means of an examination at the end of the term, and in my case my Professor explained to me that mere knowledge was of no use, it had to be shown to be logical and to be properly displayed. He was helpful and kind and I managed to enter the School at the second attempt. Our subjects were, of course, Geography in the main, with compulsory French because our set books were mainly in French. Compulsory French lasted for one year but we continued with History and Economics for two years. The first-year course in Geography, which was of great importance and embodied the whole of Professor Roxby's teaching, was based on Vidal de la Blache's book on the *pays*. Fortunately there was an English translation of the first part of the book which enabled us to understand the gist of it and I fear that none of us read the whole book. The course was based on this, and we learned of the relationship between geology, soil, climate, trade and agriculture, with regional differences in architecture and customs springing from the natural environment and cultural contacts. ... As far as Britain was concerned, he would develop his theme with generous quotations from living authors, past poets, etc. I remember in particular when referring to Asia how he quoted Matthew Arnold's 'Sohrab and Rustum', and on Yorkshire he cited J.B. Priestley. The course itself was a great widener of education and has given me, for the rest of my life unending various interests.

In the second year, we had Course B, which was on the movement of peoples and the beginning of nations, and gave a general summary of the world as we know it, its geology, climatic regions, trade routes, migration routes, etc. In the third year we had to write a thesis and we had our best loved course, one on China and the Far East, a subject on which Professor Roxby was an authority. It is sad that he appears not to have written books on the subject. A number of Chinese scholars, however, came to Liverpool and we benefitted from talks given by these men.

In addition to these three courses which were taken by Professor Roxby himself, we had courses on economic geography from Mr Smith, on historical geography from Mr Baker, and work with plane tables, etc, with Miss Winchester. We also went across to the Geology Department where Professor Read lectured to us on geomorphology. It was a pity that between the very greatly extended lectures which Professor Roxby gave us and the lecture on Geomorphology there was no time to eat, and we had a horrible habit of buying peanuts and littering the floor of the Geology lecture room with shells, a habit to which Professor Read quite rightly objected. Professor Veitch taught us history in the Arts Building and we were also taught economics over in the Social Sciences Department. Our French lectures were in the Arts Building, with a secondary lecture by the French tutors of the time, young women of our own age, which we enjoyed more. The French lecturer had a great scorn for the English use of their own language and I remember vividly some poor student being held up to ridicule for saying that he took a morning bath. The French lecturer, who admitted that he had not been as long in Britain as the student, neverthless insisted that it should have been 'matutinal ablutions'. This man had a habit of spitting out his s's to such an extent that when a new acquaintance told me, many years later, that she had had a French lecturer in protection from whom she had donned a sou'wester hat, I gave the poor man's name and it turned out to be the same person. I am afraid that the young in those days too were unkind. ...

In addition to his lectures, Professor Roxby took us on occasions into the country to see geological formations, the petrified forests on the coast, geology in Frodsham, and, in the summer, Helvellyn and the Peak District. ... He was completely unaware of the effect he had on anybody, and I remember that once he stopped us in our walk along a country path in Ireland when we came across a group of very poor gipsies whom he immediately began to lecture on, much as if they had been a whole family of waxworks, to their entire astonishment but courteous acceptance. I suppose in our second year we were still very young, and Professor Roxby, who seemed to be terrified of womenkind in general, was heartily relieved at the horseplay that we preferred to indulge in, rather than any romantic episodes.

The family aspect of the School of Geography was reflected in our communal lunches. Most of us had about £1 per week for spending money. To give some idea what a £1 would do, we could buy a pair of court shoes for 10s. In the Union we could buy a main course for 9d (that would be a meat and two vegetables), soup for 3d, coffee for 2d, sweet for 3d, but this was too expensive for us and we managed to buy 4d or 4½d lunches for ourselves. This meant that one would go up to Mulberry

Street to a cheap little grocer's shop on the corner, and buy an unspeakable bright pink brawn, some fresh white bread, and margarine or New Zealand butter. When we were fairly 'flush', we would buy some bananas and some condensed milk to make a horrible mush, which to some tasted delicious. It took us nearly six months to save a few odd pennies from the change of our 4½d, and with these pennies we eventually bought a dozen lead spoons. On the first day that we were going to use them, one of our practical jokers, whom we didn't easily forgive, twisted each spoon into a knot and hung it on a line across the table.

Another piece of mischief was the use of the water from the rain-gauge in the garden to tone down the paint we used to colour maps. From time to time one or other of us would have a guilty conscience and refill the rain-gauge. This ultimately resulted, to our great shame, in an article by Miss Winchester, who was in charge of the weather station, written in *The Geographical Magazine*, on 'the peculiar weather of 1932'. Our lectures amounted to eleven hours per week and as there were no set books and practically no library we spent most of our time at the Picton Library in town. Here we could gather information from articles and chapters in various books, and collate the material for our essays. On these visits, the height of extravagance was a poached egg with cheese at a tiny cafe on the edge of Lime Street Station, and we would survive the day with this until closing time at the Picton at 9.30 p.m., when we would start walking towards the hostel, getting a tram if possible, and stopping at a chip shop for 2d worth of chips. This would give us an enormous parcel to take home for our evening meal. Occasionally we would go into Coopers for some flamboyant ice cream which we found needed a subsequent penny cob [bun] from the counter to enable us to digest the kaleidoscope of colour and taste which we had so recently absorbed. ...

In about 1930, Professor Hetherington, our Vice-Chancellor, told a meeting of freshers in the women's residential hall at Holly Road that they would gain much from each other and that time spent talking over cups of coffee and cocoa would not be wasted. I heard about five or six years later, but was unable to verify it, that students were now importing glasses instead of cheap crockery and that drinks of alcohol, etc, were more fashionable than coffee and the unspeakable old-fashioned cup of cocoa. ... Unpleasantness occurred at the various 'hops' (as we called our small dances) when the men would go out to the nearby pubs and come back distinctly the worse for wear, while the girls were expected to continue dancing and enjoying the evening. It appeared that not just our own School of Geography but the general feel of the University was growing against the unpleasantness and the dangers of alcoholism. When Frank Kerr and Mary Shone became President and Lady President the whole problem arose in Guild meetings. An end was made to the pass-out tickets which enabled men to go out to the pubs and come back into dances - whether in all dances or only in a few I don't remember. It was also at this time that we were discussing the plans for a new Union, and a later President and a friend proposed and seconded a scheme for a bar providing drinks, in particular wine which we could have with our meals, and the other members of the Guild vetoed it. It was again at this time that the kitchen supervisor found that there were small bottles of milk available, I think ⅓ of a pint, and put them up for sale in the Union canteen which was at that time in the old architects department called 'Reilly's Cowshed', one large dining room for both male and female students. The rugby captain and soccer captain decided that this was a good thing for their team members, and drinking milk at lunch time became quite popular.

About this time, following Oxford and Cambridge, there was considerable interest in 'King and Country' debates, at which pacifists argued as to whether they would or would not fight for king and country if a war broke out. In the university, pacifist sympathies were strong. We published a Panto *Sphinx* in which there was a very good cartoon showing a schoolboy amongst skulls and crosses. The *Sphinx* was banned by the City Fathers but this of course made it an immediate success in terms of sales. We were astonished at the anger with which it was received by the public. I suppose that both the pacifism and the attempt to control alcoholism arose from the background of orthodox religion which most of us experienced as we grew up. We argued about our beliefs, and they appeared to be rather tenuous at the time, but we went to international services at the cathedral. Evangelical Union and Student Christian Movement societies held their own, even though they did not flourish. All in all, life must have been much simpler for us, with fewer choices in our social activities, and with a taught background of religious principle which translated into simple moral codes of behaviour. Sex was a risky affair and not likely to be entered into casually. However, apart from parental and church influence, probably another factor was that of having very small grants and very little money so that our economic situation limited the excitement.

In our day the privileges of the Union were very jealously guarded by the students. Unless lecturers and professors were old students they could not enter the Union buildings, except presumably by special invitation. The Union was controlled by administrative staff with remarkable tact and patience, and run by different committees, with students as the secretaries and chairmen. I was given the post of Kitchen Secretary. This turned out to be extremely interesting although I knew nothing whatsoever about catering or administering staff. For the first time a manageress was appointed who had been trained at the Colquitt Street Domestic Science School, and she was young, lively and imaginative. She produced good meals, she managed to keep them cheap, and it was she who introduced to the Union the idea of small bottles of milk. ...

At this time I wrote to all the universities and university colleges then in the U.K, in order to find out how much their student unions were spending, how they controlled their committees, and so on, and in every case was informed that the matter was not in the hands of students. We were very proud when we realised that we were then the only university where students were running their own affairs. We of course ignored the fact that it was our very able though small administrative staff that was really running the Union on our behalf. I think the experience of trying to run things ourselves was very valuable to us in later life.

In 1933-1934 I became Secretary of a new International Society. The first thing I did was to see all the wealthier and more popular foreign students, Indian, Egyptian, Persian, etc, and I asked them to assist me in putting the International Society on a firm footing so that it was a smart thing to join. They readily agreed to support any event which I could launch. I had joined the School of Social Science. (I had been frank with Professor Carr-Saunders and told him that it was simply in order to have a further year. I was not prepared to study education since a career in teaching would require me to challenge the apparent colour bar.) Professor Carr-Saunders was very sympathetic and actually took me down to the ground floor of the Social Science building and showed me a delightful small room with chintz curtains and white paint, copper kettle and tea set, which I could have for my exclusive use when I found students who needed to sit and talk. We did not use it very much in the event but I was most touched with this assistance.

The programme was planned so that there were lectures, dances, picnics, etc. for everyone. There were special evenings for different nationalities but we were able to go as a group to a Quaker evening held every second Tuesday in their premises. This, however, was not very satisfactory as it was swamped with Esperantists who did not realise that their particular language was of little use to Chinese, Indian or Egyptian students. We contacted various firms in Liverpool and suggested that international trade could be assisted to their advantage if they invited us for tea, biscuits, and an inspection of their factories. This worked very happily. ...

During the summer, we got to know the foreign students quite well. There were only 140 at the time and we were considerably helped by a Mr and Mrs Scott, friends of Professor Roxby, who invited us in groups to their house. One day two of the group, a Persian and I think a Chinese, approached me and told me that the hostel which had been set aside for foreign students was a very unpleasant place to live in. The then warden appeared to be a respectable man until he was drunk, when he would call them yellow pigs. I went to see the Registrar and was sent immediately to the Vice-Chancellor. It didn't take me many words to explain what had happened and he was most courteous. The warden of the hostel was dismissed that same night.

Leta Jones, Geography 1929-1933, Social Studies 1933-1934, writing from Wrexham

1920s

During my pre-admission interviews I met Dorothy Swift, whose home was an isolated Staffordshire farm, when she was retrieving her umbrella from a chair on which my mother was sitting - the first of several coincidences from which lifelong relationships sprang. We went together to see Miss Chapman, Principal of University Hall, who later allocated a double room in the house, 289 Edge Lane, situated in a corner of the grounds overlooking the Botanical Gardens - I believe it has now been demolished. There was a reminder of home for Dorothy in the verse I wrote for the Hall Magazine (with apologies to Thomas Gray):-

Botanic tolls the bell of parting day,
The bleating sheep wind slowly down Edge Lane,
The students Hallward plod their weary way
And leave the world to darkness - and to rain.

For the next three years we shared a double room in Herdman Wing, chosen by us because of its reputation for an almost inexhaustible supply of hot water! ...

Miss Dorothy Chapman, whose headquarters in Holt Wing included a tasteful sitting room-cum-office, deserves a special mention. She was a tall, sylph-like figure of quiet dignity, regarded with respect and affection. Taking turns at dining 'high' was considered by the students as a privilege, and those who were fond of music had the occasional bonus of accompanying her to Philharmonic Subscription concerts for which she had a spare supply of tickets. The rules of Hall were few and effective, including the need for late leave after 10.30 p.m., and strictly silent hours for study from 8.00 p.m. to 10.00 p.m. We were allowed to invite male students for the three annual dances, Carol, Hall and Flannel, and also for small tea-dances arranged by the students themselves. I used to feel that residence in a Hall added another dimension to one's education - preparing one for life in society (with a small 's'), and that students who lived at home missed some of this benefit.

Subject-based student societies helped to fill the above-mentioned gap by providing both educational and leisure activities. In the English Society there were debates, play-readings supervised by a tutor, and various social gatherings. I took a music course as an optional extra subject, but it appeared to be in an embryonic stage - mainly easy class-choir works and elementary theory. However, membership of the Music Society from all Faculties provided free admission to the rehearsals (every other Tuesday afternoon during the season) of subscription concerts given by the Liverpool Philharmonic Society. Only ten male and ten female students were permitted to attend at any one rehearsal. Residents in Hall had an advantage as Mary Mitchell, the conductor of Hall Choir, was the student in charge of the notice to be pinned on the wall board in the Victoria Building. Thus we were able after breakfast to follow her (at a discreet distance) and ensure our places on the list.

The students of English used their Class Library and the Tate Library in the Victoria Building. 'Going to the Tate' was to me a solemn act, not to be undertaken lightly, as its size, elaborate decor (compared with the plainer architecture of the New Arts Building) and the realisation of the quantity and quality of knowledge stored on its shelves, filled me with awe - not lessened should the silence be broken. A dropped pen could create the effect of a gunshot! ...

W.D. Goodman, B.Sc. (Hons. Physics), M.Sc. ... Suffice it to say that after the separations and vicissitudes of the Second World War we were married - on Panto Day! By this time the latter event had been moved from cold winter to the month of May. The wedding breakfast was held in Reece's Restaurant (where I had lunched on my first Panto Day). The Faculty of Arts was well represented, including my friends Dorothy and Phyllis as bridesmaids. The fates were unkind to the Procession which received a soaking in a continuous heavy downpour in the afternoon. By then the happy couple had escaped to the sunshine of Wales. Our subsequent years proved that Arts and Science can live contentedly together, being both supplementary and complementary to each other.

Mrs Constance Gwendolen Goodman [Haigh], born Burton-on-Trent 1908, English 1927-1930, and Education 1930-1931, school-teacher Liverpool 1931-1947, writing from Coventry

It was my honest opinion at the time, though I was careful to keep it secret, that the food provided at Rankin Hall was quite palatable. The fashion, however, was to hold otherwise. Before dinner the gowned students, at the ready in the entrance hall, inevitably chanted the refrain: 'Waiting, waiting, waiting, always bloody-well waiting!' And when Mr Angus, at the High Table (at the opposite end of the dining-room from the present one) in due course pronounced the grace, 'For what we are about to receive', the standard response from the students was, 'Oh God!'

We had a magazine entitled *The Blue Pigeon*, and there was a ritual at dances, smokers and the like, in which, to the alternate raising of both arms above the head and bending forward to touch one's toes, one chanted 'Three Blue Pigeons', ending with a Prolonged 'sh-h-h!', which was presumably meant to indicate that the birds were flying away. Smoking concerts one remembers in general as feasts of wit, and in detail as fairly banal. At the first of the year, freshmen underwent an indoctrination of mild humiliation, including the compulsory smoking of a dubious cigar. At most of them the legendary Professor Roxby was prevailed upon to give his famous impression of a shy small child reciting 'Mary had a little lamb' before guests under parental compulsion. There was invariably a great deal of noise, shouting and singing, but I recollect no rowdyism and only a very tolerable level of vulgarity.

Many memories flash into one's mind and it would be tempting to dwell on them given the time and the space. Some should at least be mentioned: the spells of conscience - or masochism - that from time to time forced one out of bed for the stimulating torment of a run round Sefton Park Lake before breakfast; the occasional sprints to the Croxteth Road tram terminus to catch a no. 15 to the end of Bedford Street, and the more frequent and thrifty walks to no. 46 in which one could profit from one's misspent youth; the blessed last resort when one was broke of being able to lunch at Rankin and have it put on one's bill, even if it entailed walking from the University to Ullet Road and back again in the middle of the day, and the tempting jugs of barley-water set out on warm summer evenings which were generally believed not only to slake the thirst of parched young men, but also to include a secret and sinister medicinal ingredient guaranteed to impel even the most lethargic into motion.

William Barker, later Sir William Barker, Russian 1927-1930, diplomatic service, eventually H.M. Minister to the U.S.S.R., Professor of Russian 1969-1976, extracts from the account in A.R. Allan, ed., Rankin Hall 1922-1972, *Liverpool, 1972*

My first contact with the Faculty of Arts was when I was interviewed by that wonderful man, Professor Campagnac. ... I was successful and did the educational year at Abercromby House, and thoroughly enjoyed the lectures given by Campagnac and his staff. At the first lecture on the History of Education, the speaker implored us to form a habit of keeping notes in a booklet as our memories would deteriorate in time. This I commenced to do and my current book is marked F6, the sixth notebook of the sixth series i.e. my 162nd notebook. Some years later, I applied to do research and was interviewed by Professor Collinson. I did not know at the time that Collinson was the John Buchanan lecturer in Esperanto. ... A few years later, I became interested in Esperanto and got to know Collinson personally, and have been an enthusiastic student of the language ever since.

Norman Williams, born Liverpool 1908, Physics 1927-1930, Education 1930-1931, school-teacher, headmaster 1941-1970, writing from Manchester

I was a student of Professor Roxby's Honours School of Geography and the Department of Education. Abercromby Square was not yet surrounded by University buildings, so we had no access to the Square. Geography was in no. 10, with Egyptology next door. Some of the houses were privately occupied. ... In 1927 or early 1928 Miss Winchester succeeded in installing a Stevenson Screen and its accompanying thermometers and rain gauge. I became the Weather Man, making daily observations and sparking an interest which is still strong today. Early in 1928 we had a 'cold snap' with temperatures of 20° F (postively balmy by Eastern Canada winters!). I was in the habit of walking to no. 10 each morning, joining some friends on the way. In the middle of the cold spell the Indian member of the group appeared with overcoat buttoned up, and a university scarf wrapped around and over his head, the whole outfit topped by his hat. This kept us happy for days. ... My extra activities were S.C.M. [Student Christian Movement], where I landed up as Student Verger in 1929-1930. ... We were all poor. Many, myself included, received £26 annually as Education students, and yet we scrounged and saved to join an Easter (2-3 weeks) Geography trip to Brittany in 1928. Each term we had a trip to a nearby source of geographical interest, always ending in a tea and singsong. As far as I can gather, many of our 1926-1929 group are 'passed on'. I still soldier on into my 90th year.

Alfred Douglas Jones, born Liverpool 1907, Geography 1926-1929, Education 1929-1930, writing from Brockville, Ontario, Canada

(a) Life was not easy in the poverty-stricken '20s and '30s. I met my Varsity fees by having a loan from the local Council and and the rest from my parents. I travelled daily by tram-car to the Varsity, even going home for lunch as I could not afford to eat out. Student life in those days meant constant serious study ... The routine was a very sober Puritanical one and students were highly respected. ... After sixty-five applications I became an assistant master ... I had met Margaret Riding at Liverpool Varsity in 1928 and we married in 1935. My wife and I still remember the balcony in the Victoria Building where we had many an interesting chat. We'll always be indebted to our University which launched us into long successful careers, and a happy married life.

(b) How I hated the 12 noon lectures! I left before 8 a.m. to travel from Ormskirk, so by 12.30 I was ravenous. But Prof. Roxby was immersed in e.g. China, so time had no significance for him. Education Department - comments better left out. P.S. Our house is named after the Varsity courts at Wyncote.

(a) William Killen, born Bootle 1908, Ordinary 1926-1929, Education 1929-1930, school-teacher 1930-1942, 1946-1987 (at the same school); (b) Mrs Margaret E. Killen [Riding], Ordinary 1928-1931, Education 1931-1932, school-teacher 1933-1935, 1940-1974; writing from Chatham

At the beginning of October 1925, with an 'Intending Teacher Scholarship', I became a student in the Faculty of Arts and was accepted provisionally into the Honours History School. For intending teachers there were no fees and we had a grant of £26 per year, supplemented in my case by a three-year scholarship from my old school, worth an annual £25. The University was approached from town either by Browlow Hill or by London Road, the former then a poor residential area, the latter lined with shops, large and small. The University buildings varied from the purpose-built to the adapted, and Abercromby Square was the most attractive area, where the Education Department faced Geography across the centre garden, at that time reserved for the private residents who had keys. The buildings were clean and warm, and I remember no graffiti and very little carving of initials on desks or seats. In the cloakrooms one could safely leave coats, bags, cases; to my knowledge there was only one incident of pocket thieving in my four years there.

In the Arts Faculty lectures began at 9.30 am and lasted about fifty minutes; the last was normally at 4.30 pm. In the History Department the professors and lecturers were somewhat remote and formal, and tutorials and interviews were few. Professor Veitch was not a particularly good lecturer but he did each year entertain the History students at his house, as did Mr Routledge, one of our lecturers. The best lecturer by far was Professor Coopland on Medieval History. Of the ladies, Miss Lackland would sweep in, gown flying, already talking and the flow continued unabated as she departed. Miss Howden would come in quietly, present her better profile to the class and softly murmur her medievalisms. Garmon Jones, a charming man, was also Dean of Arts and lectured on Tudor History. There was only one really poor lecturer, an unfortunate young man who taught a course in Social and Economic History; he was the dullest of the dull and the students simply chatted quietly to each other. In my third year I took a course in Historical Geography with Professor Roxby, an enthusiastic and delightful lecturer who looked like a primitive man! My fourth year was in the Education Department for the Diploma; here Professor Campagnac presided. He took great pride in the building and students were enjoined to move about quietly and carefully, which we invariably did.

The students I knew could afford few books and we used the libraries a great deal, including the Picton in town. The main library was the Tate where could be seen, moving with slow tread to and from his office there, the corpulent and white-haired John Sampson. The departmental libraries were well used but only rarely were the books one needed unavailable, for the number of students was small by today's standards.

Students were soberly dressed, blazers and sports jackets were rare, but some architects wore plus fours and the women supplied a little colour to a rather drab scene! We addressed each other rather formally unless with particular friends. Most of us came in daily from a region bounded roughly by Southport and the Wirral to the west, Bolton to the east, Preston to the north and Warrington and Widnes to the south. Consequently student life, except for the few hostel residents, was rather different from that in the modern residential university. One's contacts were confined very much to the Students' Union, strictly segregated, with on the men's side, a ground floor lounge, first floor dining room (for the more affluent), second floor coffee room, very popular and crowded at lunch time, and in the basement a billiard and snooker room. Over the Union presided the dignified head porter, Mr Wright, with his assistant, Mr Tanner. The most popular foods in the coffee room were pies, chips, buns and cakes, with the usual beverages, but no alcohol. Prices were low and in the dining room reasonable.

The first University event I recollect was the memorial service for the late Vice-Chancellor, held in the Anglican Cathedral and attended by a large congregation of staff, students and others. His successor was Professor Hetherington from Scotland, for whose arrival a song was offered by two students, Ellis and Roberts, who often performed as a duet. The chorus of their song was:

Hoots man, the brainy Prof.
Och hie and his haggis,
He wears a sporran and a dirk
An' a kilt instead of baggies.

It was generally understood that Professor Hetherington was *not* amused. Ellis (English) and Roberts (Geography) sometimes performed at the coffee room piano after lunch, but more often this chair was occupied by Kitchen (Science), an excellent jazz pianist as he might be called today, who for half an hour or so would improvise on the popular dance tunes of the time. In the lounge would be seen a few pairs intent on chess games, but the room was rarely crowded; for most students it was lectures, libraries, laboratories and home. After 5.30 p.m. the University and the Union were almost deserted. There were occasional tea-dances held in the coffee room from 5.30 pm to 7.00 pm, rarely well patronised by men, with music supplied by some student band. In the Arts Building the various societies sometimes had meetings at 5.30 pm, with tea and cakes followed by a short talk and discussion. Few commuters supported these activities which were almost wholly organised by resident and local students. I was rather an exception as I was regularly in - often buying the student magazine, the *Sphinx*, to which I contributed the odd item, under a pen name!

Wednesday afternoons were generally free, and sporting activities took place at Wyncote, as they did on Saturdays, but once again commuters had little part in this. Most went home, though I rarely did so, spending the time in a library, sometimes going up to Wyncote or, when funds allowed, attending some tea-dance in town, for this was still the 'Dancing Twenties'. But most students preferred the cinema matinees.

An important annual occasion was Rag Day, or Panto Day as it was known at the time, because the hospital collection was ended at the Empire Pantomime, when some student turns were included in the show. Men collected in fancy dress of all kinds, the women in cap and gown. However the pantomime tradition came to an end after the occasion when George Robey was shouted off the stage and the stalls were deluged in flour bombs. The Guild had to pay the cost of the damage, of course. The effigy 'Sister Jane' (named after the character in the Freshers' Song) was awarded to the Faculty which had collected most on the day and was handed over to the winners usually in the Quad, whereupon a small mob of students fought over possession of the trophy. Victory was signalled by getting the doll into your department; the contestants were usually Rugby enthusiasts suitably clad for the fray and the usual winners were the Engineers. In spite of this frivolity, on the whole I would say we were a conscientious and hardworking body.

I enjoyed those years from 1925 to 1929. Coming from a smaller town and from a somewhat narrow background, I certainly gained much from the experience. A residential education would no doubt have added to it, but travelling daily saved one from an 'ivory tower' outlook and maintained contact with one's roots. As Professor Coopland used to say, 'Walking up Brownlow Hill every day keeps you students in touch with reality'.

[Postscript: from a letter to the editor of 29.8.1996] At the age of 90, I have many happy recollections of my time as a History Student and, as is usual, looking back over the years, the Victoria Building seems in my mind to have been always bathed in sunshine, though I know the reality was somewhat different!

Charles Lowe, born Wigan 1906, History 1925-1928, Education 1928-1929, M.A. 1934, school-teacher 1930-1940, 1946-1970, writing from Wigan

1910s

I became a student at the University of Liverpool in October 1912. In my first few days I went to the University Book Shop which conducted business either on the ground floor of or in a shed attached to a building that remains in my memory as a rectangular block of blackened stone in pouring rain - which is odd, for I must often have seen it in fair weather. I had then no idea of its historical importance, but it was the lunatic asylum that originally housed University College, Liverpool. It stood in the quadrangle, near the doorway to the New Arts Building, which was already going up on Ashton Street. I have no recollection of its demolition. This probably took place in the Christmas vacation in 1913-1914 for, if I remember right, classes moved into the New Arts Building in January 1914 before the official opening in May 1914.

During the session 1913-1914 I read a course in Economics. Lectures were given by Mr Macdonald in a room on the first floor of this old building. The room was overheated by an open coal fire which Mr Macdonald kept generously stoked from a well-filled open scuttle. The room was dusty and had a peculiar smell, compounded I suppose of rotting timbers and dirt. The fire risk must have been appallingly high. ... Mr Cecil Sharpe, collector of folk songs and pioneer of folk dancing, came to give a lecture to students. He was allotted a first floor room in the asylum. Fired by his enthusiasm, some of us announced our intention of starting a Folk Dance Society. He responded by teaching us on the spot the dance 'Gathering Peascods'. This energetic dance proved to be too much for the old structure, and we literally went through the floor. I recall no repercussions from this damage to fabric, but when Mr Roxby returned from his Travelling Fellowship adventures in China, he called a meeting of *all* students of Geography at the beginning of Session 1913-1914 and we met in this room with Mr Roxby on one side of the gap in the floor and we students on the other.

It was not only the fabric of the University College that remained in 1912. If Lady Stocks deplored the amenities for women staff in the 1930s, she should have experienced the lot of women students in my first term. The Victoria Building on the first floor ended in a wall just beyond the Clock Tower stairs to the Old Arts Theatre. Opening off the balcony that extended from here to the stairs leading up to the Tate Library was the Women's Common Room. It had a coal fire and some dilapidated easy chairs. Around 3.30 p.m. a very old lady, as a purely private routine, sold cups of tea at 2d a cup. There was no provision of a rest room or a sick bay. Our cloak room was the balcony rail, which was always draped with our coats and macintoshes and hats - and every woman student wore a hat. These hats tended to slide down into the Victoria Hall, then not a thoroughfare but the stamping ground of men students. When a hat fell, some man, during a temporary absence from Victoria Hall of Parrington, the Head Porter, would pick it up, scale the life-size statue of Christopher Bushell that stood in the Hall on a high plinth and place the hat on its head, where it remained until the owner could persuade Parrington to fetch his step ladder and rescue it. The New Liverpool University Students' Songbook of 1913 had a brief Spanish song to which were set the English words:-

> If I meet you on the balcony
> Please will you cast a glance my way?

This referred to 'balconising', an activity indulged in by students of advanced 'ideas'. A man came up from Victoria Hall and conversed with a woman leaning on the balcony rail at the foot of the stairs to the Tate. Scandal making and not done by the best people!

In January 1913 the women entered into possession of their half of the first Students' Union. Theoretically the Men's Union and the Women's Union were separate entities divided by the Gilmour Hall. In the entrance hall of the women's side sat Mrs White, usually engaged on our mending which she did for small fees. If a woman wished to speak to a man, e.g. on Society business, she gave his name to Mrs White who took it to Wright, the ex-naval man who was steward of the men's side. When Wright had located the man he informed Mrs White and the man and woman were then allowed into the Gilmour Hall where they conversed with both doors open so that Mrs White and Wright could see that propriety was maintained.

Theory soon ceased to be practice, for other things were changing. Women no longer had the so-called Refectory. This was a dismal room in a house in Bedford Street where hot milk drinks and sad-looking buns were the only fare. It was little patronised and of course it disappeared when we had our dining room in our Union. There was also a room where one could dine with a man on the men's side!

In my first term I was admitted to the practice team of hockey for the elevens. Our playing field was at Knotty Ash. We went by tram to the terminus at Knotty Ash and walked by field paths to a small farm where we changed into boots and into skirts so scandalously short that they fell only to our calves. The fascinating feature of our changing room was a wall map, framed, of *The Straight and Narrow Way and the Primrose Path that leadeth to Destruction*. Eschewing drink, cards, dances, and theatres, the righteous could arrive almost at the Gates of Heaven and then by taking a Sunday train arrive after all in the very jaws of Hell! In January 1913 both men and women moved to new playing fields at Calderstones Park. Here we shared a tea room. It soon became possible to arrange to catch specific trams so that men and women could travel together to the grounds. And it became fashionable in the summer term for men and women to walk down to Penny Lane along Menlove Avenue, inspecting in some detail the progress of houses rising there.

The library at the top of the Men's Union was used jointly by men and women for meetings like Mass Meetings, Sing Songs, and rehearsals of plays. And here too we held Informal Dances. Dress was not informal and we had dance programmes on which men asked for the honour of inscribing their names as partners. But to dance more than twice with one partner was frowned on. We were chaperoned by the wives of Senate and staff and they generally brought their husbands. As their programmes had to be filled with partners this became a very pleasant way for Staff and Students to meet. The dances had a small orchestra and there was always a sit-down meal in the Men's dining room. And the cost - believe it or not, one shilling and sixpence! There was no doubt about it - University College was dead and its lingering traditions were dying fast.

Mrs Edna Rideout [Leach], born Rochdale 1893, Modern History 1912-1915, Education 1915-1916, from an account written in 1976 for the University history, which cited a few sentences

In 1912, the Victoria Building had been occupied for twenty years: the first members of the University to move over from the Old Building in the quadrangle must have felt that their feet were set in a large room, but by present standards of accommodation it was a miniature. Yet it had to house central administration, quarters for corporate student life, the university library, and a place of assembly to be used on ceremonial occasions - all these, as well as lecture rooms and class libraries for the Arts Faculty. The other buildings round the quad - those devoted to biology, chemistry, engineering, medicine and physics - had, of course, their own clerical and common rooms. The Victoria Hall on the ground floor of the Victoria Building, with the room down a few steps at the eastern end, was in 1912 the common room of men students, while women had two rooms on the balcony above. However, for meetings of societies, Christmas soirées and so forth, the whole of the accommodation was made available to both. The gallery round the hall was at all times common ground, and the niche framed by the ceiling, two columns and a balustrade was surprisingly convenient for private conversation - hence the term 'balconising'. The wide staircase with its shallow risers was another place of concourse.

As one entered the Victoria Hall by the main entrance, the corridor on the left divided the space unequally between smaller rooms for administration (facing Brownlow Hill) and lecture rooms (facing the quad). The Registrar, Mr Carey, had the first office. Himself a law graduate of the University, and formerly a student leader, he was a friend and counsellor to the Students' Union, and was particularly interested in student debate; however, though his manner spoke benevolence, he never wasted words. Beyond his room was that of the Vice-Chancellor, Sir Alfred Dale. He was mainly seen on ceremonial occasions, but his character was known and felt throughout. At the height of the militant suffragette campaign, a woman student [Margaret Ker], the daughter of a pioneer woman doctor, set fire to a post-box; she was arrested and taken into custody. It was no surprise to anyone when Sir Alfred visited her in prison, taking with him some of the books she needed to continue her work. ...

The plan of the first floor was similar to that below. The large lecture room on this floor was used for English Literature and Modern History, and the professors of Mathematics, Latin and Greek had their private rooms opposite. I believe the History Class Library adjoined them.

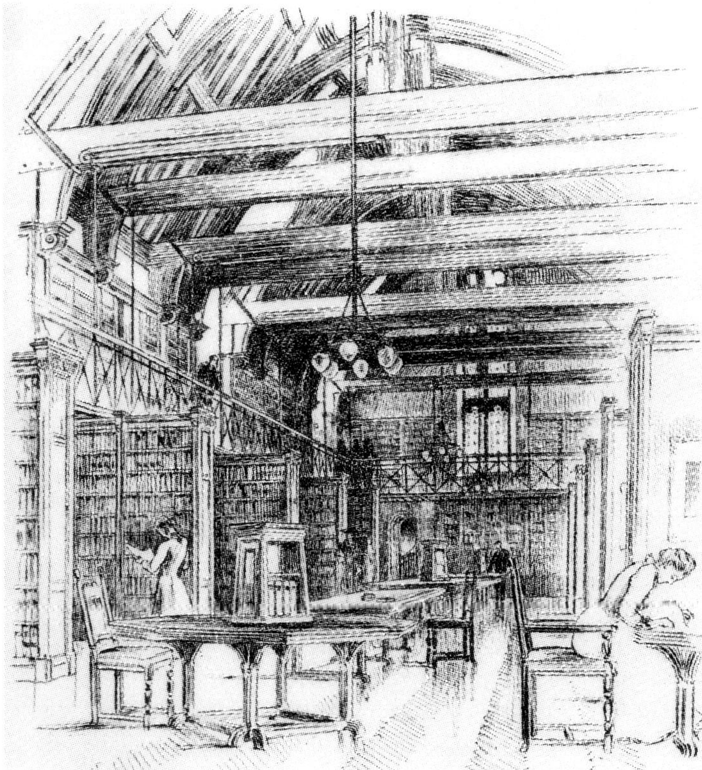

The Tate Library in 1892

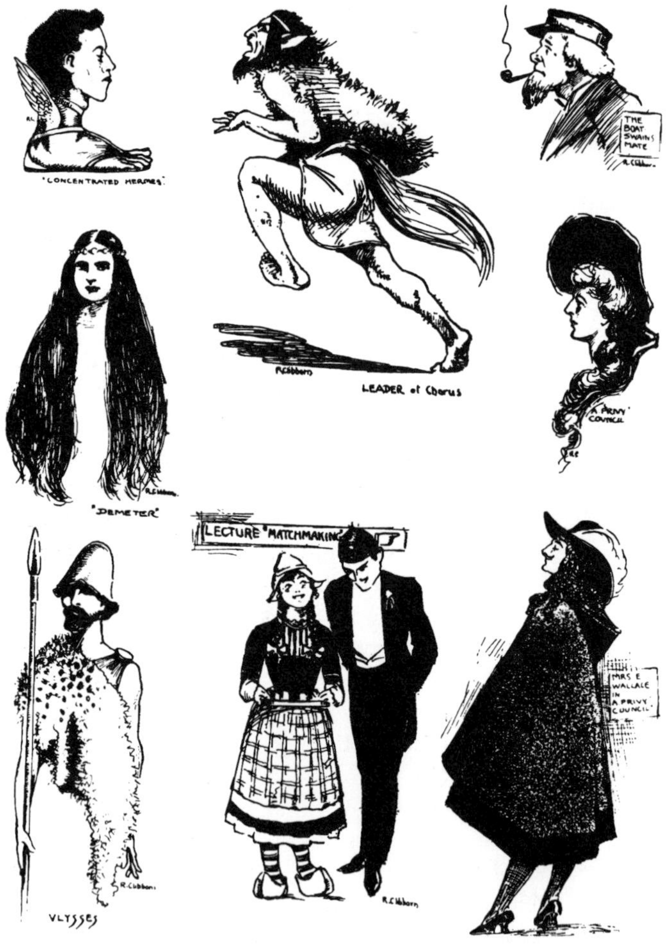

Scenes from tableaux at a students' 'Soirée' in 1909

Drawing from *The Sphinx*

What other quarters were allocated to members of staff, I did not ask at the time, and now cannot work out. There must have been 'doubling up', and for several years accommodation must still have been available in the Old Building, the disused lunatic asylum. Obviously the Academic Department must have had a puzzling time, drawing up the schedule for the use of lecture rooms, when the total number was so limited - a large and a small on each of two floors, and no more.

The staircase led up again to the floor which housed the Tate Library, the Arts Theatre, and the private room of the Professor of Modern History. The Library communicated with a set of private rooms beyond for the Library staff. My main recollection is of the Chief Librarian, Dr Sampson, whose two great scholarly concerns were the poems of William Blake and Romany life and culture. ... One recollects his large, light-stepping, Augustan presence, passing down the Library, looking neither to right nor to left, and even the glint of his pince-nez was intimidating. But those who knew him well protested that he appeared formidable merely because he was shy, and indeed there must have been another aspect, for he published a little collection of his own verse and prose, some romantic and some comic: one series, the utterances of an imaginary Liverpool Irishman called Mr Dooley, is racy with Liverpool humour. In its early days, the Arts Theatre had many uses, for examinations, for degree ceremonies, for public lectures, and even for plays. As an amphitheatre, it was especially suitable for Greek drama, but it had also an inner stage, usually closed off by folding doors, which would have made possible an Elizabethan-type Shakespearean production. I remember a presentation of 'Iphigenia in Tauris' ... .

A dark and angled staircase led up to what was then the English Literature Class Library, a large square room, with a further door which opened on to the clock-balcony in the Arts Theatre. The rooms for the professor and the lecturers were contained within the library. Its remoteness gave a delightful feeling of seclusion and intimacy to the English school, which was, in fact, a closely-knit group. ... One's earliest recollection of Professor Elton is of his stately entrance into the lecture room, and the ceremonious removal of his cap (to be resumed as ceremoniously when he departed). The delivery of his lecture was a model of utterance and his occasional discriminating glance at his audience showed that in spite of his reserve, he was neither cold nor solemn. His speaking of poetry was itself illuminating criticism and could be a celebration of great moments. One day in the Great War, he paused in his lecture to read Collins' short but exquisite 'Ode Written in 1746', which commemorated the English who fell at Fontenoy, and it became a living tribute to the dead of our own armies. He had approached English literature as an Oxford 'Greats' man, and regarded it as the province of any excellent English writing, not only imaginative, but religious, philosophical, historical or scientific. This approach was something different from the use of criticism for political, sociological or religious propaganda. His knowledge of many languages enabled him to set English Literature in a European context, whether classical or modern, and made him covet for his students this wider view, as when he sent them to the lectures of that great Latin scholar, Professor Postgate, or to those of Professor Fitzmaurice-Kelly on what was then the avant-garde of French poetry. He himself seemed to warm especially to the heroic or chivalrous strain - from the Icelandic sagas (which he had translated) to the lays and novels of Scott. By contrast, he often referred to Jane Austen as 'Miss Austen', perhaps with a shade of irony. ...

The Students' Union, designed by Professor Reilly, was opened in 1913. My most enjoyable memories of it are connected with sing-songs from the new Liverpool Students' Song-book, published in the same year. These were held, like many other sizeable gatherings, in the hall on the top floor of what was then the Men's Union in Bedford Street. The circulation of the book may never have recovered from the second world war, but in its nearly 30 years of currency, it must have given a world of pleasure - thanks to the work of many members of staff, and student officials, who chose to be recorded under their contributions by initials only. In this connection one fiery figure stands out - that of Professor Pares [Bowes Professor of Russian History, Language and Literature], who not only was a chief begetter of the collection but usually took the chair for sing-songs, for which he had his own ritual, perhaps traditional: 'Silentio' - 'the song rises' - 'the song falls'. In 1912, the sound of jazz - 'Alexander's Ragtime Band' - first reached the University, played by a student group in the Arts Theatre, in the course of a social.

The last development which comes to mind within those old years was the opening in 1914 of what was then the New Arts Building, an extension of the Victoria Building. The top floor housed the Education Department under Professor Campagnac ... . One realises now that the Professor's concern was to show education as an art and not as a box of tricks. The visual arts and music were only beginning to receive their due importance in the curriculum and his influence was directed towards emphasizing it. He once gave an audience in the Abercromby Square building the memorable pleasure of an exhibition of William Morris's arts and crafts presented by his daughter, May Morris.

Elsie Kneale, born Liverpool 1895, English 1912-1916, Education 1916-1917, M.A. 1919, school-teacher, from 'Recollections of the University', published in The Recorder, *1972*

1900s

Once in the Tate Library I saw a procession of Ragging students rather sheepishly following their leader and just as sheepishly retiring hurriedly when the figure of Sampson [the Librarian] appeared. Garmon Jones liked to tell us how in his student days he was having a little flirtation in one of the niches of the Tate when Sampson appeared like an avenging angel and drove Garmon and his partner out of their paradise.

William Garmon Jones, History 1904-1908, M.A. 1909, lecturer, etc, History 1909-1937, Dean of Arts 1916-1920, 1926-1928, University Librarian 1928-1937; the extract from an unpublished account by Professor W.E. Collinson

[Answers to Correspondents.
Mrs G. [= Grundy?] No, it is not usual for students to kiss young ladies in the Library. Very occasionally, however, Arts students offend in this direction.

The Sphinx, 5, 1898, p. 201]

1890s

[a] I entered the University College, Liverpool, in 1889, as a stage in my training to be a Presbyterian minister. But even as a student I realised that I was involved in no less an enterprise than the building of a new type of university. ... The college was only seven years old, and was just beginning to take root. ... The main part was housed in a disused lunatic asylum, in a slum district, with a high workhouse on one side, and the other the Royal Infirmary ... Across a corner of the derelict quadrangle ran a deep railway cutting which belched forth clouds of smoke. ... The founders of the college had been offered an alternative site in a rather beautiful small suburban park, which was privately owned. They had refused the offer because they wanted to spend the money on men rather than site and buildings. ... In my first year only about a dozen students entered for an Arts degree. ... But as yet the college was no more than a mere knowledge shop. It had not begun to be a focus of intellectual life. There were almost no opportunities for the students to meet one another or to carry on the vital, if often shallow, talk which is the most valuable element in university life. They all lived at home, and scattered to every part of a wide area when lectures were over. There was, indeed, a common-room, but it was a dark comfortless cellar which few ever entered; there was a Refectory, but it was only another cellar where you could buy poached eggs and meat pies and cups of coffee. ... [I felt that] the [forthcoming] university must be something more than a mere knowledge shop ... it must be a well of intellectual life. ... What could I do towards the attainment of this aim? ... I wrought out the idea of establishing a Students' Representative Council. ... We formed, by invitation, a provisional committee. We summoned a mass meeting of all students, and to them I made, with some success, my first public speech. ... The Students' Representative Council was floated. Meanwhile I had been active in another way. I had often contributed to the *University College Magazine* ... I was asked to join the editorial board ... I resolved to change the whole character of the journal, including its heavy name, and to turn it into a means of awakening a corporate spirit among the students.

(b) In 1889, when I made my first acquaintance with this University, it can scarcely be said to have had any 'student life'. The students numbered not much over 300, and those of different faculties saw very little of one another. Perhaps the most vigorous aspect of their life was the athletic. Tennis throve greatly when we had a team of Careys to win the championship of Lancashire; and there were two cement courts in the quadrangle - one was on the site of the Thompson Yates [Laboratory], the other still protrudes from beneath the art sheds. Lacrosse also was vigorously played, but cricket and football languished. The Athletic Club was then largely maintained by the indefatigable energy of Professors Strong and Carey. But apart from athletics, student activities were few and unsuccessful. There was a Medical Students' Debating Society; and there was an Arts and Science Debating Society, which had boldly hired a club-room for itself in a house in Browlow Street. I am ashamed to say that I only attended one of its meetings. The other members present on that occasion were the President and Secretary. There was also a Literary and Historical Society, whose meetings were usually very solemn and improving. Those who desire to understand its mode of procedure are referred to an article entitled 'The Alliterative and Pre-historic Society,' which appeared in the first volume of *The Sphinx*. This journal has never published anything wittier. All the Societies combined once a year to organise a 'Soirée', from which the modern soirée is a lineal descendant. The first soirées were very humble affairs, but they formed the only co-operative social efforts in which students then engaged.

Men students had a cellar in the old building (the Victoria Building not being yet erected) as a common-room; it is not easy to imagine a drearier place, and it was never exactly crowded. The cellars of the Old Building also contained a Refectory, where (if my memory is sound) we chiefly consumed mutton pies and poached eggs. It was presided over by Miss McCubbin, who continued for years to be the presiding genius of the Refectory, even after it was removed, in 1892, to the disused Mortuary of the Royal Infirmary, which stood where the Physics Laboratories now are. Women students had as their common-room the room now used as the Education Class-Library.

The only other student institution that needs notice was *The University College Magazine*. This was a ponderous quarterly, modelled in style on the *Fortnightly Review*, and containing articles on 'Women's Suffrage', 'The Immortality of the Soul', 'The Approaching Exhaustion of the Coal Supply', and 'The Poetry of Byron'. The magazine was run by four editors, who filled up vacancies in their own number. They were financially, as well as editorially, responsible. This meant that when they found themselves in debt (as they always did when they drew up their balance sheet), some of them resigned, and the rest went and collected the money from the Professors. In 1891 I was invited to become an editor. I was immensely pleased with the honour until the remaining editors resigned, and their successors, on examining the books, found that we were responsible for £70 of debt to the printer.

Faced by this situation, we resolved to take bold action. 'We' included Miss Silcox, now Headmistress of the East Liverpool High School, Miss Barrett, now Mrs Speechly, and resident in Canada, and W.E. Henderson, now in Ceylon. ... We determined to write about nothing but the college and its students, and to change the form of the magazine, turning it into a two-columned sixteen-paged paper. Unfortunately the printer was resolved to use up his existing stock of paper, and as we were at his mercy, we had to consent. We therefore came out in an enormous form, about the size of the *Graphic*, which made our sixteen pages seem rather thin. The printer, also, could not be persuaded to publish punctually: as we couldn't and didn't pay him, he is scarcely to be blamed for giving precedence to other work, and we generally came out three months or so late. Nevertheless, the magazine in its new form had some success. Its circulation doubled, and to our increased audience we preached in every number the necessity of organising student activities by establishing an elected Students' Representative Council to look after all student affairs.

Meanwhile the Victoria Building was rising; it was to be opened in the Autumn Term of 1892. Some of us were resolved to make this opening the occasion for a new move. So we formed ourselves into a Committee of six members, including carefully-selected representatives from various departments. The Committee drew up a scheme, obtained Principal Rendall's approval in an interview during which we all sat on the edges of our chairs; and summoned the first students' mass-meeting ever held in this University. It took place in the brand-new Arts Theatre, on

October 18, 1892, and that may be regarded as the date of the beginning of student life in Liverpool. The mass-meeting decided to establish a Students' Representative Council, and elected a Committee to draw up its constitution.

While this Committee was sitting, stirring events happened. The authorities of the University had decided that the public opening ceremony of the new building should be held in the Arts Theatre. Lord Spencer was to perform the ceremony; Mr Bryce, the Chancellor of the Duchy of Lancaster, was to be present; and many distinguished guests from other universities were expected. Anxious to bring in as many Liverpool people as possible, the authorities decided that, as the space was limited, students should not be admitted. The news of this decision somehow became known to the students. At once a strongly-worded petition of protest was organised. It was signed, I believe, by almost every student in the College; and the Senate and Council decided that the gallery of the Theatre should be reserved for students. But the students, who were just 'finding themselves' and were elated by the victory they supposed themselves to have won, were not satisfied with this. They resolved to signalise the occasion in a way that would surprise people, and they did. ... A wire had been rigged up from one horn of the semi-circular gallery to the other, the middle of it being immediately over the head of the Red Earl, in the august splendour of his robes as Chancellor of Victoria University. When the procession had filled the platform, and just as the Chancellor took his seat, an enormous biscuit, about three feet in diameter, specially baked for the occasion, was run along the wire, and amid the breathless attention of the whole audience, gradually lowered until it hung right in front of the Chancellor, completely obscuring him from the audience. It bore an inscription stating that it was for the Senate, which took the biscuit for its impudence in trying to exclude the students. The idea was amusing, but it was in abominably bad taste on such an occasion, which was not the moment for washing dirty linen. ...

I cannot stop to narrate all the events of the unimportant session of 1892-93. But one important event still remains. The *University College Magazine* had been the source and origin of the whole movement. But it was in a very unsatisfactory condition. As soon as the S.R.C. was fairly launched, we resolved that the magazine ought to be transferred to it. But the printer, with his debt of £70, was a lion in the path. We decided to proceed without regarding him, and to raise the money 'somehow' to pay him off later. We got estimates from other printers who promised punctuality. Our old printer thereupon told us that we had no right to do so, the copyright of the title 'University College Magazine' being his property. Thereupon we all solemnly sent in our resignations of the editorship of his paper, and looked about for a new title. It was not easy to find. We held an 'At Home,' and compelled everybody present to make suggestions. Professor Herdman suggested that 'Amunyssle' would be a good title - alluring by reason of its mystery. But we were much too young to dream of being so flippant; and after the solemn consultations, we chose the title of *The Sphinx*. We had shaken off our printer, but of course we could not leave him unpaid. To raise the money we organised a great entertainment of tableaux, principally arranged by two professors' wives, Mrs Gotch and Mrs Raleigh. Its profits were so large that the whole debt was paid off, and a balance of £22 remained to the credit of *The Sphinx*, after a single performance.

J. Ramsay Bryce Muir [Ramsay Muir], born Otterburn 1872, History 1889-1893, lecturer in history, then Professor of Modern History, 1899-1913, Dean of the Arts Faculty 1905, 1906-1907; (a) from Muir's autobiography, published posthumously 1943; (b) from an essay in The Making of the University, *Liverpool, [1907]*

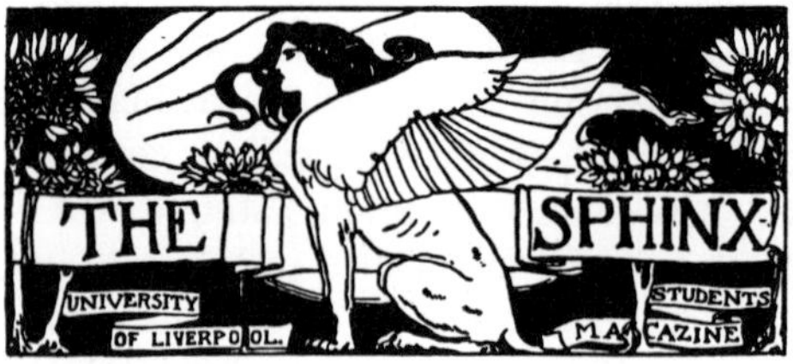

Vol. XIII. No. 12. May 16, 1906 Price Threepence

FORMER STAFF

Since members of staff normally spend longer at university than students, the reminiscences of former staff of Liverpool University regularly cover lengthier periods of time - and can run to book length. Given the limitations of space in the present volume, living contributors were asked to be succinct on specific topics and earlier printed accounts are represented only in select extracts (generally chosen to encourage the reader to seek out the original and read all). Furthermore, it was felt necessary and proper to concentrate on the reminiscences of those most involved at a formal level in the Faculty machinery. This concentration on former Deans means (regrettably) a professorial bias - as also represented in the official histories of the university - and the recollections of less senior staff are under-represented. Many living former staff who might have contributed are asked to accept this explanation for their not having been individually invited.

1890s-1920s

Walter Raleigh, Professor of Modern Literature and English Language 1890-1900 (extract from his contribution to a 1914 tribute volume)

The staff of University College, when I first knew it, consisted largely of young men, chosen, with such warrant of ability as was available, not so much to carry on University education in the North (for the thing was new) as to invent it. In any such staff the majority will always be individualists, content to be clever each in his own way, clinging to any freedom that the machine allows of him, incurious about the mechanism, and willing to pay a reasonabale respect to the duties put upon him by time-tables, registrars, principals, and the programmes of committees. Such an institution develops quite naturally and normally into a fairly efficient and useful High School, shaped, without any great reach of imagination, by men of method, and officered by a discontented staff, who do their duty in term and live for the vacation. The small group of men whose acquaintance I first made in Liverpool were much unlike this. I will only mention R.A.M. Stevenson [Professor of Art 1888-1892], Kuno Meyer [Professor of German 1894-1911, Honorary Professor of Celtic 1908-1911, 1913-1914], and Mackay [Professor of History 1884-1914]. There was no common creed uniting them, except that they cared for life and art, and for a University only so far as it could be made to reflect life and art. Stevenson was frightened by the University of which a strange accident had made him a Professor - frightened as a small woodland creature is frightened by a steam plough. Civic life was to him a succession of heavy shocks. He was compelled to speak at a public banquet, and he made some remarks on the French School of painting. The Chairman (to whose mind the word French conveyed obscurely immoral associations) said that he hoped no more would ever be heard, in this place, of French art.

Ramsay Muir [J. Ramsay Bryce Muir], lecturer in History 1899-1906, Professor of Modern History 1906-1913, Dean of Arts 1905, 1906-1907 (extracts from his autobiographical account, written c. 1940, published posthumously 1943)

The part-time post at Manchester suited me very well. ... But my heart was in what I was doing in the other four days of the week at Liverpool. Feeling that it was necessary to spread the idea of the university throughout its area, I started, with the aid of Theodore Brown and others, a University Extension Society, with a subscription income of about £500 a year. I was secretary of this body, at a small salary. The professed object of the Society was to start lecture centres in every part of the area, through which the Professors of the College could be made known to the public. The real object was to create a body of opinion friendly to the university idea. I went about hunting out people who would undertake to organise courses, with the backing of modest subsidies from the Society; I hunted also for suitable halls, and I tried to organise a team of lecturers within the College. Alas! the Professors either despised this sort of work, or did it very badly; Mackay [Professor of History 1884-1914], for example, utterly refused to touch it - and rightly so, for he could not possibly have held the attention of a public audience. ... So I had to do a large proportion of the lecturing myself, and I found that my training in the Arnold Society had given me a useful facility. This work, even in the first year, more than doubled my income. But it made it impossible for me to do the solid work which was necessary if my university lectures were to be good. I became dangerously skilful in 'vamping' both university and popular lectures. I was working very hard; but I was not achieving sound scholarship, which I had always lacked. I was not unaware of the sacrifice; but it seemed to me worth while for the sake of planting the idea of the university throughout its province. In this first year I succeeded in establishing, almost single-handed, thirteen lecture-centres in Liverpool and its district. ...

I then obtained an assistant-lectureship in history at the noble salary of £150 a year. ... My time at Liverpool, which I had hoped would last for the rest of my life, actually lasted for fourteen years. They were the happiest, on the whole, and certainly the most industrious of my life. They fell into two almost exactly equal parts, separated by a lecturing tour in America. The first part, which lasted from 1899 to 1906, was filled with the struggle for the establishment of an independent university, and with its organisation. In this I was completely absorbed, so that I had neither time nor thought for anything else; and that kind of absorption makes for happiness. I hoped that the second period would be a time of fruition, in which I should be able to establish my reputation as a scholar. This hope was doomed to disappointment, and in the end I was glad to escape from Liverpool, to which my heart had been given.

When I look back from a tired old age upon these full and active years, I am amazed by the courage and energy with which I tackled an immense range and variety of work. To begin with, Mackay expected me, as his assistant, to do for him all the drudgery of marking essays and examination papers. He also expected me to crystallise and to put into form the vague and hazy notions about university development which floated in his brain. I rejoiced in doing this, for I still regarded Mackay as a prophet; and the doing of it brought me into close contact with the university movement, in which he played a leading part. But I also had to do a vast amount of teaching. Mackay had almost completely neglected medieval and modern history, seldom lecturing on any modern period except the Tudor age, on which he considered himself to be an authority. I thought this a very serious defect, especially in a modern university. I set myself to remedy it, lecturing on the whole course of medieval and modern European history, on the constitutional history of England, on imperial history, and on the critical age since the French Revolution, and the Industrial Revolution. For all this I was but ill-equipped, and it ought to have required a vast deal of preparation. How I had the impudence to tackle these tasks I cannot imagine, especially in view of my other occupations. Often enough I had to 'vamp' lectures on very insufficient material. But I got through, thanks to the facility of speech I had acquired at Oxford. The students unquestionably liked my lectures; my classes grew rapidly in size, while Mackay's remained very small. But, under the system of payment then in vogue in Liverpool, he received two-thirds of the fees paid by all students attending my lectures as well as his own; so he was not dissatisfied.

Remembering how little social contact the students had had with their teachers in my own student-days, I did my best to remedy this. I tried to encourage community singing among them, holding a sing-song (with refreshments) for all my students once a term, for which I had song-sheets printed. I took a few of them, as my guests, on reading-parties in the Lake District; and I got some of them to come to my rooms for talk. I was still keenly interested in student-organisations, and tried to disseminate my keenness. Some of my students always played a leading part in such student-life, as there was; and I was in touch with all the student leaders, even if they did not come to my lectures. Meanwhile, I was still carrying on the public lecturing which I had begun before I reached Liverpool: I continued doing this until the university was established, when I dropped it, to find time for more serious work. Usually, two or three evenings in the week were devoted to public lectures all over the district; I also gave long courses in the University to pupil-teachers and to working-men who, having night jobs, were free during the day. This was the beginning of the Workers' Educational Association, in which A.L. Smith was deeply interested and into which he drew me.

These activities almost inevitably cut me off from social intercourse with my academic colleagues, most of whom were, I think, inclined to regard me as a popular tub-thumper rather than as a serious scholar; and the fact that my family had no part in the life of the university supported this view. I regretted this, but I thought that I ought to go on. I was also in considerable demand for prize-givings and such occasions; I was consequently better known to the general public in the district than most of my colleagues. But I had no intention of allowing these multiform activities to divert me wholly from the independent work of research which every university teacher might pursue. I had chosen my subject, the history of Liverpool; for I held that one of the services which a university ought to render to its community was to make it aware of its history. ...

University teaching, popular lecturing and private research did not occupy the whole of my time or thoughts during these strenuous years. In the first four of them the agitation for an independent university was in full swing, in the next three the university was at work creating its new system; and in both of these activities I eagerly took a far larger share than corresponded with my humble status as an assistant lecturer. My incessant public lecturing gave me opportunities, which I did not neglect, to popularise the idea. I also did a vast deal of writing on the subject. I kept up a constant correspondence in the three local papers, writing under many pseudonyms, and sometimes carrying on a controversy with myself: at one time I was using eleven different signatures. Long afterwards a town councillor told me that what had made him support a civic grant of £10,000 a year to the university was the evidence of public interest given by the correspondence in the Press. It was an entirely fictitious interest; university education is one of the things in which the supply must precede the demand; most of the letters in the Press came from my pen. I also contributed to two of the papers long series of articles on the university problem. One of these series, reprinted (at my own expense) in a slim paper-covered volume, under the title, *A Plea for a Liverpool University*, was actually my first published work. Whether it was good or bad I can't judge; I have not seen a copy for many years. ...

During the days when the Privy Council was considering our case, we produced in the College a sort of modern morality play in verse, entitled *Everyman's Education*, in which Sir John Gorst, robed in blue-book covers trimmed with red tape, was called upon to pronounce upon the rival claims of the various universities to educate Everyman's sons and daughters, while Knowledge, a bedizened flirt, and Wisdom, a stately dame robed in white, proclaimed their ideas of what the Universities should teach. The Victoria University was represented by three beauteous damsels, chained together and incessantly quarrelling. I wrote and spoke the prologue to this amusing piece. There was quite a stir of excitement when, on the last evening, I came on with a big official envelope, which 'perhaps contains the news' - but must not be opened until the Vice-Chancellor returns. Sure enough, next day the news came that Liverpool had attained the dignity of an independent university.

Then came a very strenuous period of organisation, when new Professors and Lecturers had to be appointed, and new regulations and courses had to be passed. I was made the first Dean of the Faculty of Arts, an office which kept me busy interviewing students and drafting courses of study. I was also promoted to the dignity of an Independent Lecturer in Modern History, and my new terms of appointment gave me full control over the medieval and modern periods. But Mackay still remained Professor of History, and the relations between us were not defined. Moreover, under the very unsound method of payment which then existed, I now drew the share of fees which had previously gone to Mackay. As my classes were large and numerous, and his were few and small, this meant that his income shrank and mine grew, until it was larger than his. I tried to amend this very difficult situation by bringing, as Dean of the Faculty, all the pressure I could exercise upon the students to drive them into his classes. But unfortunately he had a bad reputation as a lecturer, and I had a good one. The result was a strain in the relations between us, which grew steadily during the following years. I was glad when the invitation to lecture in America gave me an opportunity, for a time, of escaping from this unpleasant position. ...

When I became a full Professor, we [his mother, sister and himself] found a pleasant house in Liverpool, with large rooms suitable for entertaining. I hoped that, quietly at first, we should be able to play our part in the social life of the university. It was a severe wrench for my mother to give up the retired life she had lived for twenty years ... and our new home promised to become a place to which many professors and their wives, many junior teachers, and many students willingly resorted.

We had jolly students' parties, in which we laboured to break the ice of their shyness. One of our devices for this purpose, however, had an unfortunate result. We caused the students on arrival to draw cards from trays, those for the men bearing the names of widely advertised articles, while those for the women carried the recognised descriptions of these articles, and then they had to find their partners. Unfortunately an almost white-haired lady, who had undertaken a university career rather late in life, drew the description of Mazawattee Tea - 'recalls the favourite blends of fifty years ago'; a plump, red-faced girl found herself labelled 'pure fluid beef'; and an untidy girl carried the inscription, 'Won't wash clothes'. After this experience we had to change our method! ...

My first preoccupation on returning from America was to get out my three pieces of work on Liverpool history. Before leaving I had lent my highly condensed V.C.H. [Victoria County History] essay to Miss Platt, and had forgotten that I had done so. I searched in vain, and had to write a second version ... . When this was almost completed, I met Miss Platt in the street, and she asked me in a casual way if I wanted my MS back! On comparing the two versions, I found that each in some respects excelled the other; so of course I had to write a third version. This delayed my work on my *History*, the last section of which needed a good deal of extra labour, for it had been hastily written. But it had to be out in time for the seven-hundredth anniversary of King John's Charter in 1907.

The first of the three books to appear was the *History of Municipal Government in Liverpool*, including Miss Platt's documents, and my introduction, long enough to make a book by itself. The whole thing was in type; and the printer was pressing for payment. I had begged Mackay until I was tired to send out an appeal for guinea subscriptions as President of the School of Local History. He would do nothing. Finally I had to send out the appeal myself, unsigned. It brought a good response, but not enough to cover the costs, and I had to find £100 out of my own pocket. Mackay was wildly angry with me for having acted without his express authority, though I had got the assent of the other nominal officers of the school. He actually demanded my resignation from the school. ... My *History of Liverpool* was the next to appear. The edition was sold out, and it has long been regarded as the standard book on the subject, though it has been out of print for many years. I never made a penny out of it. ...

Of all this ferment of intellectual activity which distinguished Liverpool in the years preceding the war of 1914, and which gave hope that the city was going to become a real centre of civilisation, the University was the focus; and, thanks largely to the new recruits who came in after the foundation of the university, the variety and colour of its life was greater than it ever had been, and its membership included many vivid personalities. Among the older men, I recall with affection John MacCunn, Professor of Philosophy [1881-1910], salt of the earth and most modest of men; his brilliant wife taught many of us what good talk could be. I was very fond of the genial economist Sir Edward Gonner [Professor of Economic Science 1891-1922], who was lackadaisical but energetic, and always understanding, though a little prone to loquacity: there was a story, perhaps apocryphal, that a deputation to a committee of the Cheshire County Council (of which Gonner was a member) was kept waiting for two hours. They complained of the delay, and were told that Professor Gonner had been explaining the extreme urgency of seeing them at once. Oliver Elton [Professor of English Literature 1901-1925] was a critic of real distinction, whose clear judgment and chiselled style was reflected in the carved lines of his cold, handsome countenance. Kuno Meyer [Professor of German 1894-1911, Honorary Professor of Celtic 1908-1911, 1913-1914], a German, who had spent most of his life in England, was an outstanding Celtic scholar, both in Welsh and Irish, and his translations of early Irish poems, such as 'The King and the Hermit' were really beautiful. English as his sympathies seemed to be, his loyalty was to Germany. Summoned to a Chair of Celtic in Berlin three years before the outbreak of war, he sent over a stream of stalwart goose-stepping students of Celtic, who studied the dialects in the Aran Islands and other places, which subsequently became centres for the supply of submarines. Soon after the war began he wrote to A.L. Smith, among others, asking him to send him an occasional letter with news of his friends, and promised that, if he would do so, Meyer would guarantee his house and property when the Germans occupied Oxford. Nevertheless, one remembers him as a model of hearty good fellowship combined with exact scholarship.

Among the newcomers there were outstanding personalities. Charles Bonnier [Professor of French 1905-1913] was one of the best types of

Frenchmen. He listened to our academic squabbles with an amused smile on his jolly countenance. He painted pointilliste pictures; he wrote rather precious verses and essays in French, which he had privately printed in green type on large yellow sheets; he produced a monumental history of his native village near Lille; and he professed an interest in the English popular drama, which took him, with a number of us as his rather uproarious companions, on many visits to popular melodramas at the Star Theatre, which later became the house of the Repertory Theatre. I remember one of these plays, in which the heroine, a lovely Russian prima donna who had sung before all the crowned heads of Europe, rashly visited St Petersburg, where she was claimed as his property, because she was the daughter of one of his serfs, by the villain, a wicked Baron, who carried her off to his castle in the depths of Siberia. But we knew that all was well, for she had won the love of an English naval lieutenant, who pursued her to Siberia. The great scene of the play was in a dungeon in the villain's castle, where the hero, manacled but undismayed, was faced by the villain, armed with a revolver, which he aimed at the hero's heart. But the hero somehow contrived to throw open his jacket, and showed that his manly chest was covered by the Union Jack. The villain staggered back, foiled; even he dared not fire at that; and the gallery cheered uproariously.

Charles Herbert Reilly, later Sir Charles Reilly, Professor of Architecture 1904-1933 (extracts from his autobiographical account, Scaffolding in the Sky, *published 1938)*

I started work in Liverpool after the Easter vacation in 1904. I found my cabman did not know the way to the University, then only two years old. When discovered it was seen to be mainly housed in a red and brown brick and terra-cotta building inherited from University College, designed by Mr Alfred Waterhouse and looking like a less prosperous Prudential Insurance one. Its colours of mud and blood and the harshness and its outlines and detail were a great shock after Cambridge and even after King's College, London. It was a greater shock still when I saw the inside of the main block and found I had to teach there. The ground floor and staircase were lined with glazed tiles of the general colour of curry powder, relieved with a narrow line of Cambridge blue. The entrance hall had a Gothic fire-place with a hood over it supported on little arches and columns like an outsize Victorian over-mantel, modelled in a glutinous mass of the same material. Facing this, and very bleak and uncomfortable there, was a large white marble statue of a worthy in a frock coat. Above was a gallery running half round the hall in the same yellow glazed material, softened later in my mind when I discovered it was where the students started their love affairs. Behind this rose the main staircase similarly glazed. Up this stair and past this pastrycook's architecture my handful of students had to go three or four times a day to reach their studio under the roof. The approach to the University buildings from the centre of the town was through the mean streets behind the Adelphi Hotel, and chiefly by one called Brownlow Hill, then clearly a sort of ghetto. That was depressing enough. That the little Department of Architecture, not yet called a School and certainly not worthy of such a name, should be so housed was worse. ...

In one wall of the studio of this first home of the School was a small mysterious flush door always supposed to be locked. One adventurous student, Adrian Berrington, afterwards to win all sorts of scholarships and to end up as Professor of Architecture at the University of Toronto, where, sad to say, he died from effects of the war, managed during part of his two or three years at Liverpool to possess himself of the key. The door opened on to a little gallery above the clock facing the audience in the main lecture hall of the University. On the occasion of a public lecture, and they were all held there, he and his friends, including, I like to think, my successor, Professor Budden, used to creep out and hang over the balcony railings posters on which they had written such encouraging things as 'Cheer up, he won't be long now' and 'He is not such a stick as he seems'. It was a crude form of joke no doubt, but some of the audience found it amusing and the lecturer, who could not see what was happening above him, probably thought he was wittier than he really was. Architectural students with their long hours on, rather than at, the drawing-board, not always entailing intense thought and especially so when repeats are being drawn, need relief. Hence the broken windows from which all Schools of Architecture suffer. ...

It was in this Bloomsbury area [around the university], when I first arrived, that most of the professors and lecturers lived, which meant that they were near to one another and that therefore some sort of university life was possible. Now ... they mostly live in Cheshire at Hoylake or Meols, or far away to the north at Formby or even Southport, and contacts, except at lunch or at formal meetings, are rare. I remember how disgraceful it was thought when Edward Gonner (later Sir Edward), the economist, moved out to Hoylake. He was the first to do anything so unpatriotic and, needless to say, he belonged to the wrong party in the university politics. ...

There is no doubt that the one great and undoubted genius with whom the University of Liverpool has been connected in its short career is Augustus John. ... When I came up, John himself was still living with his growing family in Chatham Street. In that semi-slum, where I was to live myself later on, at that time were three men to whom it would not be too much to apply the word 'genius'. The Corporation should note the numbers of the houses where they dwelt. They were Eugene Goosens the composer, John Sampson the Romany scholar and University Librarian [1892-1928], and Augustus John. John as I knew him then was a glorious-looking young man of about twenty-five, tall and graceful with longish hair, big magnetic eyes, bearded like the pard, picturesquely dressed with big hat, sailor's jersey and earrings and with a fine springy walk. ... I think John Sampson must have helped him with his Romany, though he always had an uncommon power of acquiring languages and was gathering his sixth when I stayed with him a few years ago. Anyhow, there was North Wales and its gypsies close by for both of them to study from their different angles. Liverpool in 1904 was still arguing about a caravan on its way there going down Bold Street at the fashionable hour with the Hon. Mrs Dowdall, her one aristocrat, seated stockingless - a first-class event in those days - on the steps and behind her the Sampson and John families, with Dowdall, a rising young barrister now the County Court Judge, and John riding on nags behind. ...

John Sampson had discovered Doonie and introduced her to John. Some of his most beautiful drawings of the Liverpool period are of her. Doonie, who had held a bursary at Edinburgh University, was and is a good linguist. When, therefore, Albert Lipczinski, arrived in Liverpool, knowing no English but with an introduction to John, it was natural the latter should use Doonie as an interpreter and that later she should give him lessons in English. It was also natural, I suppose, that she, then little more than a child, should marry Lipczinski, who is still a fine-looking man and was very handsome in those days with his big black beard and upright figure. Very naturally too, John and her other Liverpool friends did not appreciate the outcome at the time any more than, a few years later, the members of the Sandon life class appreciated her seeing so much of me and spending so much time at the Dingle. She was, they said and rightly, very much one of them - 'one of the boys' - and they feared, I suppose, she might lose this happy characteristic. ... When the war came how she and her husband were to go through very difficult times, and, from our British point of view, very disgraceful ones. ...

Pondering these things [about Liverpool architecture] as I was walking down Brownlow Hill one evening from the University, and perhaps moved thereto by the sights and smells of the meat market and the other delights of the neighbourhood, I turned into the University Club and wrote to Lever. I pointed out what was happening and the need for reconnecting the words 'town planning' with architecture in the public mind. I think I said it was in the main an advanced form of architecture as it is or rather should be. I have no doubt I reminded him how he had practised it himself at Port Sunlight. I wound up my letter with a suggestion of an endowment for a Chair, for a Lectureship and for a Journal in the subject. By return of post I had an encouraging letter asking me to come and see him. Could there be anything more exciting? The deed was done in a few days. ...

I first met Shute through getting to know the Reynolds family, the leading Roman Catholic family in Liverpool, which is the town with the largest Catholic population, and I first got to know the Reynolds family through my first public lecture. Seated in the front row was a dark handsome woman in, I remember, a white dress with a long white coat over it. I was nervous and shy and felt that my lecture was going badly, but this lady at any rate seemed to be interested. When I discovered that I gave the rest of the lecture to her. Afterwards I was introduced and she told me she liked my adjectives. She then called on my wife and a friendship which has lasted ever since was started. She was the young and beautiful wife of Sir James Reynolds, Bt. (plain Mr Reynolds he was then), the leading cotton broker of the town and senior partner of its oldest firm, Messrs. Reynolds and Gibson. At that time they were about to buy a house and estate at Woolton, called Dove Park, later given to the town by Sir James and now 'Reynolds Park'. In it are some gardens screened with yew trees and trained limes which I designed for the lady in white. In another part I made for her with clipped yew hedges a place where she could give outdoor luncheon parties in summer time, with the footmen to disappear through the hedges as actors through the wings, and not spoil the freedom of conversation.

It was here that Leila Reynolds entertained what Jimmy, her husband, healthy, prosperous and golf-playing, called her 'corpses'. I was privileged to be a corpse and so were John Sampson (poet and librarian), Oliver Elton (critic and Professor of English Literature [1901-1925]), Dixon Scott (writer), Norman Wyld (everything, and officially University Extension Secretary), Alexander Mair (philosopher [Professor of Philosophy 1910-1927]), Lascelles Abercrombie (poet), and occasionally the great Mackay himself. Seated at table eating her peaches and sipping her wine, perhaps reading verses to our hostess or listening to hers, discussing books and people but never cotton or stocks and shares or politics, we use to feel, or certainly I did, under the inspiration of our lovely patroness, that we were having much the same sort of escape for the time being from Liverpool and its affairs that Boccaccio's story-tellers did from Florence six centuries before. That was one side of her life, another was with her handsome family of a dozen of so children living the freest open-air life and riding through the house on their ponies ... The Reynoldses, like the Holts, the Rathbones, the Rankins, the Booths and a dozen other rich Liverpool families, lived up to a great tradition of good works in addition to public ones and instilled it into their partners and business associates as well as into their families. ...

In the University there are today, below the more developed Faculties, such as the Faculty of Arts, Boards of Studies consisting of all the teachers in a group of allied subjects, such as the History Board, the Classics Board, the Modern Languages Board, the Board of Architecture and Civic Design. This was a later development of the constitution which took place in my time and is highly important, for it means where it exists that each teacher, down to the humblest grade III lecturer and studio instructor, sits on a university body and can initiate proposals for legislation in his subject. It means when the Boards of Studies are properly conducted and meeting regularly, that every teacher can feel he is part of the government of the University and responsible for its success. It should and does, under sympathetic heads of departments, foster a great feeling of loyalty and fellowship to the institution. I have often thought that, with its grades of salaries and grades of responsibility, a university organized like Liverpool is today a very fair indication of what the Socialist State of the future might be like. Some think the democratic idea is carried too far because each step can theoretically be debated on Board, Faculty, Senate and Council with the delay involved before anything is done. That is not my view. One can always act quickly if one has the confidence of one's colleagues, and the best way of gaining that confidence is to share ideas with them.

William Edward Collinson, lecturer 1913-1914, Professor of German 1914-1954 (from an unpublished memoir entitled 'Portraits from the Past', written c. 1965)

Professor Reilly has left such a richly embroidered portrait of himself in *Scaffolding in the Sky* that there is little to add. He was flamboyant and dynamic, a demon for treading on other people's toes, as when he once called the non-academic members of the University Club the 'townees', but at least never dull or boring. I like to think of him swinging down Brownlow Hill flourishing a fine ebony stick surmounted by a silver knob and how forlorn he looked when the students purloined it in some rag. ... In Faculty he was a nuisance for he was always tinkering with the regulations for his Department and was not even a law unto himself. The astute Garmon Jones and Reilly's sacrificial victim, Budden, had their work cut out extricating him from his self-made messes and bedecking the Faculty minutes with 'Notwithstanding Regulation so and so and in the exceptional circumstances of the case ...'. Once his unsubtle and often outrageous candour led him to the brink of disaster. After World War I, a new Ph.D. degree was instituted in Liverpool as in other universities to lure foreign (especially American) postgraduates to Great Britain rather than to Germany. One year Reilly spotted that an unusually large number of Ph.D. degrees had been awarded in certain subjects of the Faculty of Science. Acting on impulse he wrote a letter to one of the two professors concerned practically accusing him - without any cogent evidence - of lowering his standards. The upshot was that this professor and his colleague took legal opinion and threatened an action for libel. At a special meeting of the Senate Reilly stuck to his guns till Campagnac [Professor of Education 1908-1938] placing his hand on Reilly's shoulder and making a persuasive and diplomatic speech, including the phrase 'I am sure my good friend R. will behave in a gentlemanly way etc.' brought him to the point of a tardy and grudging withdrawal and apology. Camp's good neighbourliness, however, merely evoked from Reilly the remark 'One finds oneself with strange bedfellows'! In spite of our exasperations we were all genuinely proud of Reilly's great achievement in building up the Liverpool School of Architecture into a world-famous institution. In 1933 I made a Farewell Speech to him in Faculty and we all felt that we were losing a significant and picturesque, even picaresque, personality. He elicited our sympathy, too, for the fortitude with which he bore the prolonged absences of his wife at sanatoria in the United States. Finally he showed great courage when he had to confront his own fatal illness. He was indeed a colleague no one was likely to forget. ...

Professor Henry Cecil Kennedy Wyld [Professor of English Language and Philology 1904-1920] came of a Fifeshire land-owning family. He was Liverpool's best all-round philologist after Kuno Meyer's departure in 1911. He had been a pupil of Henry Sweet of Oxford in whose memory he edited a collection of striking and original papers on linguistic matters by that scurvily treated pioneer scholar. When he came to Liverpool as Lecturer in 1899 he had contributed to the history of the English 'gutturals' and after his appointment to the Baines Chair of English Language and Philology in 1904 he published several works of major importance ... He himself gave the general introductory course on the History (since 1953 Science) of Language still taken by all the Honours students offering a modern language. He was an excellent phonetician and could imitate all sorts of queer sounds such as the nasalized vowels and unrounded 'u' of Scottish Gaelic and he made a determined effort to convert his Northern listeners from their retracted 'a' in 'hat,' their over-rounded 'u' in 'butter', and their insertion of 'g' after -ng- in 'singing'. He was so ferocious in his campaign that some of his girl students were reduced to tears. ....

Though a keen member of the N. T. and progressive in his academic views, he liked to give others the impression that he was a hard-bitten Tory squire. This aspect of him was enhanced by his rather pugnacious bull-dog face and his habit - for he was very short-sighted - of peering hard through his glasses. His permanent home was a manor-house at Alverscote in Oxfordshire. During term he shared rooms with the aristocratic- looking professor of Spanish, Fitzmaurice-Kelly [1909-1916], in the Old Hall, now demolished but once standing near the corner of Mersey Road and Aigburth Road. ... Wyld was a great stickler for the proprieties and he was once genuinely shocked when he saw Professor Petsch [Professor of German 1911-1914] and me rowing on the Sefton Park lake in our shirt-sleeves. He disliked seeing on a coat-cuff buttons which had no corresponding button-holes, but were merely relics of an older genteel type of coat and I remember hearing him say 'Only a cad of a tailor would do a thing like that'. It was easy to pull his leg. He had been airing his views about the 'lower' classes when I chipped in with Tennyson's 'Kind hearts are more than coronets', just to see the effect. ... I enjoyed talking to him and was much amused when he said to me soon after I had been appointed to the Chair, 'Now you'll be able to get a horse and ride in Sefton Park'. After I returned in 1919 he seemed to have fallen out with some of his, I dare not say, 'comrades' of the N. T. for he was consorting with Professor Campagnac, one of its opponents. In Faculty he was not too popular when he acted as 'Elder Statesman' and kept intervening. On one occasion the Dean, Garmon Jones, simulating indignation as he could easily when required, jumped to his feet and said to the Chairman, 'MUST we go on putting up with all these pin-pricks?', which reduced Wyld to astonished silence. ...

Outside the New Testament group, the most distinguished scholar on the Faculty of Arts during my earliest years in the University was Professor John Percival Postgate [Professor of Latin 1909-1920], author of a famous Latin grammar, a sound comparative philologist and a man both exact and exacting. It really hurt him to hear a false quantity and when

Professor Garstang once stressed *senatus* on the first syll out *senātus*. Once he caught me out when I made the firs *sabulum* 'sand' short instead of long. In the Senate he c 'snarleyow'. Once when chairs in the Faculty of Engineering were being founded thick and fast, he turned in his seat towards his Engineering colleagues and snapped out, 'Are all the privates in your army to be generals?'. He was reputed to be a ruthless examiner in Latin. ... It was said that as a true Roman father he insisted upon his children talking Latin at table under penalty of having to go without what they wanted. One day his daughter could not think of the word for 'sausage' and was in some distress till allowed to compromise with the correct use of *istud* 'that near you'. His die-hard conservatism must have been affronted when his son Raymond - now known to a wider public as an author of treatises on social history and gastronomy as well as some excellent thrillers - joined the Labour Party and married the daughter of George Lansbury, and when his daughter Margaret married G.D.H. Cole. ... The family lived in a large house in Linnet Lane and Postgate used to cycle in to the University. After he retired to Cambridge in 1920 he continued to use his bicycle and was riding on it when he was run down and fatally injured by a lorry on Magdalen Bridge. He had willed his money to his Cambridge college which, however, refused to accept it. The second beneficiary, Liverpool University, took it on condition that his wife should have a life-interest in it.

1940s-1980s

Frank William Walbank, lecturer, etc, in Latin 1934-1946, Professor of Latin 1946-1951, Professor of Ancient History and Classical Archaeology 1951-1977, Dean of Arts 1974-1977, FBA

I came to Liverpool as an Assistant Lecturer in Latin in January 1934 (at £250 p.a.). At that time the Arts Faculty was, quite literally, at the centre of the University. Apart from Architecture and what were later Social Science subjects, already in Abercromby Square, we were all housed chock-a-block, often three lecturers to a room, in the Victoria and New

Arts (now Ashton) Buildings, alongside the University Administration, including the Registrar and the Vice-Chancellor. The University Library was upstairs in what is now the Tate Hall and the Senate Room, with its large soporific fireplace, lay just at the end of the first floor corridor above the entrance hall. True, if you looked at student numbers, Liverpool was a 'science-based university'; but out of 59 chairs, 19 were then held by Arts professors, nearly 33%, compared with 18 out of 107, a paltry 17%, when I retired in 1977.

Such statistics, however, would have meant little to a young assistant lecturer hesitantly confronting the great men in the common room on the ground floor of the New Arts Building, where (male only) academic staff from the whole precinct came to drink coffee at 11.00 a.m. I have a vivid recollection of approaching a slightly forbidding Allison Peers (later to be revealed as 'Bruce Truscot', inventor of the term 'Redbrick') for information about the Pyrenees prior to a hiking holiday in the Basque provinces and with difficulty evading his pressing invitation to enrol as a member of the summer school which he ran annually (and profitably) at San Sebastian. Here too I approached Professor A.M. Blackman on a point of Ptolemaic chronology and was obliged to evade *his* attempt to inveigle me into a hostel he ran for Middle East students in Sefton Park - 'like an Oxford College, my dear chap'. Blackman was a fine scholar, who entertained lofty pretensions, which were ultimately satisfied when, as a sort of proto-Rastafarian (or, as he probably saw it, as a latter-day Aristotle), he was taken on as tutor to the son of Emperor Haile Selassie. It was all very democratic (up to a point); and I certainly recall with pleasure the hilarity of J.F. Mountford, when around 1947, shortly after he became Vice-Chancellor, I reported to him that the German colleague I had introduced to him in the coffee club the day before had previously enquired nervously whether he should address J.F.M. as 'Your Magnificence'.

In 1934 what could be called the mythological age of the Faculty was just over. Academics love gossip and stories still circulated about the pre-war 'New Testament', conjured up by the famous painting now in the Sydney Jones Library, but then (and until late in the war when it was damaged by the chairs of fire-watchers) in the New Arts Building common room, especially stories about Mackay, Reilly and the Librarian Sampson.

Reilly's 'Cowshed', the architecture building in Ashton Street, had been vacated only a year ago, when Reilly himself retired from the chair; and the gypsy connection initiated by Sampson (the 'Rai') and Augustus John, was still vigorously pursued by Dora Yates. I remember calling on her one day in the library only to have a small bright-eyed Romany lady introduced to me as 'descended from kings on both sides'. Dumbfounded to find myself for the first time in such lofty company I could only mumble 'That's fine!'. It was a relief when the gypsy lady showed herself quite satisfied by my response.

If asked to mention one event that stands out in my memory of those pre-war years, it is the Greek play. In February 1939 a group of Faculty staff and students put on Aeschylus' *Agamemnon* in the lecture theatre in the Victoria Building. The translation was that of Archie Y. Campbell, then Gladstone Professor of Greek, of whom many stories were told. He was a poet of no mean quality and author of several books of verse. In one he had included a poem to be entitled 'Nympholepsy', but through some momentary abberation had headed it 'Nymphomania'. When he corrected this in the Library copy, Garmon Jones, John Sampson's successor as Librarian, recognising the hand-writing, threatened to denounce him in Senate as a defacer of library books.

To return to the play, Archie himself played the leader of the chorus. Clytemnestra was a professional actress, whose name escapes me. Cassandra was played by Dorothy Knowles (French), a talented ballet dancer; and Eric Colledge (English Language) both produced the play and took the part of Aegisthus. A.M. McIlwraith (English Literature) was Agamemnon and entered the theatre majestically to his doom, installed on a chariot, which was in reality a disguised wagon kindly loaned by the stationmaster at Lime Street Station (who was rewarded with complimentary tickets). Colledge divided his chorus into old and young men. My old friend Harri Hudson-Williams (Greek) made a most handsome youth with a fine sun-tan, but I was less fortunate. As an old man I was given a white face, ruddy nose and several blacked-out teeth. My wife in the audience was struck with horror. But happily my daughter, who was born three months later, proved to have been unaffected by this disagreeable pre-natal experience. The tragedy was adjudged to have been a great success.

Six months later the war broke out. Most arts departments were split, half their staff and students going to Coleg Harlech, whence they returned in 1940 just as the bombing started. But of those staff-members who stayed on in Liverpool several became involved in an important activity - the University Fire Service and the Tower Watch. Both were soon incorporated in the Auxiliary Fire Service (AFS) later the National Fire Service (NFS). Fire appliances were housed on the ground floor corridor of the New Arts Building alongside the Arts Faculty Office (then two rooms to the left of the staircase). A common room was made available adjoining Ashton Street. Later, after the raids died down, we were moved upstairs. The Tower Watch consisted of academic staff and research students, roughly four each night and working on a six-night rota. Whenever the siren sounded, two of us made our way up to the balcony below the Victoria Tower clock, where there was a sighting instrument and a direct phone to Hatton Garden, the fire HQ. Our job was to take a bearing on any fire started by incendiary bombs and report this on the phone. A second team reported from the Cathedral Tower and the fire was thus located where the two lines intersected (always assuming we were reporting the same fire). On really busy nights of course we had to concentrate on major outbreaks. High up above the city, as if on Olympus, we enjoyed a wholly false feeling of immunity and a splendid view. Some nights, especially during the March and May raids of 1941 we witnessed some quite spectacular disasters. I recollect in particular the burning of Lewis's, the destruction of the Argyle Theatre in Birkenhead and the collapse of the dome of St Catherine's church in Abercromby Square.

The Fire Service was a great social and faculty leveller. Through it I made several friends in other faculties whom in the normal run of things I might never have met. My own colleagues were Gordon Rawcliffe (Engineering), Donald Coult (Botany and later Warden of Rathbone Hall), Trevor Goodwin (Biochemistry) and Joseph Rotblat (Physics). There were lighter moments. Rawcliffe's professor, he reported, had recently delivered himself of a passionate outburst against the enemy, beginning 'Those swine, those foul swine . . . ' and this struck us as understandable but a little off-beat. We therefore decided to adopt it as our private chant and henceforth we would ascend the stairs to the tower intoning *con brio*: 'those swine, those foul swine, etc. etc.' Later a curious remark by an assistant on early duty in the Harold Cohen Library provided a welcome variant. One morning, after a particularly nasty night, I had enquired why she looked so disconsolate, whereupon, to my surprise, she burst out with the weird complaint: 'Last night's blitz was a disgrace to the Corporation of Bootle!'. (She went on to explain that the tea-wagons had come round late.) In future, whenever bombs fell frequently or closely, we consoled ourselves with the reflection that tonight's blitz was a disgrace to the Vice-Chancellor (or the Lord Mayor, or whichever other dignitary came to mind).

Some nights were undisturbed and we slept comfortably on beds in a room near the Ashton Street entrance. The strategy of burning tar in a tar-wagon so as to blot out the city from the eyes of enemy pilots made the atmosphere rather acrid; but one got used to that. Meals (sausages, black puddings, etc) were sent in by the Fire Service and we had breakfast in the Students' Union. There was a cooker in our common room, but because it served a succession of teams, it was no one's job to clean it and eventually it became indescribably filthy. Still, I think all surviving members of the Tower Watch must remember it with nostalgia. It provided several anecdotes. Here is one, told me by J.F. Mountford, who answered the phone one night when on duty to receive an enquiry from some dockers, who had been arguing about the meaning of a word and had decided to ring up the University for a decision. Mountford felt this trivializing use of the University was to be discouraged, so replied: 'Sorry, mate, we're only the fire-watchers.'

Since 1945 the shape of the University has completely changed. As part of the vast post-war expansion the Arts departments shifted gradually to their present location. Figures notable in my early days, such as Collinson, Peers and Campagnac, retired and eventually a slimmed-down Faculty, shorn of Education and what is now SES, and with its administration housed in the much larger office in Abercromby Square, has taken on the shape familiar to us all today. The above paragraphs are an attempt to recall a little of what is now a piece of history.

Irene Collins, lecturer, etc in Modern History 1947-1986, Dean of Arts 1980-1983

When I arrived in Liverpool in 1947, the term 'Faculty' meant very little to me. As a student at Oxford I had been aware of the College and the University, but a Faculty was merely something one read about in connection with medieval universities. At Liverpool, where I was the only female member of the staff of the Modern History Department, I soon discovered that the five or six other females dotted about the Faculty were to be my closest associates. For the first couple of years I seldom saw my Modern History colleagues. They were housed in the 'New' Arts Building, where space was so restricted that only senior members could have separate rooms; since it would not have been considered proper for me to share a room with a male colleague I had to camp out in the Palaeography classroom in the Victoria Building and find accommodation for tutorials wherever I could. Along with the staff of the Medieval History Department, we were scheduled to gather together twice a term for Board Meetings; but these occasions were tailored to last as short a time as possible - ten minutes was usual - on account of the tension existing between the respective Heads of Department, Mark Thomson [Professor of Modern History 1945-1956] and Geoffrey Barraclough [Professor of Medieval History 1945-1956]. These two gentlemen carried on the tradition of the Ramsay Muir and Mackay era by being at complete loggerheads with each other, with the result that business for the Board was best arranged beforehand by the unfortunate Secretary (first Cyril Northcote Parkinson [of Parkinson's Law later fame] and then myself) running backwards and forwards between the warring parties.

Recognising my isolation, Mark Thomson made the unnerving arrangement whereby I was to call on him in his room each Monday morning at 10.45. In his extraordinary voice he would bark a few well-meant but often unanswerable questions at me from across the mahogany table. After an uncomfortable fifteen minutes or so, we would both of us escape for our respective coffee breaks. Men and women members of staff had separate commonrooms. The men, it was said, were practically fighting for spoons in theirs, whereas we handful of ladies were liberally supplied in ours. The room itself was dreary enough; the only seating accommodation I can remember was an antique horsehair sofa under which 'Marie V' (or 'Vicky') de Lara from the Spanish Department, who was the comedienne of our group, insisted on hiding her umbrella each day, lest marauders from Brownlow Hill should see it and take a fancy to it.

If we wished to speak to one of our male colleagues during coffee break, we had to lie in wait outside their commonroom for someone to enter and ask the individual to come out. At lunchtime, groups of men could dine together at the University Club at the bottom of Mount Pleasant, but women were not allowed to join. Their wives had formed a University Women's Club for afternoon meetings, but female members of staff were not allowed to join that either. Why didn't we protest? Lexie Zaina, then in the French Department, used to say it was because we had more to do. We certainly did a lot of lecturing. Even the bigger Departments of the Faculty had few members of staff to cover the broad topics fashionable in those days. I think, too, we were more amused than irritated by the ludicrous situations in which we sometimes found ourselves - as when my colleague John Rowe and I, invited to dine with Parkinson at Derby Hall, learnt on arrival that I had to eat my meal from a tray in our host's room whilst the two men ate at high table.

Relations between staff and students were cordial and mutually respectful. Many of the students were ex-servicemen with several years' experience in the armed forces (and sometimes in prison camps) to their credit; they found it remarkably difficult to cope with administrative details such as timetabling arrangements and were surprisingly in awe of classmates who had come to university straight from school. As was the custom, we addressed them all formally. This unwritten rule applied also between junior and senior members of staff - certainly in the two History Departments and I think elsewhere in the Faculty. A change in this respect came with the advent of Christopher Brooke as Professor of Medieval History in 1956 [1956-1967]. The news rapidly spread around that he had addressed a number of colleagues by Christian name. A discussion took place as to how suitably to respond. Dorothea Oschinsky, who was older than he was, decided that she would wait and see if he called her 'Dorothea'. If he did, she would respond with 'Christopher'. 'After all,' she argued, 'I am not the old family retainer'. Christian names thereupon became usual.

A change in male/female relations came as departments moved away from the Brownlow Hill site to separate houses in Abercromby Square. Mark Thomson resisted such a move for his department as long as he could, on the grounds that historians needed to be able to nip across to the Harold Cohen Library between lectures. I had by then acquired a handsome room with parquet flooring and elegant furniture, high up in the Clock Tower, and had no wish to leave it. However, Mark finally accepted the last of the houses likely to become available in Abercromby Square rather than be driven into what he suspected would be some unedifying purpose-built accommodation, and we were installed there, along with a few familiar departmental treasures such as our two bronze statuettes of Burke and Sheridan (or Burke and Hare, as generations of students preferred to believe) in time to welcome Professor David Quinn as our new Head.

In Abercromby Square, I welcomed the comradeship of my History colleagues (in a single commonroom at last) whilst regretting my separation from friends elsewhere in the Faculty, most of whom moved into the Modern Languages Building. The Faculty Board was a closed shop until one became a Senior Lecturer. My arrival at this distinction in 1964 coincided with the beginning of a period in which it became *de rigueur* for every committee to have a woman member. There were more women around now, but few were considered senior enough to be eligible, hence Miriam Allott and I found ourselves coxing and boxing with our advice on every conceivable subject. At about the same time, the onset of democracy resulted in my election as representative of the non-professorial staff of the Arts Faculty on Senate. Here too I was welcomed as a 'statutory woman', in which capacity it became my unhappy lot to serve on the Discipline Board which sat for a week in 1968 in judgment on the ringleaders of the sit-in. I was afterwards, along with my male colleagues, hanged in effigy in the Students' Union.

My appointment in 1980 as the first woman Dean caused anxiety among Senate House officials as to what I would do in graduation ceremonies at the point where male Deans doff their caps to the Chancellor or his deputy. Vice-Chancellor Whelan entered into the fun of pretending that we had arranged for me to blow him a kiss. Doreen

Bowsher, experienced as Sub-Dean of the Faculty, dismissed fears regarding the wellbeing of a Faculty run by two women with the good-humoured retort, 'I don't think there'll be a problem. I believe the Science Faculty has two men, and they get on alright.' Unfortunately, grimmer times set in with the first round of government cuts in funding. Two small departments, Linguistics (recently established to meet official demands for innovatory policies) and Italian (lovingly fostered by my friend Lexie Zaina), were scheduled for immediate destruction. Others were expected to lose so many staff by 'natural wastage' that they were likely soon to become unviable. An attempt to shield them by grouping Departments into Schools was described by a speaker at Senate as 'a piece of nifty footwork by the Dean of Arts', but it proved ineffectual in the long run. Of course we all hoped, and I think even believed, that the crisis was temporary. Some of us took early retirement under the illusion that it would help colleagues to ride out the storm. All in all, we did our best to buoy each other up, and morale was still high in the Faculty when my term of office came to an end.

Reginald T. Davies, lecturer, etc in English, 1948-1986

As a soldier, and then as an undergraduate who was paid for by a grateful country, I smoked like a small chimney, but had to stop on becoming an assistant lecturer because I could not afford it: such, in 1948, was University pay. Enjoying the good fortune of the post-war need for new staff and the particular requirement of our department of English Literature for my own, at that time, rare specialism, I had been appointed to teach the later medieval period. Newly arrived, I walked from the steam train off the platform at the old Central Station in a triumphant dream of greatness, but tickled that no one about me had the slightest idea of it.

A new colleague had taken me after the interview some months before to celebratory tea at what was Fullers, on the corner opposite that same Central Station, down Brownlow Hill on the open top-deck of a tram. She warned me earnestly, in the exultant sunshine, that I should have to have something published within three years or my appointment might not be renewed. At the interview Dean Ormerod, Professor of Ancient History [1928-1951, Dean 1945-1949], whose first name I was never to know let alone use, gigantic, and with knuckles swollen by arthritis, had played with me, reassuring and dangerous at once: 'Of course, at Oxford, your study of literature stops at 1832, the year of the Reform Bill!'

On my first Saturday, our Senior Lecturer, Archie McIlwraith, with warm and crusty kindness, entertained me to lunch at his home. He declared criticism was in so uncertain a state that a literary academic of integrity could only edit texts to enable truer reading. On his papers, scattered and still, as he had left them on his table in the Staff Reading Room of the Harold Cohen Library, in his subsequent last years dust gently settled: his eye-shield lay where he had dropped it, unused. After lunch, a snooze in arm-chairs on either side of the fire, and afternoon tea to revive us, Archie flung a cocktail party. There among others was James Mountford, every inch the impressive and effective Vice-Chancellor, and never any other, even when talking of his favourite football club which, if I remember right, was Wolverhampton Wanderers. To him, who was to become Sir James, I was introduced, callow new-boy that I was, so much smaller was the University and so much more a college. In the same Victoria Building, academics passed administrators on the grand stairs, the Vice-Chancellor himself having time to stop and talk about our latest publications, which he always knew of, or the Registrar, in the gents, time to try to dissuade one from some unwise enterprise that had come to his ears.

For several years I had to share a room, my first with that same Senior Lecturer: a gothic chapel, just beneath the clock in the Victoria Tower and to its right as you look up from below, it gave access to the flagpole on the roof, from which the flag, when removed, hung dripping over the banisters of our attic stairs to dry. The second was shared with a woman, appointed even more recently than I; and, though there was no alternative to sharing, the propriety of us two doing so was questioned by the Vice-Chancellor. So short of teaching rooms were we that, for one year, the Harold Cohen Library had to provide me a room for a seminar, much to the chagrin of the Librarian, Kenneth Povey, eccentric and an excellent scholar, who, when I deferred to him once, being the younger and junior, as we came together to the front of his library, said, 'Oh no! after you - otherwise you might think you owned the place'. He devised a system to classify his books such that, one evening, when we were making up new words over dinner in Hall, we invented the verb 'to povey', meaning, 'so to arrange books on the shelves of a library that they cannot possibly be found'.

My first head of department was Leonard Martin [Professor of English Literature 1929-1951, Dean of Arts 1934-1937], a gentle, thoughtful, immaculate scholar, who published even more in his eventual Scottish retirement than when in his chair - and in that, as in all things, he was an example to us all. He was delicate in body, but by taking every care of himself, especially by a little sleep every day for half an hour after lunch, he lived into his eighties; and he was delicate in moral sense, so that he would never talk with a young lecturer about what went on at the Board of the Faculty or at Senate, and it was as inconceivable that he should show him their minutes as that, at that time, 'openness' of government, academic or other, should ever become a matter of principle. The fight for all who teach to be on the Board of Faculty and their representatives on Senate was yet to come. The right was conceded with regard to the pioneering Arts Faculty by the Chairman of the Senate Committee considering the proposal, a Professor of Law, Freddie Odgers [1965-1977], brilliant lecturer and first-class company, High Tory as I believe he was, saying, 'I cannot conceive why anyone at all should want to be on Faculty, but, since you do, I can see no reason why you shouldn't.'

Most members of our departmental staff ate lunch one day or more a week at Staff House, and in the company of members of other departments. It was, for me, a substantial lunch, too, even though there was to be an equally substantial dinner that evening in Hall. Eating habits have changed, and there was more time for such intercourse, more general inclination, a larger consciousness of being at University. Official contact time with undergraduates was normally some eight hours a week, principally in lectures and tutorial groups ranging from an exceptional one to eight (but actual contact, in one way and another, many more). For some ten years we ran an 'Undefined Group' of some twenty or more, likewise from across the University though it was among members of the then undivided Arts Faculty that it began. It met once a month and at each other's homes, the subject of the next meeting and its leader making themselves apparent at the end of a session after refreshments. Discussion was of a range of topics including educational ones, issues in the news, personal problems and questions philosophical, religious or cultural, whatever we felt moved to discuss, yet we never fell out but grew in understanding and confidence. A chief reason for its demise was that their careers had called so many members to work in senior positions in other universities.

One topic was massive university expansion, particularly after the Robbins Report of 1963, and with that a new era began, the less desirable consequences of which I personally, never envisaged, unlike one or two of my more percipient colleagues. Most of us welcomed the implementation of Robbins' recommendations with enthusiasm, having an eye on our future advancement, but also as believers in equal opportunities for all who had the ability. For most of us, that principle was incontestable.

Richard Lawton, lecturer, etc, in Geography 1949-1970, Professor of Geography 1970-1983, Dean of the Faculty of Social and Environmental Studies 1977-1980

The Faculty to which I returned after service in the Royal Navy (1943-1946) was similar in academic structure to that of the early 1940s but very different in personnel. Few pre-war academic staff remained and many young, bright and often research-motivated scholars were taking up posts. Increasingly it was to be the strength of individual departments and their Special Honours schools on which the Faculty's reputation rested. Distinguished Heads of departments, often building on pre-war eminence, enhanced the reputation of their subjects: Walbank and Brink in Latin; Muir in English Literature; Thomson then Quinn in Modern History; Barraclough then Brooke in Medieval History; Budden and Gardner-Medwin in Architecture; Holford, Stephenson and Myles Wright in Civic Design; Whale and Shackle in Economics; Simey in Sociology; Darby and Smith in Geography; Hearnshaw in the newly established Department of Psychology. Of pre-war survivors, Mountford, a distinguished Latinist and

Dean (1941-1945), went on to become, arguably, the most able of the University's Vice-Chancellors to date (1945-1963) and the sharp-tongued Allison Peers (Gilmour Professor of Spanish, 1922-1952) achieved posthumous fame (notoriety in the view of those who saw themselves pilloried in the chapter on 'The Leisured Professor at Bay') in his *Red Brick University*, written under the pseudonym of Bruce Truscot in 1943-1945 and one of the most informative insights into the Civic Universities of pre-war days, not least their Arts Faculties. Despite Peers's strong views on the necessity for research in a university, sound teaching, with a strong emphasis on tutorial supervision, dominated the ethos and academic emphasis of many departments, especially some of the smaller ones. In retrospect it might have been to their benefit and longer-term viability had there been reorganisation into stronger Schools of studies with a greater research emphasis. As it was, such association was confined largely to the Boards of Studies that organised academic arrangements for students in closely related subjects.

The undergraduate population of the 1945-1951 years was also very different. The many ex-servicemen and women brought a breadth of wartime experience and, in many cases, varied previous careers in commerce and industry. They were demanding students whose commitment stretched small staffs to their limit. But they also provided a rich pool of talent for new posts being provided, not least in the newer social sciences. The Department rather than the Faculty provided the focus of activity, especially in those with a strong student society. While as an undergraduate (1946-1948) I played in the soccer XI, as a junior member of staff (from 1949) I occasionally turned out (along with Stan Gregory) for Geog.Soc. Many ex-servicemen saw their degree as a passport to a new career. Thus, while teacher training continued to provide the major outlet for many subjects (including most humanities and geography), for many of the social sciences jobs in business, social work, technical departments of central and local government and such increasingly graduate professions as accountancy encouraged the teaching of practical skills. This was particularly so in the departments that later formed the Faculty of Social and Environmental Studies, whether through practical, laboratory and field classes, or in such skills as statistics and computing or methods of economic and social survey. Some of these last had been pioneered in the pre- and war-time Social Survey of Merseyside pioneered by A.M. Carr-Saunders (Charles Booth Professor of Social Science, 1923-1937) and the Survey's Director, D. Caradog Jones. Increasingly the idea, sometimes even the designation, of 'Applied' came into certain of the courses given in SES Departments. It was a small but, in retrospect, significant contrast in emphasis between them and most of the humanities subjects, perhaps a symbol of their drawing apart.

Within the student body there was also, I think, less inter-departmental contact as the faculty grew in size, in particular as the result of larger age-cohorts and increasing numbers staying on in the sixth forms to take the 'A' Levels that replaced the Higher School Certificate in 1953. My teaching, even in the 1950s, was mainly focused on the Geography Honours students, apart from a regional course specially designed for the Part II of the General degree, mainly because of the increasing difficulty of background for the advanced final year options. The decision, in 1953, to admit students to a Preliminary Honours year, rather than, as previously, to the introductory year of a general B.A. from which Special Honours were recruited, led to a rapid progression to dominance of the Faculty by large Honours Schools. This was especially the case when, subsequently, students could take two out of the four first-year courses in their Honours subject and then concentrate entirely on them in both Part I and Part II. Within the general studies degree there was increasingly a tendency to focus on related subjects and, in the case of the social studies group, this was to lead to a new degree and an Honours School of Social Studies. Such developments pointed to academic changes in the Faculty in the 1950s which also reflected changing relationships between departments and which were leading to differences in the academic objectives and the resources needed to achieve these.

Thomas Kelly's history of the university up to 1981 is curiously silent on the reasons for the prolonged battle for independence - though this term may overstate the process - of the social sciences. Writing without access to the various reports which incorporated the arguments for and against the division of the Faculty of Arts, my impression remains that the fundamental reasons were academic. First, the changing agendas and the differing philosophies and concepts in both research and teaching. Secondly, an increasing focus on departments that reflected both specialisation of knowledge and learning and the organisation of much larger Honours schools. Thirdly, the increased demands on both physical and human resources needed to meet these, especially in science-like field and laboratory subjects, demands that certain senior figures in the Faculty seemed either unable or unwilling to secure (or, on occasion, even to press for) from the University's capital development programme and its non-recurrent (essentially for equipment) and recurrent departmental grants.

The first initiative in pressing the case for a new Faculty for the social and environmental studies (henceforth referred to as SES) came from a group of young staff from economics, geography, politics, psychology and sociology. The concept behind the degree in Social Studies was of a core course in the Preliminary year with three other subjects leading either to a single honours course in one of the participant departments or to a more broadly based social studies degree. Even within the participating departments involved (Economics, Economic History, Geography, Politics, Psychology and Sociology), however, there was no unanimity on the idea. Geography and Psychology had strong links with the Faculty of Science in which they had Honours Schools dating, respectively, from 1953 and 1963; Economics was interested in developing closer ties with Mathematics and Statistics; several feared weakening of longstanding links with, for example, History; Architecture and Civic Design stood outside both frameworks. But the situation clearly demonstrated the changed situation within the Faculty. The senior professors who argued the case for a new Faculty made too much of the growing administrative problems of a large, rapidly growing and increasingly diverse Faculty: the then Dean, Kenneth Muir (1958-1961) found little difficulty in demolishing the administrative burden argument by pointing to his substantial publications during his Deanship! Thus, although the new School of Social Studies brought a valuable new Degree and concept to the social sciences, one that mature students, in particular, were anxious to explore, the major objective was lost for a decade during which fundamental changes occurred in British universities.

I still regard this as a lost opportunity for the SES group to play an even fuller part than they did in the Robbins expansion of research and graduate schools fostered by the Social Science Research Council (SSRC) and the Natural Environment Research Council (NERC). The revision of the University's Charter in 1961 could have provided the opportunity for a new Faculty had the vision not been lacking. The Arts Faculty benefited less than it should have done from the relatively lavish funds - as these look in retrospect - that followed the Robbins Report and the great capital projects and much increased grants for equipment and recurrent costs that accompanied it. The fear, on the part of some in the Faculty, that SES would take funds away from the Humanities was, I am sure, misguided. The combined case from *two* Faculties for a bigger share of a larger cake would, I believe, have been of benefit to both. However, neither was there much enthusiasm in other faculties for such a development. Student recruitment was proving more difficult in the Sciences than in the Arts, and the Faculty, which was second in size to Science with nearly 1,400 students in the early 1960s, surpassed it in the next few years: by the mid-1970s the combined student numbers of Arts and SES as compared to Science was 1.4:1 and the two provided one-third of the University's students. However, the greater part of that growth came from expansion of big departments, especially those within the SES group: the ratio of Arts:SES changed from 2.4:1 in 1960-1961 to about parity by the mid-60s and was 1:1.4 by the mid-70s.

Far more significant than mere numbers, however, were changes in the backgrounds of those coming up to read in the respective Honours schools. Fewer and fewer had studied classics or even a modern language in the sixth form. Many wishing to read economics or architecture would have taken maths; those entering geography embraced a wide range of subsidiaries from history to geology or botany, quite apart from those who came from the 'science sixth' to read Geography Honours in the Science Faculty, a situation paralleled in Psychology. As 'A' Levels were developed in 'new' subjects (economics, then politics, sociology and psychology), the very idea of Arts and Science sixth-form studies changed and demanded greater flexibility of courses to meet the needs of a different type of sixth-former. As Academic Sub-Dean for the SES group of subjects (1960-1963) I was well aware of these changes and the new inter-and intra-faculty relations that they created.

The contrasts in the type of research being undertaken in the SES and Humanities departments forcibly underlined such academic divergence.

Many SES departments needed relatively expensive laboratories and equipment; they were, increasingly, heavy users of computer time; some used field equipment and vehicles and recurrent grants to support undergraduate field work. In short, many SES departments were no longer 'classroom' subjects but were science-like in their research and teaching methods and their staffing requirements, not least in the need for laboratory technicians and other support staff. It often seemed much easier for a post of lector to be approved than for a technical post to be created. The differential needs of departments within the Faculty of Arts could not have been more clearly demonstrated than when, belatedly, new accommodation was provided. Arts had lagged far behind Science in that new accommodation came only in 1965 in the shape of the Modern Languages and Social Studies (now Roxby) Buildings. Their internal layout reflected different needs. I well remember spending hours on the Joint Buildings Committee discussing the layout and furnishing of lecturers' rooms (to create the right ambience for tutorial classes) when, for me, more important was the problem of adopting the architect's module to the needs of cartographic and physical laboratories, including that of laying on services for these and the photographic department (there was no gas in the building, for example, and the ducting, inadequate for fume cupboards or computers, subsequently needed much costly adaptation). Nor were such differences in need confined to Geography. *De facto*, the Arts Faculty was divided by 1965 when the new buildings were commissioned.

By the time the Faculty of Arts next discussed its future organisation in 1968-1969 the case for separation of the humanities and SES was overwhelming. The arguments for and against the proposal, which came from the SES subjects, were presented, respectively, by Robert Steel (Geography) and David Quinn (Modern History [1957-1976]) at a special meeting of Faculty. The vote was tied, but I declined to use my Chairman's casting vote since, as I told Faculty, the pattern of voting gave clear evidence of the reality of the situation: SES representatives voted solidly for the split while the Humanities, which were in a majority on the Faculty, though mainly against, provided some support for it. In agreeing to forward the proposal, Faculty had to persuade Senate of the validity and viability of the new structure, many of the Senate members being suspicious of both the academic standing of some of the 'new' SES disciplines and, not least, of the radical - and as some thought - leftist attitudes of many of their staff. But the persuasive advocacy of the then Dean (Professor Basil Smallman [Professor of Music 1965-1985, Dean of Arts 1968-1971]), of Robert Steel (Geography and a Pro-Vice-Chancellor in 1971-1973), and of Ron Parker (Economics and shadow Dean in 1970-1971, then the first Dean of the new Faculty from 1971-1977), ensured that the new Faculty of Social and Environmental Studies came into being in 1971. The cumbersome title was itself a matter for considerable debate. Those departments in the new Faculty with a strong involvement in physical and natural science, such as Geography and Psychology, and in environmental matters, such as Architecture, Civic Design and again Geography, pressed the case for the inclusion of the word in the title: from the outset the more appropriate term 'Sciences' had been abandoned, not least because of the Faculty of Science's sensitivity over its use, in favour of the anodyne 'Studies'.

In retrospect, this long drawn-out and factious (often fractious) chapter in the history of the Faculty of Arts must surely be seen to have provided more gain than loss. Losses there were: for example the severance of old ties such as the unilateral decision of the Board of History to abandon the joint degree in Modern History and Geography (though happily students were able to follow a similar course in the Arts Faculty's new (1971) degree in Combined Studies); also the gradual loss of regular contact between colleagues with common interests in the humanities. The gains were many: a greater academic focus in both teaching and research; stronger and more widely representative presence on University committees and in Senate; enhanced and more equitable access to funding of capital and recurrent needs and of both academic and support staff; a stronger research drive, not least in the many new interdisciplinary developments of the 1980s.

One benefit, originally the object of great suspicion in Senate House, was the decision of both Arts and SES to become 'open' Faculties on which all members of the permanent academic staff had a seat and on which there was some student representation. Far from proving politically disruptive, this infusion of young blood brought energy and new ideas. Certainly, as Dean of SES (1977-1980) I had no reason to fear the 'broad

Left', the target of suspicion in other parts of the University, whose contribution to academic affairs and whose often policy-orientated research was substantial and whose involvement in the community and the problems of Merseyside was to the benefit of both the University and the region. In due course many of the reforms suggested by the social studies departments were adopted by the 'new' Faculty of Arts. In the 1980s, under pressure to cut back activities, fewer and stronger 'Schools' integrated many smaller (and sometimes weak) departments. Meanwhile new relationships were forged in Area Studies (for example Latin American, African, Central and Eastern European, Irish and European Population Studies) and in new interdisciplinary degrees. The dual strength of the Faculties in university affairs is evident in their presence amongst Pro-Vice-Chancellors and committee chairmen in the past two decades. Sadly, the delay in deciding the future cost both Faculties much in resources to fund such developments. By the 1972-1977 Quinquennium, Government funding lagged behind need and the cuts of 1974 were a foretaste of the stop/go attitude of successive governments towards the universities. The pathways subsequently trodden by all departments - whether Arts or SES - have been rocky, not least in this centennial year.

Robert Walter Steel, Professor of Geography 1957-1974, Dean of Arts 1965-1968, Pro-Vice-Chancellor 1971-1973

I arrived in Liverpool in January 1957. The Arts Faculty provided a new university world for someone who had never come across Deans before and whose concept of a Faculty was restricted to the quite ineffective Faculty of Anthropology and Geography in the University of Oxford. Geography in Liverpool was firmly in Arts but was associated with Science. As head of department I had therefore to deal with two very different deans, Herbert Fairman in Arts and Alan Burges in Science. Never having anticipated such a translation, I found myself a Dean of Arts within eight years of arrival in Liverpool. I followed immediately two very distinguished deans - Albert Sloman, who left the Faculty to become Vice-Chancellor of the University of Essex, and David Williams, who became a Pro-Vice-Chancellor and was chairman of some of the key

Senate Committees such as Staffing and Departmental Grants. In my experience, the Arts Faculty representatives always made a major contribution to the deliberations of Senate and hence to the smooth running of the university.

What struck me at once was the multiplicity and diversity of departments in the Faculty. In terms of staff and student numbers some were very small, while others, like English, History, and my own department, were large and complex. Thus early on I could see, first, the need for additional administrative assistance in the Faculty Office and secondly, the possibility of a division of the Faculty into two parts. Geography, Civic Design, Architecture and Economics, for example, were so different in the nature and complexity of their needs and problems from the traditional Arts subjects such as Modern Languages, Classics and History. I tackled the first matter forthwith and came to deal with the second later on, some years after I ceased to be Dean but when I was a Pro-Vice-Chancellor.

When faculties had relatively small departments, deans could cope with the varying needs and demands of many of these, especially as there was a well-established tradition in the Faculty that part-time Academic Sub-Deans (of which there had been some excellent ones over the years) should exercise discretion, if not authority. But what we now needed was a permanent and full-time administrative Sub-Dean - someone who was always in the Faculty Office and who could represent the Dean at meetings with other Faculties (nearly all of which had their permanent full-time Sub-Deans). There was some resistance in the Faculty. And there was, of course, the usual fear of the spread of bureaucracy in the university! The Faculty had a stroke of good fortune when F.T. Mattison was recruited from the University of East Anglia as its Sub-Dean. Frank endeared himself to nearly everyone very quickly, and 'made' the post for his successors, including Doreen Bowsher. Frank was able to listen patiently to all who called on him, whereas I as Dean had had only limited time for each head of department (and for others). Believing in personal face-to-face contact, I had found - and Frank confirmed this - that the amount of time needed for an interview varied inversely with the size of the department. David Quinn and I, for example, could sort out Modern History's problem vis-à-vis the Faculty in five minutes; but some of the smaller departments needed much more of the Dean's time. What the Faculty achieved in my time as Dean could not have happened without his help, support and understanding. After my time, Frank was eventually succeeded as Sub-Dean by Doreen Bowsher, one of the Faculty's own graduates and a former Lady President of the Guild of Undergraduates.

I continued as head of the large Department of Geography, at that time as its only professor, but I had wonderful support from senior colleagues (notably Richard Lawton and Mansell Prothero, both of whom became professors in due course). It was some years before the publication of the so-called 'Steel Report' on the 'Organisation and Administration of Departments'. As chairman of the Senate committee that produced the report in the early 'seventies, I was able to draw on my knowledge of the workings of Faculties, especially that gained from being Dean of Arts. But the strain of two jobs was considerable and I was very glad to return, full time as it were, to Geography in 1968.

However, by the time I retired from being Dean, I could see the need for a split in the Faculty if its parts were to compete with the other very well-organised faculties for funds and for representation on Senate committees. I suppose I played a leading role in bringing about the split which I know is still deeply regretted by some of my former colleagues, even after twenty or more years. There seemed, to many of us, very sound sense in the proposal for a Faculty of Social and Environmental Studies, though we in Geography were especially sorry to be separated from our colleagues in History. In the event, I believe both the old Faculty and the new benefited from the administrative change. But I still recall very vividly the verbal battles fought in Faculty and elsewhere - though they never disturbed long-existing (and still maintained) friendships. I remember particularly the debate in the Faculty where David Quinn was the advocate of the *status quo* and I spoke on behalf of those who were regarded as 'rebels'. I regretted the Quinn v. Steel debate not only because he was a much better debater than I was (the Irishman in him came out very clearly!) but because we had been close friends and associates ever since coming to Liverpool. We each reached Liverpool in 1957 - he from the University College of Swansea to which I eventually went as Principal.

Others will deal with the split and its consequences and will no doubt emphasize the continuing good relations that exist between the two

Faculties that represent the 'Arts' side of a very large university. I hope that someone will also write about the working out of the Steel report's recommendations about headship of department. This all took place after my move to Swansea in September 1974. My memory of the Faculty Working Party on the issue was of the great support that I had from Kenneth Muir. He had been Head of English Literature for over twenty years, and I had been Head of Geography for about sixteen years, so we kept very quiet when some issues were raised - notably, I recall, when one of the younger members from Social Science proposed, in all seriousness, that each department should elect by democratic vote who should be head of department for the coming term at a meeting held during the last week of the vacation!

I have many happy memories of the Faculty of Arts in Liverpool, and I am pleased to be associated with the celebrations that are taking place more than twenty years after I left Merseyside.

Paul Edward Hedley Hair, lecturer, etc in African History 1965-1979, Professor of Modern History 1979-1990

Even although I was only a bystander, two events which occurred during my first five years at the university perhaps deserve recording, even if only from a personal and no doubt idiosyncratic viewpoint. The student 'troubles' of 1969-1970 are competently discussed in the official history of the university and Kelly provides a very fair assessment of their origins, a genuine if fuzzy idealism on the part of a tiny minority of 'radical' students, allied to a post-adolescent derring-do on the part of a larger group of hangers-on anxious to cock a snook at any element of authority. What was perhaps more puzzling at the time, and perhaps more significant, was the studied indifference of the vast majority of students, only anxious to keep their heads down. The major disturbance arrived late at Liverpool, copy-cat activities having moved gradually northwards from university to university, and as it happened, more or less terminating nationally after the Liverpool authorities' response. As Kelly points out, humanities students were considered to form the backbone of the radical movement, especially those from the 'social science' departments soon to break away from the Arts Faculty. A rehearsal of the later large disturbance occurred when the Vice-Chancellor was Winston Barnes. The University was developing a nearby street of slum houses and moving the tenants elsewhere, and the radicals described this as an instance of capitalistic expropriation. From my upstairs window in the History School I looked down on a procession of about one hundred students, shouting and waving placards with the almost-witty declaration, 'Houses not Barnes!'. From my window I also looked across the Abercromby Square gardens. During the later disturbances a marginal 'demand' was that they should become a communal park, presumably a football field.

The major disturbance in March 1970 took the form of a group of radicals attempting to sabotage the university day-to-day administration by 'occupying' Senate House. As had happened elsewhere, there was alleged to be no possible immediate legal response, on the grounds that students formed part of the institutional fraternity (even more than the disturbances this show of impotence weakened public confidence in the universities). Eventually, however, it was announced that internal disciplinary procedures would be brought to bear on the ring-leaders; and my colleague, Mrs Collins, was involved (as she describes elsewhere). At the proceedings one student on trial produced a pistol and waved it at the panel; a Dean of Arts and other males recovered wartime reflexes and dived to the floor. Meanwhile a bishop wrote to *The Times*, deploring the disciplining of high-minded youth, but neglected to add that one of the martyrs was his son - as I then pointed out in a headline letter, somewhat heated and intemperate, to the same paper, which produced, to my surprise, two grateful telephone calls from Vice-Chancellors. (My disinclination to sympathise with violent 'Positive Action' may have had something to do with the fact that, unlike most colleagues, I had recently lived through, in a distant land, a genuine revolution; during which the poor illiterate messenger, who sat at the staff room door to bring us cooling drinks, while marketing was killed by revolutionary crossfire.)

A few days later the History building was invaded by a group of students who, failing to find Mrs Collins in her room, decorated the door with swastikas and burst into my (tiny) room, swarming up to my desk. The confrontation lasted about an hour and became more reasonable every minute; those silent at the back looked distinctly uneasy and those at the front turned from shouting to expressing politely their viewpoint, and we eventually separated, agreeing to disagree and more or less shaking hands. However, a character in dark glasses (much more unusual and threatening in that decade), with a foot on my desk, put forward what would later become New Age arguments. A new race of superior humanity was now around, he pronounced; a claim, I conceded, not unknown in South Africa.

Within the History building reactions to the troubles were mixed. A handful of students commandeered a classroom and wrote the Marxist periodization of history on the blackboard. A 'mass meeting' in a classroom was addressed warmly by the only other staff member present, who assured the meeting of the support of all History staff, which was curious, given that she was a guest visitor from North America. The whole radical scenario was then demolished by a mature student, a former Liverpool bricklayer who over many years had worked his way up the educational ladder to enter the university and was a long-term, card-carrying member of the Communist Party: in a careful, cool speech he denounced undisciplined bourgeois shenanigans. Among university staff a group had formed a radical society, and some close colleagues sympathised. It seemed right to counter this with a 'moderate reform' group, and with limited support across the university such a group was formed. We discussed certain changes, some of which in fact were to come about, notably the greater participation in university committees of both junior staff and students. I put a great deal of effort into this society, but as the disturbances passed into the distance it declined and died. The *coup de grace* was given deviously. On the advice of one of the executive group, a distinguished elder statesman among staff, with known mild-leftish leanings, was invited to be chairmen, to give us a less reactionary flavour. He agreed, and then chaired the next meeting at such a slapdash, dismissive speed that the society was killed off instantly.

The aftermath of the disturbances was equally unpredictable. The most patent change to come about was the introduction of a system of student representation on university committees, and this (it seems to me) failed. I believe that it was intended as more than a neat device to take the steam out of student protest, but, as predicted by many reactionaries, students had little to contribute to staff debates. Regularly the election

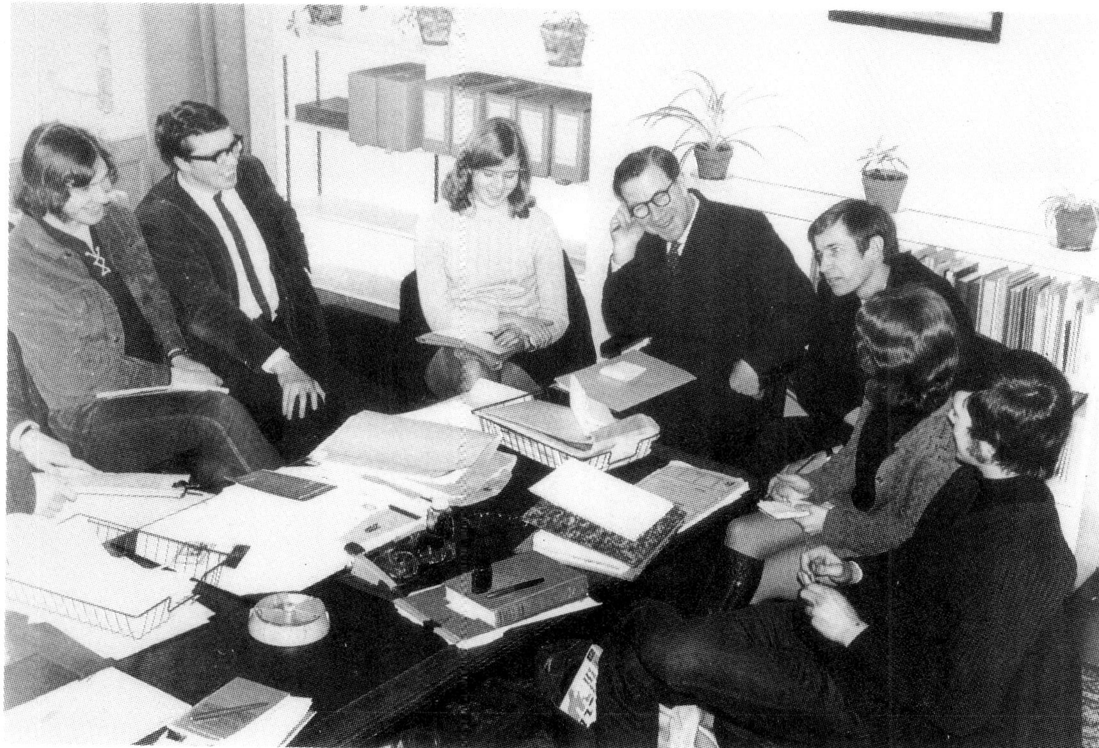

A seminar in progress in the History building 1969

Professor A.R Myers conducting the seminar

WE OCCUPY ...... WE STAY ...... UNTIL ......

At 2.30., 350 students in protest against the refusal of the Vice Chancellor to give satisfactory answers to various questions, occupied the Senate House of the University of Liverpool.

The occupation has now formulated five points, the meeting of which will be condition for withdrawal.

The demands are:

1) That Senate Council and the Court proclaim their opposition to all forms of discrimination on racial grounds, and consequently disassociate themselves from the views of the Marquess of Salisbury and call for his immediate resignation.

2) That Council and Court order a detailed Schedule of all university investments - to be published in the Staff Newsletter - and Guild Gazette.

3) That an independent public enquiry be held into methods used at all university levels for keeping data and information of staff and students.

4) That the Vice Chancellor gives satisfactory answers to the questions of political files and chemical and biological warfare.

5) That there be no victimisation of any people taking part in this occupation.

Text of a notice from 'occupying' students affixed to Senate House, 1970

The text transcribed from part of the original which was later torn down. The five points referring to (1) Rhodesia, (2) sanctions-breaking oil companies, (3) student dossiers, (4) and (5) as stated.

procedure among students failed to be operated because of lack of candidates, regularly any students elected failed to attend the committees, or attending the committees failed to break silence. Even at departmental level, where staff-student committees were resumed or installed, the procedure tended to be kept going more by staff initiatives than student enthusiasm, any novel or really significant issue being put into the mouths of students to raise, by caring or discontented staff. Meanwhile, as the decades passed by, one of the disciplined ringleaders of the disturbances became a prominent media figure. I monitor his utterances and fear that he has declined to a mere light pink. However, fifteen years after the disturbances, on a train from London I sat opposite two young-middle-aged business men, immaculately dressed and enjoying some light refreshment. Perhaps it was the latter that set them reminiscing, and lo!, they were activivists in the disturbances. As they talked the capitalistic veneer peeled off: their language began to acquire the simplistic codification of Marxist discourse and the tone of their voices modulated to one of one venomous rectitude and dedication. Interesting.

At the time of the disturbances my head of department, David Quinn, was on study leave in America; but he played an important role in the division of the Faculty, in 1970. As explained elsewhere, he led the opposition to the split in the final debate, and this made sense because the History School was probably the entity in the rump Arts most affected. The 'rump Arts' vote was divided, with some of those supporting the split doing so because they felt likely to be unaffected or because they welcomed getting rid of some turbulent elements and having more of their own way in getting on with their own thing. The case for the split is well put elsewhere but it is suggested that both subsequent Faculties gained. This strikes me as debatable. Completely unimportant as my voice then was, I felt at the heart of the argument. Geography had a research and teaching interest in Africa, and I had been recruited, in Africa - my first contact being as it happened with Robert Steel, the Professor of Geography - in order to teach a joint Geography-History course dealing with that continent. Hence, shortly after my arrival, an Africanist in Geography (Mansell Prothero) and myself started up an African Studies Group. If I found it odd that Robert now campaigned for a Faculty barrier across the History/Geography course, I also was unhappy in respect of the second string to my bow, the social and demographic history of Britain, a newfangled 'quantitative' study, where my contacts lay more with seceding than retained Arts Faculty elements.

I cannot of course challenge the view that the SES Faculty largely did well out of the split. It was assumed that the prime motive was to appear by name more eligible for money from various outside bodies of a 'social sciences' disposition; and the departments involved succeeded. As regards the rump Arts Faculty, to my mind its subsequent development bore the marks of the attitudes displayed during the split. After all, the Arts chairs and departments were almost all long-standing, indeed more or less *ab ovo*; whereas the vast majority of SES chairs and departments were not only relatively recent but had proved open-minded to fission, renaming, and multiplication. Moreover, a number of the oldest departments were in requirement decline. Compulsory Latin and Greek only in the 1950s, a modern language course for all Arts disciplines only in the 1960s - before being dropped in such very recent decades, these requirements for student admission to the Faculty or to all courses therein had lasted a long time. Staff of the relevant departments cared for both their subject and their job security. So it is not surprising that, in defence of a set ring of disciplines and at times in sympathetic defence of the apparently threatened staff members - exhibiting an old-boy (or even an old-girl) network mentality - 'Arts' staff tended to be traditionalists, eager to man the barriers for the status quo at the drop of a hat; or that the future SES staff noted this and were disgruntled. More positively, as Professor Lawton notes elsewhere, there were genuine or asserted doubts about the standards of some of the 'new' disciplines; and also, in some quarters, about the motivation of some of their staff, thought to be too 'leftish'.

I opiniate that after the split the Arts Faculty suffered. It might have gained more money in a large Faculty as a spin-off from the genuine large claims of the 'social sciences' departments; and it might have been sheltered from the extreme staff cuts of the 1980s. But its appalling slowness in the 1970s and 1980s to obtain - or even to entertain the thought of operating - advanced technology, its disinclination to recognise new disciplines, and its determination to be perversely defensive, surely owed something to the dominance of traditionalist attitudes, undiluted by the more vigorous if sometimes loud youthfulness of the 'social sciences' - and not merely to external factors such as lack of funds. (To be fair, change was inhibited by the inability to remove individual staff whom time had proved inadequate to fulfil their contractual duties, locked in as academics were to a beloved but publicly indefensible life-tenure system.) It is true that within the rump departments some experimentation took place, some advances were made, and existing high standards were in some parts maintained. But in general it took a couple of decades and the next generation of staff before the trauma of the split was on a wide front overcome.

On the other side of the divide, perhaps all was not complete joy. Now that environmentalism and feminism have replaced Marxism as the morally uplifting flavour of the day, the following comment may not be too hastily spat upon as McCarthyism. Covert political indoctrination is always practised in academia, not least by traditionalists, and cannot be stamped out; but certain SES courses, particularly some with an alleged historical content, practised overt political indoctrination, which in a broader faculty would probably have been suitably corrected. Again, after the divide History and Economic History found themselves next door but in different faculties, with quaint results, such as that, in the same year, one state council awarded more staff to the latter and a different state council decreed far fewer to the former. No overall view of the discipline of History was ever taken. 'Social history', practised in both departments, floated uneasily - at least as far as external finances were concerned - between the two. Economic History regrettably limited its time-perspective to recent centuries (yet wisely attempted world coverage), History rather uncomfortably spread itself over almost two millenia. But when it was suggested that all History courses should incorporate an element of economic history a senior colleague boasted innumeracy and hence *non possumus*, and this was accepted as a telling excuse and the end of the matter. Another generation of staff thinks very differently. Both departments have latterly been State-recognised as having high research and teaching profiles, yet I am not persuaded that, unified in a united faculty, they would not, over the intervening decades, have done even better, more broadly. Certain other departments found the split unhelpful: not everyone in Architecture, for instance, became reconciled to the SES mould. If the split is to be somewhat tendentiously described as one between 'humanities' and 'social sciences', we must be grateful that nevertheless some 'science' seeped through into the Arts Faculty and some 'humane studies' persisted in SES - for instance, notable historical studies in Geography.

All the above is water under the bridge. Concentrating understandably on the present and future, many of the present shift in the two faculties think this episode of the past better forgotten. One last opiniation is therefore forward-looking. If academic contacts are never easy to achieve over a recent Faculty divide, Arts exists even further apart from Science and Medicine. All sorts of attempts to overcome the barriers to integrated knowledge have been made over the decades, often on the initiative of concerned Arts staff, but success has been limited and generally short-term. My own attempts are perhaps typical. In the early 1980s, following a promise in my inaugural lecture, I played a part in founding societies for the History of Science and the History of Medicine, whose existence has helped to introduce these subjects, eventually and on a very small scale, into the curricula of Science and Medicine. Apart from a handful of thoughtful, dedicated and cheerful individuals - God bless them! - support in those other faculties for even this trifling inter-faculty exchange of ideas has verged on the negligible; support in the Arts Faculty has been, more or less, on a par. Good reasons abound. But perhaps a modicum of the wild enthusiasm of the founders of the Faculty for Learning in general would be in order.

Doreen Bowsher [Arthur], English 1948-1952, Education 1952-1953, Lady President of the Guild 1952-1953, Sub-Dean of the Arts Faculty 1971-1984

Eighteen years after graduating from it, I came back to the Faculty of Arts in January 1971, to the administrative post of Sub-Dean. There were major differences. No longer was the Faculty centred on the old quadrangle, no longer in the Victoria Building and the New (1914) Arts Building, with only outposts in Abercromby Square. Now the School of Architecture marked its northern boundary; the end of Bedford Street and the southern side of Abercromby Square were wholly Arts and behind the square were three new tall buildings which housed all other departments. There too was the Arts Reading Room, the first separate addition to the University Library, with lecture rooms on the ground floor and an undergraduate reference collection on the upper floor (plus, for a time, a selection of carefully placed buckets when it rained). There were many more members of staff. There were many, many more students and, as in the rest of the university, no longer were the majority from Merseyside and living at home but from the rest of the country and needing accommodation. The degree structure had changed: all B.A. degrees were honours degrees and the Freshers were admitted to their chosen honours schools at the beginning not the end of the first year. A further major change was imminent. In September 1971 the Faculty divided, with the 'humanities' remaining as the Faculty of Arts and the creation of the nominally self-explanatory Faculty of Social and Environmental Studies.

The seventies were a period of optimism and stability. The spirit of Robbins still ruled; even if we were never given all that we wanted, the expansion which had so accelerated in the sixties continued, at a gentler pace. The Faculty was able to establish some new chairs and several new lectureships, and its student numbers continued to increase. Towards the end of that decade there arrived a government paper predicting, on demographic evidence, a dearth of qualified university students in the late 1990s and indicating therefore that some universities would close. The premisses on which the conclusions were based were questioned and the figures were revised; but we could not foresee, of course, the decisions taken by later governments which have produced today's very different actuality. In 1981 the horrors began: no longer were we to think of expansion but of retrenchment, of economies. Soon there was the first Premature Retirement Scheme. Departments began to amalgamate to form larger (i.e. stronger) units - or to disappear altogether. This was a very difficult time for a great many of us: the psychological adjustment was hard. The greater changes of later date I have only observed, since I left in September 1984, under another Premature Retirement Scheme.

One result of the student protests of the late sixties, which hit Liverpool in 1970, was the move to 'democracy', to more open university government, particularly for non-professorial staff. Membership of the

Board of Faculty was opened to all permanent members of staff, plus some student representatives. (Recently a Guild President was asked what students now thought about the famous 'sit-in' of March 1970, at the time so traumatic. 'What sit-in?' was the reply. *Sic transit* ... .) This change came about after much discussion of the Faculty constitution and was one of the many *ad hoc* matters which engaged the Faculty over the years. Another memorable one was the introduction of the B.A. degree in the affiliated colleges, a debate which sometimes seemed interminable. Briefer was a fierce - and effective - defence of the University Press when its closure was suggested. There were countless Faculty working parties, to make preliminary proposals on, for example, revision of the degree structure. Other matters were on agendas annually, almost marking the passage of the year. These included the allocation to departments of the recurrent (i.e. general) grant, the equipment grant, and the library grant - with much dismay when a formula was introduced for the last. (We laid bets in the Faculty Office on who that year would intone that Books were the Equipment of Arts, and who would compare the paucity of the money allocated to the whole faculty with the vast sum found necessary by the Physics Department.) Very important was the annual planning exercise, with every few years the preparation of a major plan for submission to higher bodies in the University, and if approved, to the University Grants Committee. The last Quinquennial Plan was requested by the UGC in 1971; after that we moved to quadrennial planning (including a rolling quadrennium), triennial planning, and I think biennial planning. One wondered what on earth was going on; but this mirrored the growing uncertainty of university funding.

There were moments of light relief. One Chairman on one occasion kept the Board quorate by offering a lift home to the crucial departing member. My lips must be sealed on which Dean fell asleep one hot afternoon in the middle of a committee; or which Dean, rising to address the Faculty in the Senate Room, regularly knocked over his top-heavy chair. One Selection committee was electrified when a candidate in front of them fainted; fortunately the external member of the panel was a doctor and the candidate, once revived, was offered and accepted the post.

As an undergraduate I had never given a thought to the administration of the university. I had twice been to the Dean's office and knew he had a secretary (who frightened me more than the Dean did). The Faculty Office, like everything else, grew in the sixties. Answerable to the Dean, we dealt with all the Faculty paperwork, with queries of all kinds, and with details of student admissions and other records. Our initial office equipment now seems antediluvian. A necessarily large staff did everything manually: there were manual typewriters and duplicators, and no calculators. Electric typewriters gradually crept in (but only by special pleading), it was a great day when the first photocopier arrived, and finally the general office obtained its first word processor and the Admission office its first computer terminal.

The students were - almost all of them and almost always - a pleasure to meet. The vast majority were 18+. Whatever the current fashion in dress, underneath were very likeable young people. Most who came to my office needed advice or help with minor or occasionally very serious and sad problems. Most of my memories of students make me smile. There was, for instance, the Modern Language student supposed to be spending his year abroad who had prolonged his vacation job as a bus conductor - unfortunately one day his route took him through Abercromby Square and his bus was boarded by the secretary of his department ... Again, there was the Fresher, a late applicant, who appeared for the first few days of the Autumn term and was next heard of when he wrote from Risley Remand Centre, asking if the Dean would provide the several hundreds of pounds needed for his surety. Subsequently it was discovered that at least one other university had expected him and it seemed likely that more than one Local Authority had promised him a grant. Another enterprising but more worthy student got himself a job as a part-time cleaner in the university, working the early morning shift so that he could arrive always on time at his first lecture.

There we have it. My real memories are of people, of the students and colleagues, academic and non-academic, who made the Faculty a community. It is obviously not possible to name all and it seems unfair to name only some - with certain exceptions. This limitation applies even to those who were Faculty officers. But I would like to pay tribute to the non-academic but rightly-named 'support staff'. On behalf of other departmental clerical officers and secretaries I name Margaret Burton of the School of English, Pat Brooksbank of French, and Mollie Burns of

Music, all three among the longest-serving at that time; and among the porters I name Andy Manlond of the Modern Languages Building, who was a constant support to students. Within the Faculty Office I was fortunate to be supported by Margaret Gilmour, Pam Yeomans who succeeded Pat Elliott as Faculty Secretary, and Myrtle Lewis who with superb efficiency ran the Admissions office. And who could forget Des Evans, who as co-Sub-Dean enlivened the whole place for seven years. The Deans I served were seven: those of us in the Faculty Office who worked closely with them, and for them, were fortunate indeed. Within the walls, Faculty affairs were discussed at length and seriously, yet laughter would keep breaking through. Life was good and so much of it was fun.

[An editorial tailpiece. I embroider two of Mrs Bowsher's references. First, a 1980s student with problems. During her course both parents died of cancer, one after the other; despite the home being some way out of Liverpool, she nursed them and cared for her siblings; because she tried to keep up her work, only occasional absences revealed the circumstances to her tutors; after a short break she returned and took her degree. She never complained. Second, Des Evans, a man of good cheer who carried documents between the Faculty Office and departments at such speed that he seemed to be a Mercury with winged ankles, a responsible and delightful young man who, shortly after leaving his Faculty post, was killed, with his wife and all their children, in a horrific road accident. Echoing Mrs Bowsher, it is good to have known such.]

PART TWO

ESSAYS

Informative and Critical

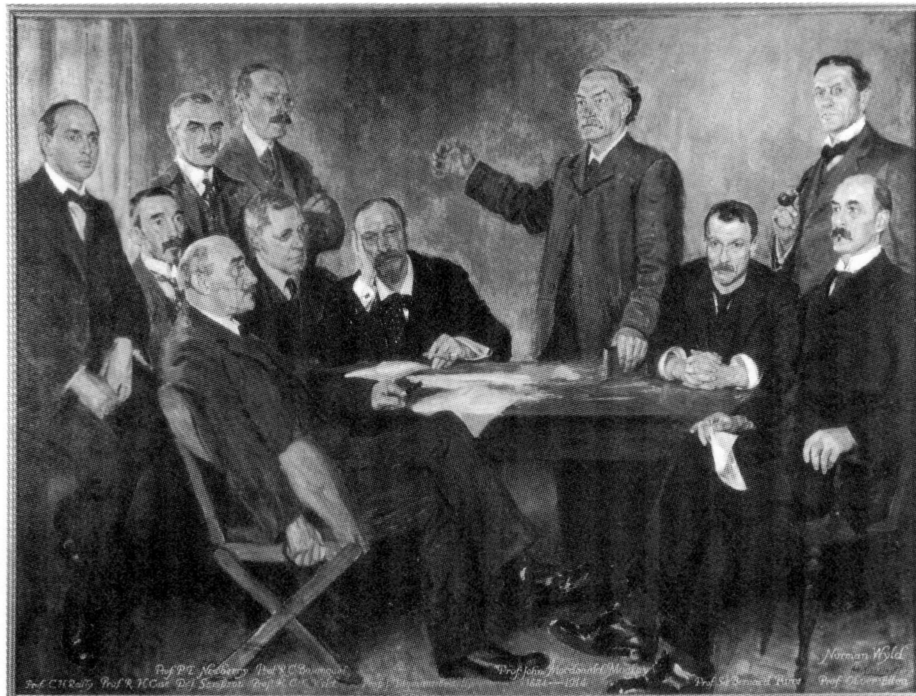

Leading members of the 'New Testament' Arts caucus, 1914

(from left to right) C.H. Reilly, R.H. Case, (behind) P.T. Newberry, J. Sampson, (behind) R.C. Bosanquet, H.C.K. Wyld, J. Fitzmaurice-Kelly, J.M. Mackay, B. Pares, N. Wyld, O. Elton

THE CLAIMS OF THE ARTS FACULTY

Bernard Beatty

The centenary of the Faculty of Arts in the University of Liverpool is celebrated in December 1996. We may recall what we are celebrating. Since the structural pattern of other comparable universities is broadly similar to our own, it is easy to think that there was some inevitability about the Faculty of Arts's existence and early development. This is not so. A picture of early Faculty members - which has been housed in various places in the past and is now splendidly sited on the stairway of the Sydney Jones Library - gives us a clue to why things turned out as they did and will give me a thread to hold together my own version, incomplete and partial as it must be, of the one hundred years now being celebrated.

In the centre of Albert Lipczinski's composition, standing with his right had raised, is the commanding figure of the Rathbone Professor of History, John Macdonald Mackay. He was by all accounts a man of 'compelling personality', and the picture gives us some sense of this. The picture was begun in 1914 and completed in 1917. It shows us Mackay addressing a group of influential academics consisting of the Professors of Russian, Spanish, English Language and Philology, English Literature, Architecture, Egyptology, and Classical Archaeology, together with the Secretary of the University Extension Board and the University Librarian. These had met as a discussion group for some years and were acknowledged as a driving force in the University under the name of the 'New Testament'. The picture helps us to recognise the part played by Mackay in conceiving the Faculty of Arts and, indeed, in shaping the character of the whole University.

Before 1896, the University (College) consisted of a thriving Medical School, some Professors, odd lecturers, and a Principal. The last was also Professor of Greek and the Registrar, when not selling text-books to students, doubled as Lecturer in Italian. Between Arts staff and the Senate there were no intermediate structures. Mackay saw clearly that two models of more complex organisation for the expanding College were possible. The first was that now adopted by American Universities. We would call it 'managerial'. Mackay spoke more straightforwardly: 'I desire to see the European University rise in England and not the repellent American type.' He disliked the 'overpowering commercial habit' of the latter which, in his view, merely led to 'a débris of classes and lectures and petty inconsequent committees'.

These words come from his opening address to the entire Arts Faculty (published in 1897). By then, the battle was won. Instead of a managerial model which cast the central officers of the University simply as fund-raisers, Mackay dreamed of a university where the Faculties exist not on paper but are 'the first organ of the University', directly controlling 'the labours of teachers and taught and their common studies.'

It is difficult for us now to see the originality and force of this conception though it derives, in part, from Matthew Arnold's suggestion (1868) about Faculty-based universities in 'Leeds and Liverpool' which might turn those 'overgrown provincial cities' into 'European cities' like Strasbourg or Lyons and into authentic 'intellectual centres'. Arnold reinforced this viewpoint in the opening address which he gave to the first full session of the University College (1882). Mackay insisted, in Arnold's spirit, that Faculties rather than notional and centralising managerial bodies should have a primary function because 'in such bodies (sc. Faculties), conscience and the love of duty increase with responsibility.' It was this impracticable dream (or so it begins to seem) that became solidly realised and it played a considerable part in influencing the development of other English universities. We should recall that Liverpool was the largest provincial city in England at the time. Certainly Mackay seems to have acted as 'midwife' to the new Birmingham University.

The Faculty of Science in Liverpool was established only in 1902, and the Faculty of Engineering only in 1903. But in 1896 a strong Faculty of Arts was considered, by the Faculty's founders, integral to the understanding of university life in the city. The more remote origins of the Arts Faculty lie, of course, in the developing cultural life of Liverpool in the nineteenth century, associated with William Roscoe and others and finding particular form in the Museum, Walker Art Gallery, Picton Reading Room, the Royal Institution, and the Academy for Arts. It was probably this huge cultural investment in Liverpool that prevented the new university from developing simply as a College of Science. For it was conceived specifically as a great European University with broadly based Faculties, founded and governed by academics of repute, and balancing cultural, scientific, and professional expertise. Mackay's energy and uncompromising insistences attracted financial investment. The noble idea came first and the necessary money followed. It attracted, too, figures of great distinction to the Faculty.

Even at its origin in 1881, there were great scholars in Arts, such as A.C. Bradley of English, but the new Faculty was the first in the country, in 1908, to set up chairs in Spanish and in Russian. It anticipated and created, rather than simply reacting to, circumstances. Always strong in English Literature, History, German, Philosophy, and Classics, it moved fast to establish strengths in English Language (chair 1904), in French (chair 1905), and in Egyptology (chair 1906). The Roscoe Chair of Art (1885) became the Faculty's Chair of Architecture in 1904. The founding of the Institute of Archaeology led to appointments and investments of such worth that the University Council could unblushingly boast in its Annual Report for 1905-1906 that Liverpool's ability to engage with the subject was 'on a scale without parallel in other British Universities'.

If we return then to Lipczinski's picture, we can understand how, by the time of its painting in 1914, the Faculty of Arts was strong, purposive and self-confident, and very well regarded. At this time, the total number of students in the University was 1,178, of whom 419 studied Medicine and 383 studied Arts. These two Faculties had two-thirds of the students. From the beginning a considerable number of Arts students were women (26% of all students in the university in 1914) and about a quarter of the students were part-time. The Faculty was so large and varied that it conceived the idea of Boards of Studies (1905) to oversee the arrangements for particular subjects or groups of subjects. They are a further implementation rather than dilution of Mackay's idea of the Faculty.

A visible sign of the Faculty's status at that time was the construction of the handsome Neo-Classical Arts Faculty building, incorporated skilfully into the main Redbrick complex in the same year as Lipczinski began his painting (1914). The building is adorned with sphinxes as an allusion, presumably, to the excellence of the University Magazine (edited as *The Sphinx* by Ramsay Muir in its early years in the mid 1890s). This building was one of the few erected at the direct expense of the University rather than through private benefaction. It opened directly out of the main Entrance Hall of the Victoria Building. When I first came to the Faculty in 1964, the magnificent common room of this Faculty building was dominated by Lipczinski's picture.

It is a danger, perhaps, to see the pre-1914 period through a golden Arcadian haze but we should understand the importance of certain guiding conceptions, insistences, and structures in the subsequent life of the University, and recognise the essential part played by the Faculty of Arts in their establishment. The period from 1914 to the 1960s was one of consolidation for the Arts Faculty, a period abounding with considerable figures and considerable scholarship. Visiting lecturers accredited to its establishment included Gustav Holst, Donald Tovey, Herbert Read, and Bronislaw Malinowski. Many holders of chairs (e.g. Allison Peers, J.F. Mountford, and A.H. Armstrong) were of the greatest distinction. The Chair of Music was established and occupied by Gerald Abraham in 1947. In the interwar years, the Arts Faculty was the largest in the University. More and more students took Honours degrees. After the Second World War, however, the Faculty maintained its character in a university whose centre of gravity was, increasingly, established numerically in medicine, engineering and science.

In the 1960s, redbrick Liverpool University expanded and took on something of the appearance of the concrete and glass institutions of that time. The Faculty would no longer fit into its 1914 premises and a new site adjacent to and partly including Abercromby Square was set up in 1966. A new Faculty office was set up in the Square itself to which Lipczinski's picture was duly moved. Since Senate House was built at this time, the Arts Faculty retained its visible proximity to the corridors of power. A new building on this site, rather timidly suggesting the idiom of a quadrangle and the fading authorisation of Le Corbusier, was designated as the Arts Reading Room though the major collection of arts books remained in the Harold Cohen Library. Later still, a new Arts and Social Studies Library, the Sydney Jones, situated at the side of Senate House, reclaimed the Arts Reading Room's collection of books and thus finalised the movement of Arts students from one side of the campus to the other. The opening of the Eleanor Rathbone Theatre (1973) provided an excellent adjacent site for the theatrical productions always associated with the Faculty (memorably Nicholas Shrimpton's production of *The Tempest* with Kenneth Muir as Prospero and Hermione Lee as Miranda). The rapid expansion of the University in these years produced larger Departments, some new Departments and, eventually, a new Faculty (Social and Environmental Studies) which took half of the old Faculty of Arts with it (1971). Many patterns of co-operation (e.g. joint courses in History and Politics, the

Institute of Latin American Studies, Communications Studies) persist across both Faculties.

During the same period, the Board of Faculty became open to everyone, and the professoriate became frequently distinguishable from the (rotating) Headship of Departments. The effect here and in the newly modified Senate was to increase consultation but to remove the careful balance between Faculty and Professoriate, between initiative, control, and representation, established in the Faculty's origins. Nevertheless the period from the mid 1960s to the mid 1980s was a time of considerable solidarity, intellectual exchange, and scholarly achievement in the reconstituted Faculty as it became used to its new environment. All students, when not otherwise engaged in the mild revolutionary disturbances of those times (Senate House was crowned with a Red Flag for a period), now took Honours Degrees in Single, Joint, or Combined Schools. The Faculty felt itself to be such.

The more recent history of the Faculty has been marked by the present crisis in British universities. Along with many other institutions, it has been shaped by the forced marriage of an uncertain *perestroika* and a more certain downsizing. 'Frozen' became a term associated with curtailed academic posts rather than with pleasing hedgerow appearances. The Faculty lost it ancient holdings in Italian, Russian, and Celtic. Departments amalgamated and large Schools formed. Departmental, Board, Faculty, Budget Centre, and Course Quality structures seem to have been superimposed on one another and alongside yet further models of radiating central control - much in the fashion of the crude sixteenth-century vaulting imposed on the more subtle structures, still discernible and pleasing, of the cloisters of what is now Chester Cathedral. We should be grateful, perhaps, to have a roof at all, however clumsily fashioned. Nevertheless, the Faculty has survived, made gains here and there, and will continue to do so.

Many of its present problems arise directly out of its success. The expansion of universities in the 1960s and the recent considerable expansion of the proportion of the population going to universities has led to unprecedented demand for Arts courses which the Government, for good reasons or bad, is determined to resist by selective financial constraints. Without such manipulations, the proportions of Arts students in the University would naturally revert to pre-War proportions. The larger Departments in the Faculty, in particular, now find themselves teaching hugely increased numbers of undergraduates and postgraduates with less staff and with a greater than ever insistence on high-level research. There being no Faculty Common Room or anything remotely like it, Lipczinski's picture has re-appeared on a stairway.

Somehow, the centre holds. Recent 'Teaching Quality Assessment' visitors to major centres of the Faculty have praised the excellence which they have found. Very major research projects are undertaken and widely acclaimed. Books appear. The energies which the present Dean and his colleagues are putting into the Centenary celebrations of the Faculty of Arts are a convincing testimony to their conviction of its continuing worth and fecundity of promise. This in a nation which seems largely to have lost the sense of its supporting institutions but still nurtures residual memories of their force, and hankers, in its own way, after that vision of collective, independent, intellectual enquiry into Arts and Letters, freely undertaken, which, one hundred years ago, set this University on course and is inseparable from the existence of 'a great European University'. Mackay's model of Faculty structure is the only form of structure generated by, rooted in, and wholly specific to universities. It is hard to see what could, either confidently or through inadvertence, replace it which would not be likely to jeopardise the primary purposes of university education. Matthew Arnold described these purposes to those assembled in our first full session as going beyond the need to establish economic prosperity by satisfying 'the need in man for intellect and knowledge, his desire for beauty, his instinct for society', so that 'intellectual culture becomes a power among you'.

A century on from these not wholly repudiated origins, we certainly have something to celebrate and can recognise gratefully something of the realisation of that power of 'intellectual culture' in the impressive history of this University's Arts Faculty. Long may the Arts Faculty thrive!

THE BUILDINGS OF THE FACULTY OF ARTS:
a barometer of changing architectural values

David Thistlewood

In common with other foundation disciplines of the university except the Medical Sciences, the Arts were initially housed in the old Lunatic Asylum, refurbished by Alfred Waterhouse in 1881-1883, which fronted towards Ashton Street, on the site of the present Quadrangle. Waterhouse had a reputation for economical, durable work, and the expenditure of £4,540 on heating and ventilation and, particularly, tiled decoration must certainly have transformed the asylum's interior. However, externally it remained unmodified, and for a decade this severe and uncompromisingly 'institutional' barrack-like building, exemplifying parsimonious charity, defeated the projection of an appropriate image for the new centre of learning. It was also grossly overcrowded and ill-equipped for other than classroom teaching, giving rise to a number of early subject departures. Chemical Science moved to its new laboratory complex in Brownlow Street (designed by Waterhouse, 1884-1887) in 1886, and Engineering Science moved into the Walker Engineering Block on Brownlow Hill (Waterhouse, 1887-1891) in 1889. The Arts were the third main academic grouping to occupy newly built premises, moving into the Victoria Building (Waterhouse, 1888-1893) on its opening in 1892.

While such relatively high prioritising of the Arts may now be surprising it had much to do with their propensity - which might well have kept them in the old asylum - for adapting to accommodation that would not have suited other disciplines. The Victoria Building was conceived as having three prime elevations (to Brownlow Hill, to Ashton Street, and to the already imagined and partly realised Quadrangle), offering no provision for the sort of 'rear' activities of commercial delivery and external storage associated with laboratory buildings. It contained a centre of administration, a galleried assembly vestibule, a large lecture theatre and a main library, which is not to say that the Arts were fitted into left-over spaces but that the non-uniformity of their requirements proved useful within a difficult interior planning exercise. Waterhouse was one of the foremost British architects of the late nineteenth century (at the time of his engagement he was President of the Royal Institute of British Architects), with recognised attributes of economy, meticulous planning, sound construction, scholarly decoration and a command of a restrained Gothic which had ensured longstanding associations with clients ranging from the Prudential Assurance Company and Manchester Corporation to the colleges of Oxford and Cambridge, as well as the confederation of embryonic northern universities to which Liverpool belonged.

On the foundation of the Faculty of Arts in 1896, then, its home was the Victoria Building which it shared with the administration, common university facilities and the main ceremonial spaces.[1] The Faculty thus identified with whatever University ideals were expressed in its flagship building, and Waterhouse's special interpretation of the Gothic subtly located these between the historic and the modern. On the one hand the Victoria Building's styling signified association with deep-cultural institutions such as the Church and Parliament: it expressed alignment with the very foundations of the State. On the other hand, its being clothed in what was considered a particularly garish red brick evoked the great commercial successes of Liverpool's mercantile and insurance industries. Extensive use of terra-cotta and glazed faience was an expression of Waterhouse's personal faith in building materials of the future, durable, decorative and highly resistant to deterioration caused by air pollution, while also betraying his affection for materials which connoted 'industry', carrying as they did the impress of mass manufacture.

Externally, the confinement of terra-cotta to window dressings and string courses struck a note of proper economy, for the skills involved in detailing and coordinating the components of large and complex expanses of this medium were both both rare and expensive.[2] Internally, the prolific use of glazed faience fulfilled Waterhouse's desire for bold, permanent and easily-maintained colouration in public spaces. The interior scheme was distinctly 'modern' and popularist: beige and duckegg blue, extensive use of chequerboard patterning, and a mixture of stylised Egyptianate, Etruscan and straightforwardly geometric decoration that would not have been sanctioned by current manuals of taste. While it is fair to say that the Victoria Building does not join Manchester Town Hall and the Natural History Museum, London, in typifying Waterhouse's finest work, it provides evidence of his abilities to arrange very large volumes on a relatively small 'footprint' (by, for example, reducing corridors to a minimum) and to combine apparently incompatible shapes and scales of interior spaces. The result was a building

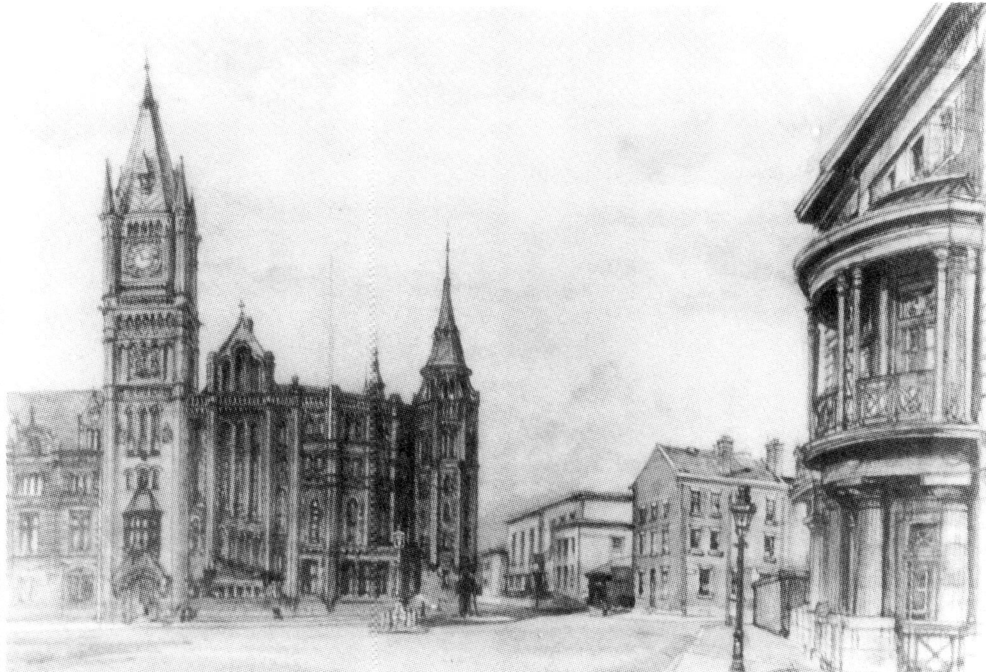

The Victoria Building, the Women's Union (1913), and (behind) the Harold Cohen Library (1936-1938), as c. 1950

The fourth building demolished, the site now occupied by the Electrical Engineering Building (1964)

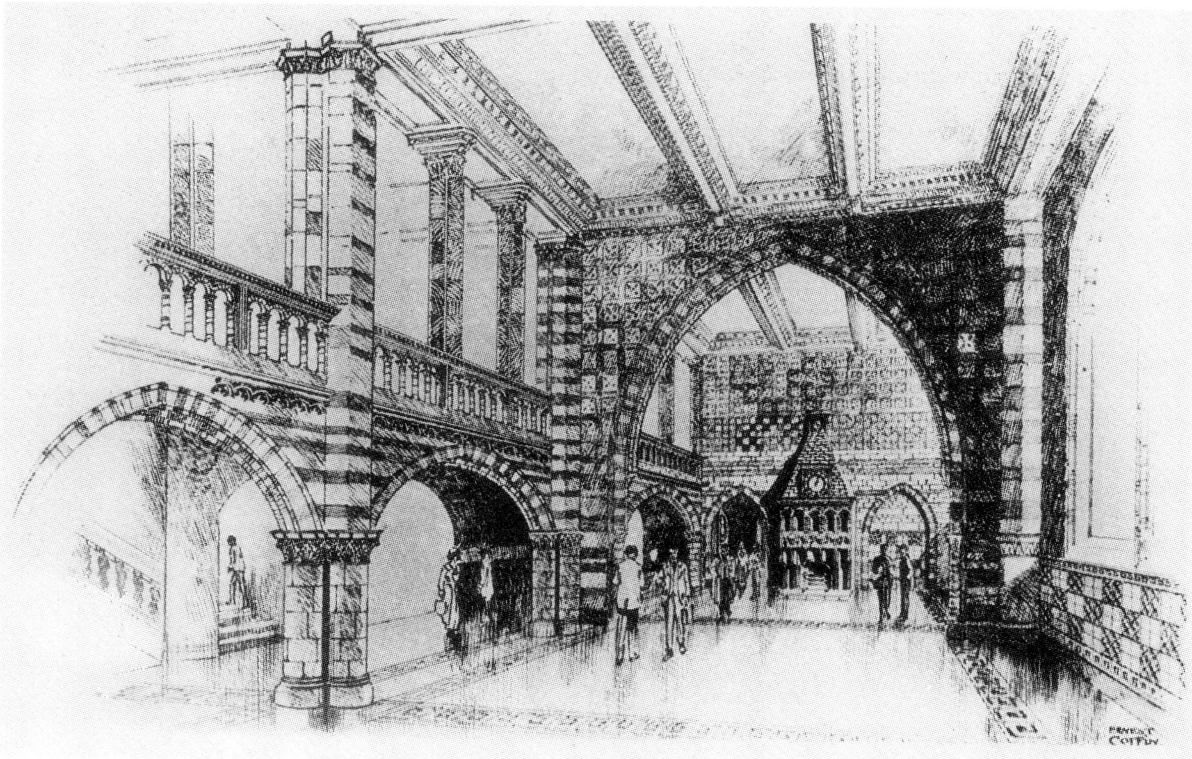

The Entrance Hall of the Victoria Building

As drawn c. 1920 but little changed since

which internally was vital and 'busy', accommodating several hundred people. Externally it signified a number of desirable characteristics: high moral values suggested by the Gothic's ecclesiastical associations, commitment to national economic wellbeing evoked by a style which had become identified with the insurance industry, a provincialism evident in its brick and terra-cotta, and stylistic identification with the generation of new national museums at 'Albertopolis' in South Kensington. But there was also a discrete distancing from Liverpool's civic centres of culture and scholarship, St. George's Hall, the Municipal Museum and the Art Gallery, clothed as these were in the Classic.

At the time of its opening the Victoria Building's Gothic historicism was much more fashionable than the Classic historicism of these comparable civic institutional buildings. But fashion was changing, and whereas the Classic had formerly been considered a tired and scholastic idiom, by the turn of the century its devotees were interpreting it afresh, reclaiming its attributes of originality and invention. In 1909 it was decided to construct a new building specifically to house the Arts, in Ashton Street, adjoining the Victoria Building on the forecourt of the asylum.[3] There was therefore a genuine dilemma as to whether the Quadrangle should be completed in a style consistent with the University's existing buildings, or in a discordant style which continued to reflect the institution's commitment to modernity. The University was vague on this question in its design brief. It ran a competition, limited to four selected architectural practices, in which it suggested three possibilities: to effect a seamless continuation of Waterhouse's scheme; to interpose a freestanding entity between the Victoria Building and the recently completed George Holt Physics Laboratory, emulating neither; or to effect a 'more collegiate' type of Gothic, presumably devoid of typical Waterhouse brickwork details and their inevitably commercial references, expressing a purer commitment to academia.

The latter alternative only makes sense in relation to a proposal absent from the brief but openly discussed during the competition, that a second quadrangle be created of which the Ashton Street elevation of the New Arts Building (later renamed the Ashton Building) would constitute the western side. Accordingly, Messrs. Briggs, Wolstenholme and Thornley, architects of the premeditated design, offered what was described as a 'late French château type of Gothic with symmetrical grouping'.[4] This would have been built but for the intervention of Charles Reilly, appointed Roscoe Professor of Architecture in 1904, who, as a proponent of the Neo-Classic, was determined that the University should patronise architectural values for which his school was becoming famous. At the beginning of the second decade of the century this meant abandoning the picturesqueness of the Gothic - now considered arbitrary in the way in which its institutional manifestations had fundamentally departed from their archetypes, the great northern cathedral churches - in favour of an idiom possessing what was considered a more apposite archetype for public buildings of the early twentieth century, the Renaissance palace. It is a measure of the versatility of the winning architects that, with the collaboration of one of their fellow competitors, they were able to redesign their scheme to Reilly's satisfaction. The result was the cameo Neo-Classic New Arts Building (Briggs, Wolstenholme and Thornley with Frank W. Simon, commenced in 1910, completed in 1913 and opened the following year). Clearly it was intended to characterise the University's next phase of development around a new square within the angle of Ashton Street and Paddington.

Internally this building was unremarkable except for the fine oak panelling of its most important rooms and public spaces and the quality of daylight filtering through the ocular lantern over the main staircase at the hub of the building's three main axes. And it is difficult to imagine that Reilly would have been satisfied with the vaulted ceilings of the entrance vestibule and corridors linking to the Victoria Building, introduced partly as a reminder that the building is of stone (and therefore disguising its skeleton of steel) and partly to effect some continuity with Waterhouse's interior finishes, by now losing their evocations of 'modernity'. Externally, however, the New Arts Building was perhaps more remarkable than its conservative clients would have wished had they fully appreciated what it signified to Reilly. Superficially, the Classic constituents of both Ashton Street and Quadrangle elevations - their pediments with decorated friezes, the rusticated stonework of their lower storeys, their Ionic consistency - simply exemplified Reilly's scholastic values. To Reilly, however, such details as their fluted pilasters signified the ultimate refinement of an idiom that had been gradually approaching perfection since its anglicisation in the seventeenth century.[5] Correct deployment of the Order respected cultural origins. A mannerist composition of seated figures over the Quadrangle pediment, by the sculptor

William Birnie Rhind, acknowledged a proper line of post-Renaissance descent. A pair of sphinxes, also by Rhind, on each of the roofs of annexes to either side of the main building, besides having local significance,[6] bore reference to Britain's strategic interests in Egypt at the geographic nexus of the Empire. This was *elitist* architecture, not merely in its reflection of the principle of stylistic perfectibility but also in its cultural imperialism. The upper-storey brickwork in the annexes, the bow front of one of these, linking it to the Victoria Building, and the treatment of the gateway attic which closes with the Holt Laboratory; these were *Georgian* characteristics which both expressed the building's pedigree and signalled the architects' ambition to rationalise the institutional as the Georgian had rationalised the domestic, that is, in an unmistakably British way.

There is little doubt that the proposed new quadrangle would have confirmed the Neo-Classic ascendancy. However, two things seem to have intervened to arrest this development. One was the Great War, the demands of which reduced the University to subsistence levels of activity. The other was the unexpected need to retain the old Lock Hospital on the east side of Ashton Street (the site now occupied by the Harold Cohen Library) which would have made way for the square but was now pressed into service as the home of the School of Architecture. Architecture had earlier inhabited the Victoria Building before moving well away from the University precinct, to the Old Bluecoat School premises in School Lane, in 1909.[7] W.H. Lever, deeply involved in architecture and urban planning at Port Sunlight and elsewhere, had secured the lease of this building with a view to purchasing it on the University's behalf, expressly to enable Reilly to install his School of Architecture and constituent Department of Civic Design in an appropriate setting. This eighteenth-century Queen Anne building was thus preserved from demolition, its principal interior space, a first storey chapel extending the full width of its main axis, serving as a studio for the whole of the undergraduate population, and its myriad small rooms providing offices for staff, postgraduates and the many visiting fellows from overseas attracted to observe Reilly's instructional innovations.

The circumstances of a disagreement between Lever and the President of the University Council have not been fully explained.[8] But one of its consequences was the cessation of the Bluecoat lease and the return of the School of Architecture to the main site in 1918, just before Reilly himself returned to the University after secondment to war work. With no money for refurbishment of the Lock Hospital, Reilly recruited a number of Australian ex-servicemen, all qualified in building trades, to receive an intensive course in architecture in return for their demobilisation training grants and their labours.[9] The wards were turned into communal studios and the central administrative block into offices and lecture rooms. As the School population grew there was expansion into temporary buildings in yards to the rear of what became affectionately known as 'Reilly's Cow Shed'. This complex was the home of the School of Architecture until 1933, when it finally moved into its present premises in Abercromby Square.

The colonising of Abercromby Square by departments of the Faculty of Arts, as houses were gradually made available through gifts and bequests, and the adoption of what was in effect a ready-made precinct no doubt contributed to the abandonment of plans for a second quadrangle. The drift began in 1920 when the Department of Geography moved to no. 10 Abercromby Square. The Department of Archaeology (previously at 40 Bedford Street North) moved to no. 11 in 1921, the year in which the Department of Education occupied the specially-refurbished and combined nos. 20-22. These premises were further enlarged in 1925 with the addition of no. 23, and the Department of Social Science joined the enclave, coming to no. 26 in 1925.

Abercromby Square had been planned in 1800 and laid out in 1816, and most of its houses built over the following twenty years to an elevational scheme by John Foster.[10] They comprised four three-storey Georgian terraces in Flemish bond brickwork of (originally) light red stretchers and paler headers, though with some individual houses, especially on the east side, faced with stucco. The terraces had different but complementary compositions, each with a central Doric portico, that of the east side belonging to the Church of St. Catherine (built 1831), derelict long before it was demolished in the site clearance for Senate House in 1966. Except for the Square's most imposing residence, no. 19 (not built until 1863), all houses had uniform heights of cornices, string courses and first-floor balconies. All were set back from the pavement by an iron-railed basement area, had a common pattern of window sizes and spacing, and displayed a regular distribution of entrances that disguised a great variety of plan widths behind their frontages. Consistent with the Arts' adaptability to non-bespoke

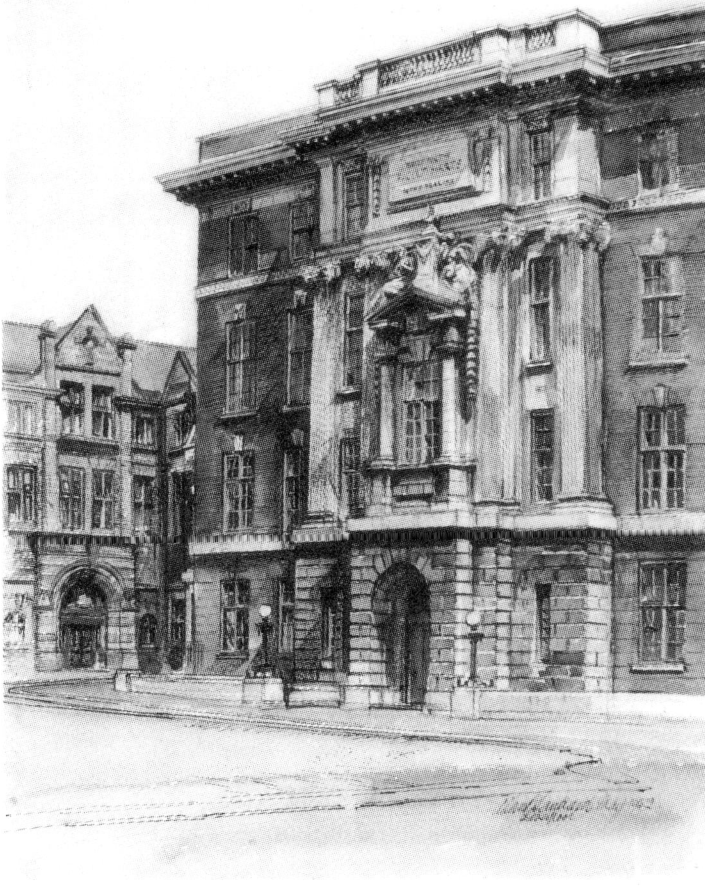

The New Arts Building (1914), seen from the Quadrangle, 1952

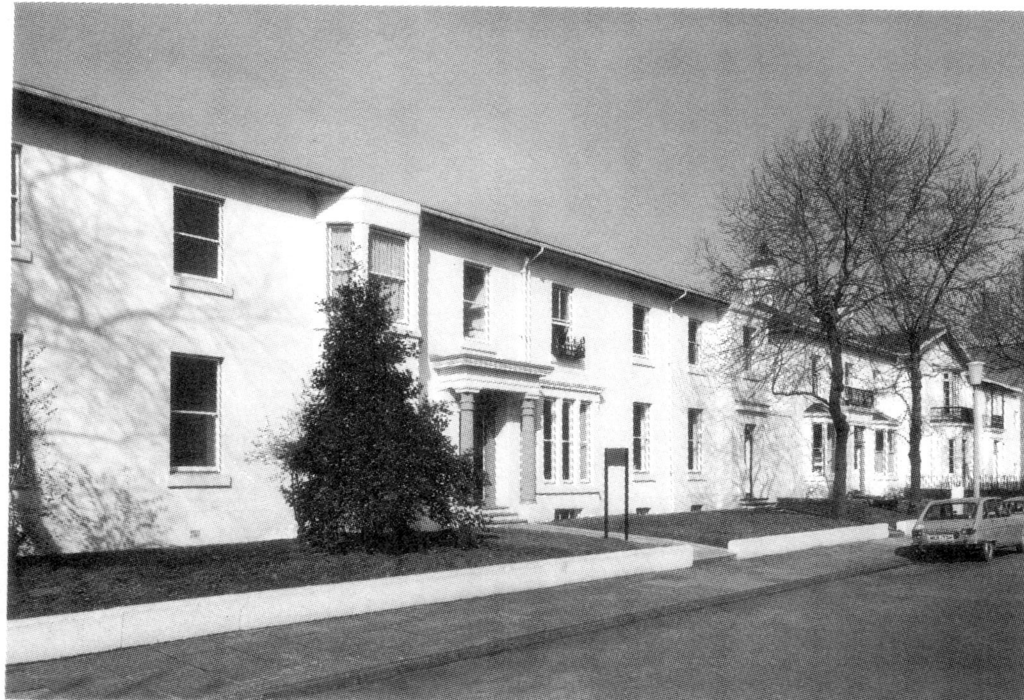

The Regency villas in Bedford Street South

Intended at one time to be demolished, now housing the Institute of Latin American Studies and the Department of Music spaces, incoming disciplines found congenial homes in houses with large entrance halls (for arrival, orientation and information display), generously-scaled reception rooms at first and second floors (for lecture rooms and libraries) and numerous bedrooms and servants' attics (for private offices and tutorial rooms). Three examples are worthy of special mention, all on the north side of the square, as instances when buildings were prepared in advance of occupation instead of being gradually adapted to their new purposes. One of the instances involved high-quality refurbishment, though in a style which bore little relation to the Georgian; another the restoration and retention of many existing features; and the third a substantial eradication of original characteristics.

The first of these was the two-phased refurbishment of nos. 20-23 (1921 and 1925) for the Department of Education, by Ronald P. Jones, brother of Sydney Jones who had presented the houses to the University. The principal interiors of the combined premises were not restored to their original condition but were clothed in a much earlier style, generally evocative of the Enlightenment.[11] Georgian and Victorian wall finishes were covered with oak panelling, and moulded ceilings were replaced with plain, decorated only with simple borders. Fluted Ionic columns made of oak and with ornately carved capitals, reminiscent of American Colonial applications of the Order,[12] were prominent in the main vestibule and other congregating spaces, giving way to simple oak-clad pilasters with box capitals in less formal rooms such as the garden parlour - though this room had its own distinctive feature in the flat-arched, segmented, clear-leaded light over the garden door. The only late Georgian or early Victorian elements which seem to have been preserved are the cornices, which have fine, stylised acanthus corbelling not entirely out of keeping with the severity of the rest of the scheme. It is apparent that in this refurbishment, as elsewhere, the fabric of the University was deliberately imbued with an informed code, in this case symbolising the rationalism and liberal humanism of early eighteenth century Western thought by association with its characteristic architecture. There was a willingness to discard original fittings and finishes in favour of achieving the right evocation. It is this which makes the second refurbishment scheme on the north side of Abercromby Square, that of no. 19, unusual because of the retention of an eclectic mixture of stylistic features which had accumulated over its sixty-year existence.

This house, also donated by Sydney Jones, was to provide a home for Social Studies (moving from no. 26 in 1931) and the cognate Departments of Economics and Commerce (though Geography remained at no. 10). No. 19 was originally owned by a South Carolinan, Charles Prioleau, who had settled in Liverpool and had become naturalised in 1863, the year he built his house.[13] Not surprisingly, as the American Civil War was currently being fought, the house was replete with Confederate references: painted, wrought and carved star symbols; ceiling depictions of cherubs astride wild turkey and rye whiskey barrel; panther heads in the cornice of the first floor balcony over the entrance hall; in the eight arches directly above, keystones embossed with female faces wearing star headbands; over the galleried staircase a great lantern containing an eight pointed leaded star; and in the main entrance vestibule a ceiling painting of the cabbage palmetto tree, state symbol of South Carolina - all of which were consistent with the function of the house as a centre of organised credit and supply for the Confederacy. Second Empire styling, popular in the southern states, is evident in the classical dress of figures on the ceilings of reception rooms and in swags decorating the deep cornice of the staircase lantern.

It is not known how much more of this overt symbolism was present in the original decor and how much was lost when in 1880 the house was converted into the Bishop's Palace for the See of Liverpool. Presumably most of the ornate ironwork was introduced at this time: Victorian cast-iron columns and pilasters, the latter having capitals with stylised acanthus leaves and lilies; the highly ornate terminal banister at the foot of the great staircase; the decorated ringbeam reinforcement to the lantern above. Any reception room turned into a chapel, an examination room, or an ordinands' retreat no doubt was stripped of temporal distractions. It is not known whether such removal from sight was in a manner benign and recoverable. What is certain, however, is that in 1930-1931 the surviving mixture of South Carolinan fancy and Victorian Gothic would have defeated homogenisation except by means of a strong and unifying colour scheme such as the one employed in the most recent refurbishment of 1986.

It is fortunate that Sydney Jones considered the stylistic hotchpotch appropriate to the new usage, though his reasons are obscure except for remarks in Sir Basil Blackett's address at the building's opening in 1931.[14] This was to the effect that the scheme had tangible founding in the world of real experience, an interpretation of obvious significance to the renamed School of Social Sciences and Administration. The same might have been said of the School of Architecture. However, in contrast and ironically, when in 1933 Architecture and Civic Design moved from Ashton Street into the vastly enlarged and remodelled nos. 24-27 Abercromby Square (Lionel Budden, Charles Reilly and J.E. Marshall, 1931-1933), the only interior decorative features which were preserved were those inoffensive to a now-prevalent architectural ideology of geometric plainness. The new home of the School of Architecture, named the Leverhulme Building in acknowledgement of the source of its funding, comprised four converted houses fronting on to Abercromby Square and a completely new and vastly larger annex built on the site of their rear gardens. The converted houses contained the secretariat, library and staff rooms, together with drawing offices overlooking Abercromby Square for the Department of Civic Design. Mouldings and other interior decorative features were retained sparsely, sufficient only to illustrate a highly discriminating Classic pedigree. The new part of the scheme contained a main lecture theatre, studios on the grand *atelier* principle which had become the School's hallmark, and a number of spaces dedicated to the Critique - a forum in which students defended their displayed designs '*en loge*', that is, under highly focused scrutiny.

If the Georgian wing of the scheme was not entirely ruthless with the past, the new extension was similarly compromising with the modern. This part of the building exemplified what was regarded, with hindsight, as having been Reilly's great mission, to encourage the development of a form of Modernism rooted in the Classic and far less iconoclastic than the European variety by now favoured by younger members of his staff. Accordingly the new studio wing was built of brick, not concrete, and although its steel frame would have permitted unlimited sizes and shapes of window apertures, its upper fenestration echoed and respected the characteristics of its Georgian neighbours. Though the modernity of its construction was expressed in the great band of glazing which enwrapped the whole ground-storey, a paramount Modernist leitmotif, the suspended 'curtain' of windows, was disregarded in favour of windows set in substantial frames. Even its industrially plain internal courtyard was planned to have a freestanding Doric column at its centre. Contemporary sympathisers called this 'urban-sociable-modernist' architecture as opposed to the 'hooliganism' of extremists.[15]

Perhaps unexpectedly then, at a time when the Neo-Classic was again becoming discredited (by, among other things, its association with totalitarian regimes), the University found itself no longer sponsoring this idiom, but acquiring a stock of buildings whose interiors could be made to suit the disciplines they housed, and whose exteriors were both civically polite and culturally authentic. The refurbishment of the north side of Abercromby Square exemplified several factions of conservation ideology, illustrating its dynamic. In one of its aspects, an 'historic' interior environment is created (as in nos. 20-23) without regard to achieving an authentic fit with its container. In another (no. 19), features are retained which memorialise the building's original treatment and subsequent remodellings, reflecting its 'life history' of changing ownership and use. In a third aspect (nos. 24-27), preservation is tangible but minimal, in this case characterising a building *type* - the late Georgian or early Victorian town-house - rather than a *specific* house with all the idiosyncrasies of taste visited upon it throughout its past. All three approaches shaped the Arts' further colonisation of Abercromby Square in the immediate postwar period, when there was much decanting of departments into newly-acquired houses on the south side, as the University strove to comply with dramatically rising UGC admissions targets while simultaneously planning the precinct in a strategically coherent way.

In 1946, William Holford, who held the Lever Chair of Civic Design, was appointed Consultant to the University Development Committee for this latter purpose. His report in 1949 both defined the area agreed with the City authorities as constituting the University's greatly enlarged site, and proposed a distribution of academic and administrative centres in constructive relationship and with regard to the quality and adaptability of the existing building stock.[16] Three things in Holford's plan were of great significance for the future positioning of the Arts and the fashioning of their future buildings. First, he recognised their occupancy of the north side of Abercromby Square,[17] and proposed the abandonment of the New Arts Building in Ashton Street to other purposes. Secondly, he maintained that Georgian houses were not necessarily appropriate for *all* Arts disciplines, for example advising that the School of Social Sciences be completely rebuilt behind its Abercromby Square facade because existing internal arrangements were 'inconvenient and uneconomic'.[18] Thirdly, he proposed that the area bounded by Cambridge Street, Bedford Street South, Myrtle Street and Vine

Street (minus the site of the present Sydney Jones Library) be allocated specifically to Engineering, thus categorising this part of the University site as appropriate for large-scale building projects. This principle took hold even though Holford's proposals were soon modified by Development Committee, which by 1954 had established the north, west and south sides of Abercromby Square and the street blocks behind them as the Arts' strategic location.[19]

This merely recognised that other departments had taken root here without the advantage of refurbishment programmes like those of the north side. The Department of Geography had occupied no. 10 from 1920 to 1936 when it had moved to no. 12.[20] Archaeology continued to occupy no.11, where in 1946 it was joined by Civic Design - a temporary response to overcrowding in the Leverhulme Building caused by the scale of the emergency programme to train architects and planners for postwar reconstruction. Civic Design left in 1951 on completion of its dedicated premises, one of the earliest postwar building projects, at the junction of Cambridge Street and Bedford Street.

The Civic Design Building (Gordon Stephenson and Norman Kingham, 1950-52) was prioritised partly in gratitude to Holford, partly because one of the most peripatetic disciplines in the Faculty needed a home of its own, and partly because it was the right scale for a site made derelict by wartime bombing and which demanded attention in the general improvement of Abercromby Square.[21] Further, it represented a realistic enterprise in a time of limited capital means. As Holford's successor to the Lever Chair, Stephenson was provided with the opportunity to design his own building - a rare but not unique event, for Lionel Budden, Roscoe Professor of Architecture 1933-1952, had been principal designer of the School of Architecture in 1931-1933. It was intended that the new building should serve Civic Design for a maximum of twenty years since Holford's proposals for this part of the precinct were still extant and he had earmarked the block bounded by Cambridge, Bedford, Myrtle and Mulberry Streets for an Institute of Mathematics. It was intended that, after eventual acquisition of the whole of this site, Civic Design would be rehoused once more, in a further extension to the School of Architecture. And the Civic Design Building would be incorporated into a large new Mathematics Building, serving as its entrance and as a transitional link between the future development's anticipated International Modernism and the Georgian characteristics of Abercromby Square.[22]

The Civic Design Building thus conjugated two quite different idioms, largely respecting domestic-scale, Georgian characteristics when viewed from Abercromby Square but institutional-scale, Modernist characteristics when viewed from the imagined Institute. In deference to the Georgian it was constructed of Flemish bond brickwork, though of uniform colouration similar to the weathered tone of Abercromby Square. Its steel frame and cantilevered walls permitted continuous bands of fenestration to all three storeys, but the sill and head heights of the most dominant of these, illuminating the first-floor studio (now the library), echoed those of the square, as did their modular subdivisions, unnecessarily small in terms of mid-twentieth century float glass production. The visual 'weight' of the main entrance, its canopy offering suggestions of a portico, the railed basement areas to the street elevations, and the set-back top storey respecting the pitched roofs of neighbouring houses - all of these features expressed familial relationship to the Georgian. However, a different architectural language was evident both within the building, where an absence of crosswalls 'opened up' the interior to an extent impossible in traditional construction, and when viewed from the west, where the most prominent feature of the courtyard elevation was a great vertical gash of glazing curtaining the main staircase. These were manifestations of steel and concrete technology. In this sense the Civic Design Building exemplified a zoning policy in which buildings at the corners of Abercromby Square were to have the critical function of mediating between the old and a gradually materialising ring of new buildings, representatives of both their time and the changing needs of the disciplines they would house, set around the backs of the Georgian houses. It was tacit that scores of Georgian and Victorian properties (in Bedford, Cypress, Heath and Chatham Streets) would be demolished, no doubt justified by belief that their replacements would themselves be conserved as examples of the very best of twentieth century architecture.

As things turned out, the most original British architecture in the 1960s was inimical to the Georgian and the Victorian. Brutalism, its representative style, was characterised by the desire to originate a fundamentally new urban aesthetic on the part of a generation able for the first time really to build after twenty years of virtual inactivity. A number of new buildings were commissioned for the Faculty in the quadrilateral to the south of Abercromby Square, and these were conceived in the Brutalist idiom, which was both praiseworthy since this was the style of the moment, and unfortunate since it exemplified rejection of the context of the site. The architect of the Arts Library and Lecture Rooms Building, later renamed the Arts Reading Room and subsequently the Rendall Building (Bryan Westwood, 1961-63), articulated such rejection: he thought 'it would be best to design an inward-looking building; indeed there was little then that would be agreeable to look out upon'.[23] The disagreeable included fine examples of Regency villas on the other side of Bedford Street South, today occupied by the Department of Music and the Centre for Latin American Studies but in the early 1960s destined for demolition.

Rejection of a traditional urban aesthetic is one of the reasons why more than a third of Westwood's plan was devoted to the entrance hall and internal courtyard, flanked on either side by blocks of lecture rooms each with a wing of the library on the floor above. This gave rise to one of the building's most appealing properties, the garden at its heart, overlooked through curtain glazing from the reading areas of the library. Westwood's other reason for providing an extravagant courtyard was that he envisaged it as an ante-space to a larger landscaped area around which he was developing other buildings for the Faculties of Arts and Law. Consistent with Brutalist ideology, the exterior of the Arts Library and Lecture Rooms was clad in elongated roughcast concrete panels, the vertical striations of which were a clear demonstration of their suspension (rather than compression), exemplifying rejection of the 'dishonest' use of this material in imitation of stone. For Westwood roughcast concrete had an additional virtue: grime would collect in the hollows and be washed clear of the ridges, exploiting the realities of the urban environment to produce a visually appropriate aesthetic. Brutalism celebrated materials which exhibited their prime characteristics artlessly - hence the Arts Library's stained glass windows, achieved by the apparently simple means of punching holes in the concrete gables. Hence also the coffered ceiling of the entrance vestibule (an aesthetic by-product of solving the loading problems of the floor above), and the unpretentious slabbed relief even over the main entrance, where convention demanded the finest of applied decoration.

In the Arts Library and Lecture Rooms the University acquired a fine example of the Brutalist genre and succeeded in promoting conservable Modernist architecture. Things might easily have been very different as the Development Committee and hence Westwood, urged by the UGC to make intensive use of land,[24] but also no doubt influenced by Holford's prospect of very large buildings in this part of the precinct, were obliged to consider whether the Faculty's accommodation problems might be resolved in a single monolithic enterprise. Sketches were prepared of a building 'in excess of twenty storeys'.[25] This was rejected only in view of uncertainty about the future groupings of disciplines within the Faculty, the first hint of a fractioning of Arts and Social Sciences.[26] It was decided to press ahead with the housing of service accommodation (Arts Library and Lecture Rooms), while developing further proposals to house distinct disciplinary groupings separately, within a scheme that would still contain a building of fifteen storeys and would also do away with the south side of Abercromby Square.[27]

In February 1960, the UGC asked the University to respond to the need to increase student numbers by almost thirty per cent.[28] The anticipated pattern of demand within this increase suggested an order of priorities for expanded accommodation.[29] Those disciplines destined to absorb most of the increase could not wait for the production of a complex, all-inclusive building, and it was this that initiated a phased community. In May 1961 Westwood proposed an arrangement of five buildings following the agreed priorities: the Arts Library and Lecture Rooms (under way); a five-storey building for English Language, English Literature, Philosophy and Modern Languages; a twelve-storey building for Economics, Commerce, Geography, Social Sciences and Political Theory and Institutions; a new building for the Faculty of Law; and a building to replace the south side of Abercromby Square, matching its scale, to house History, Classics, Archaeology, Music and Art.[30] Disturbed by intimations of disapproval, the architect asked for reconfirmation of the latter intention. 'His whole scheme was based on the assumption that the existing houses on the south side of Abercromby Square would be demolished, but that it would be desirable to retain the same scale of development ... so as to keep the character of this open space'.[31]

There is no record of the University's response but it is highly likely that the question of demolishing serviceable buildings in order to rebuild on the same scale gradually slipped from the agenda because of increasing financial difficulties. The whole project had been funded largely on initial estimates, a reasonable procedure at a time of stable prices. However, unexpectedly high inflation in the building industry in the early 1960s resulted in depleting resources for the lower priorities, and this fact - rather more than the Faculty's or the architect's ambitions - determined the characteristics of the eventual community of buildings.

However, the History grouping's loss of a dedicated building was compensated by the forced abandonment of a number of conceits. High quality, the intended hallmark of the whole scheme,[32] did in fact characterise the Arts Library and Lecture Rooms Building. Thereafter, it was achieved in the particular only by sacrificing dramatic generalities - the great tower; the proposal to build around the full periphery of the quadrilateral including over the cleared south side of Abercromby Square; the architect's desire to raise the English and Modern Languages Building and the Social Sciences Building clear of the ground, creating open air recreation spaces beneath them;[33] a central fountain;[34] one or two storeys of less necessary accommodation; and ultimately the fifth building. The four that were realised exhibit remarkable consistency in their livery of vertically ribbed concrete and dark purple brickwork.[35] They are significant for having been determined by the specifications of long-established departments and as models for comparable buildings for newer institutions on greenfield sites. But the architect's deeply-desired inward focus was never achieved: houses to the south of Abercromby Square naturally orient towards the square.

These buildings escaped demolition by the skin of their dentil friezes - literally, since such features as cornices and high mouldings did not need to be removed in the modification programme for departments now destined to stay. Nos. 12-14 Abercromby Square and the adjoining house at no. 90 Chatham Street were adapted for Archaeology and cognate disciplines; Archaeology and Oriental Studies moving from nos. 16-16a when these properties were demolished as part of the Senate House site clearance; Classics and Ancient History from no. 18, a former private hospital also demolished in 1966; and Egyptology from the old Workhouse in Brownlow Hill, to where it had moved from the basement of the Harold Cohen Library in 1954. The Department of History, from its earlier home in the New Arts Building in Ashton Street, had moved to nos. 8-9 Abercromby Square and no. 79 Bedford Street South in the mid 1950s. However, as History had not seemed destined to remain for long in these houses, they had enjoyed only minor modification, which partly explains the variety of domestic interior styling still evident in that department today. While Psychology transferred to the new Social Sciences Building, more Arts departments found homes on the west side. Thus, the Department of Philosophy moved into no. 7, and the Schools of Honours General Studies and Honours Social Studies (later renamed Combined Honours) moved into no. 6.[36] Finally, in 1966 the Department of Music occupied nos. 80-82 Bedford Street South (similarly now spared from the prospect of demolition) and the newly created Centre for Latin American Studies occupied no. 84.

The programme to refurbish most of these former houses now acquired by departments was conditioned by the possibility of a new building on reserved land to the south of the Social Sciences Building, should circumstances improve. It was therefore fairly utilitarian: rooms were partitioned, crosswalls removed, large fireplaces taken out to provide greater wall space, corridors driven through showpiece rooms, and skirtings, panellings and mouldings violated. Original features tended to survive mainly in backwaters, or where their (usually) Victorian aesthetic matched the dignity of academic ritual, as for example in boardrooms. There are still pockets of excellence. No. 84 Bedford Street South has well-preserved pargetted ceilings, encaustic tiled vestibule, great Georgian fireplace with Victorian carved mahogany overmantel in the front parlour, and bays of flat arches springing from Etruscan pilasters in the drawing room. No. 9 Abercromby Square contains a Victorian time capsule in its High Gothic entrance hall, preserved largely as the last domestic inhabitants left it because subsequent users have always entered by next door. Its rear parlour is equally fine in spite of its dark oak panelling having been bleached in conformity with modern taste for blond timbers. Nos. 6 and 12 have excellent pargetting - their ceilings, however, having suffered a common violation by industrial lighting - and the latter, in particular, has a profusion of naturalistic and stylised roses, a ubiquitous motif. In this stock of Georgian buildings with evident layers of Victorian modification there is the basis for fully authentic restoration if resources could be found for removal of the latterday institutionalisation and its replacement with architectural salvage. It would seem appropriate to commemorate the centenary of the Faculty of Arts with such a worthy objective.

NOTES

1. See Adrian R. Allan, 'The Victoria Building: Its Building, Furnishing and Use', *University of Liverpool Recorder*, No. 83, 1980.

2. For an account of Waterhouse's devotion to terra-cotta, see C. Cunningham and P. Waterhouse, *Alfred Waterhouse 1830-1905: Biography of a Practice*, Oxford, 1992, pp. 160-164. See also S. Maltby, S. MacDonald and C. Cunningham, *Alfred Waterhouse 1830-1905*, Royal Institute of British Architects, London, 1983, pp. 43-46.

3. See 'University of Liverpool Block Plan of Buildings AD 1907', S.2664, University Archives. The Asylum was to be demolished on the new building's completion.

4. 'Competition for Liverpool University Arts Extension Building', *The Builder*, XCVII, no. 3471, 14 August 1903, p. 183.

5. Charles H. Reilly, *Scaffolding in the Sky: a Semi-Architectural Autobiography*, London, 1938, pp. 118-119.

6. The naming of Abercromby Square commemorated General Sir Ralph Abercromby, killed at the Battle of Alexandria in 1801, that is, while this part of Liverpool was first being developed. The Sphinx is incorporated into Abercromby's memorial in St Paul's Cathedral, and is present in local memorials, for example, the gate piers of the Square (restored 1952). The Sphinx was adopted as the emblem of the Guild of Undergraduates on its formation as the Students' Representative Council in 1892.

7. See L.B. Budden, ed, *The Book of the Liverpool School of Architecture*, Liverpool University Press/London, 1932, pp. 38-40.

8. Reilly, *Scaffolding in the Sky*, p. 190.

9. Ibid., pp. 204-5. That 50 Australians were recruited, as often stated, is not supported by the university records. The number was under 10.

10. For a detailed account of the history of the development of Abercromby Square, see Adrian R. Allan, *The Building of Abercromby Square*, Liverpool, 1986.

11. 'Lavish late C17 style interiors', according to Nikolaus Pevsner, *The Buildings of England: South Lancashire*, Harmondsworth, 1969, p. 183.

12. See Arthur Stratton, *The Orders of Architecture*, London, 1931, Plate LXXIV 'Wood Porch at Salem, Massachusetts'. It is not known whether these columns were original features of no. 20 Abercromby Square, or came from one of the adjoining houses also gifted by S. Jones. No. 19, in particular, had previously been associated with the southern states of the U.S.A., but was not acquired until 1924.

13. For a discussion of Prioleau, a detailed description of the house during his occupancy and subsequently, see Allan, *Abercromby Square*, pp. 14-19.

14. *Opening of the New Building of the Liverpool School of Social Sciences and Administration, 20 November 1931*, Liverpool University Press, 1932, pp. 6, 12.

15. Anon., 'New Buildings for the Liverpool School of Architecture', *The Architect and Building News*, CXXXV, 21 July 1933, pp. 67-70. See also Budden, *Liverpool School of Architecture*, pp. 67-81.

16. William Holford, *Proposals for the Development of a Site for the University of Liverpool*, Liverpool University Press, n.d. [1949].

17. In a zone bounded by Oxford Street, Bedford Street North, Chatham Street, and the still exposed railway cutting to the south of the present Alsop Building: Holford, *Proposals*, Map No. 7, 'The University of Liverpool Precinct: Allocation of Site to Faculties'.

18. Ibid., p. 22. This advice was resisted although the University has not generally shirked the demolition of significant buildings. Witness Pevsner's fury at the 'ruthless destruction' of the portico of St. Catherine's Church in 1965-1966: 'How well it could have been incorporated into a design for the new Senate House!': Pevsner, *South Lancashire*, p. 183. The building behind the portico had been destroyed in wartime bombing, and adjoining houses at nos. 17-18 had been demolished behind their retained facades because of dry rot. 'Minutes of Fabric Committee', 30 October 1959, S.210 University Archives, p. 192. A similar proposal was resisted in 1965 when nos. 1-2 Abercromby Square were being considered for conversion into Staff House. The architect, Gerald Beech, suggested demolition and rebuilding of all but the Abercromby Square and Oxford Street facades: 'Minutes of the Building (General Purposes) Subcommittee, 15 December 1965', S.185, University Archives, p. 132.

19. *Report of the Development Committee to the Council and Senate of the University on Building Progress 1949-1954*, Liverpool University Press, 1955, map no. 4, 'The University of Liverpool Precinct: Allocation of Site to Faculties'.

20. Where it remained until 1965 when it was united with Social Science, Economics, Commerce, Psychology, and Political Theory and Institutions in the new Social Sciences Building (later renamed the Roxby Building).

21. Holford, *Proposals*, p. 22.

22. See Anon., 'New Building for Civic Design Department for the University of Liverpool', *Architect and Building News*, XXI, no. 4346, 3 April 1932, pp. 391-99; Anon., 'Civic Design School for the School of Architecture, Liverpool University', *Architects' Journal*, 115, no. 2979, 3 April 1952, pp. 427-32; Anon., 'Civic Design Building, University of Liverpool', *The Builder*, CLXXXII, no. 5694, 4 April 1952, pp. 513-18.

23. Bryan Westwood, 'Note by the Architect', *Opening of the Arts Library and Lecture Room Building*, University of Liverpool, 1963, [p. 3].

24. Holford's plan was predicated on an ideal student population of 5,000, but by 1964 the University had signalled to the UGC its willingness to accept an eventual target of exactly double this figure: 'Report of the Development Committee to the Council of the University for the Years 1959-1964', *University of Liverpool Recorder*, January 1965 Supplement, p. 11.

25. Ibid., p. 12.

26. That would result in the creation of the Faculty of Social and Environmental Studies in 1971.

27. 'Minutes of the Arts Faculty Building Sub-committee', 20 September 1960, S.185, University Archives, p. 48.

28. Ibid., 17 February 1960, pp. 31-2.

29. (i) English, Philosophy , Modern Languages and the Dean's Office; (ii) Economics, Geography, Social Sciences and Political Theory; (iii) History, Classics, Archaeology, Music and Art: 'Minutes of the Arts Faculty Building Sub-committee', 11 April 1961, p. 62.

30. Ibid., 18 May 1961, p. 66.

31. Ibid., 26 May 1961, pp. 72-3.

32. The Building Sub-committee noted with approval that once department-specific facilities were removed from the Arts Library and Lecture Rooms brief they were no longer constrained by UGC utility standards and overall expenditure was permitted to increase by around 10%: 'Minutes of the Arts Faculty Building Sub-committee', 22 July 1959, p. 21.

33. Ibid., 28 Sept 1961, insertions at pp. 83 and 88.

34. Ibid., 10 July 1963, p. 189; 8 October 1963, p. 197.

35. Of which Pevsner approved, regarding the rest of the University's twentieth century buildings as a zoo-like collection of different species: Pevsner, *South Lancashire*, pp. 197, 201-2.

36. The lack of exact dates for some of these moves is due to the fact that the dates given in the Fabric Committee minutes for proposed departures to Abercromby Square do not tally with the dates given for actual arrivals there in the Arts Faculty records, occasionally by a large margin. A probable explanation is that the original moves were regarded as temporary and that permanency of location was only later conceded.

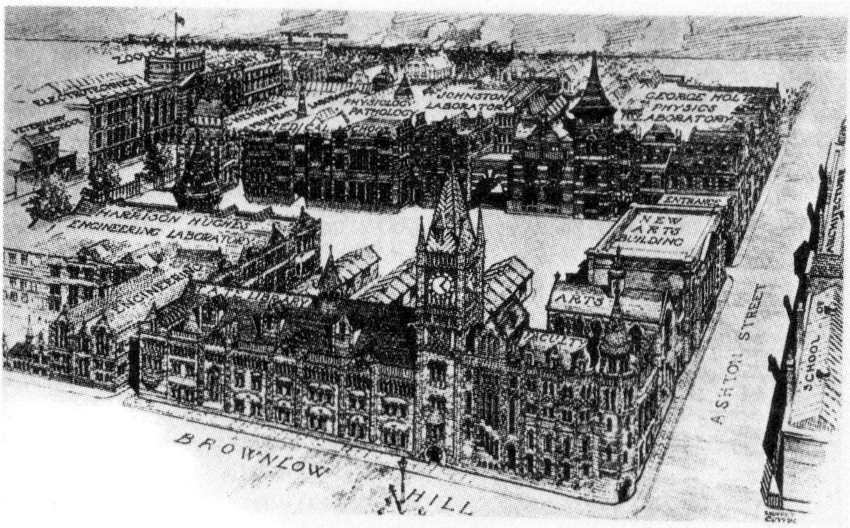

The University precinct in 1920

Note the Victoria Building, the New Arts Building, and the School of Architecture ('Reilly's Cowshed').

HOW A REDBRICK ARTS FACULTY WORKED

B. T. jnr.

Like any other institution the Arts Faculty has changed its structure and function over time. I now describe how its formal machinery operated in certain past decades not too long ago - this does not necessarily indicate the more recent operation and it certainly does not provide proof of how the Faculty operated in the previous half century or so. The Faculty is an intermediate structure between the Departments and the University. The latter consists, in power terms, of a Senate of academics notionally controlling as much as possible of what are contemporaneously considered academic affairs, and an administration made up of professional managers, notionally overseen by a Council of outside laity and academics. Between the two is - and always has been - a vast grey area, not least since the administration obtains and administers finance while the Senate attempts to dispense it. A trivial recent example of the grey area will suffice. The University, in the course of moving from a free issue to free purchase of the staff diary, has progressively dropped from its listing of academic members details of individual marital status and gender ascription, and separate listing of professors (and hived off address and telephone number into a separate publication); each step being taken by an administrator - no doubt for what seemed to him (or her) good reasons - without (as far as I can discover) any consultation with the academic staff, via Senate or otherwise.

The Departments remain, however, the base of the university pyramid. They assess applications and admit students; they assess applications and, with a little outside help, decide on staff appointments. The courses within a department to be offered to students and to be taught by staff are decided within departments. Under a Head of Department the department controls its own daily affairs. Up to a point a department is an autonomous unit. Within the period, this autonomy was slightly modified by various factors, such as the existence here and there of 'Schools' covering several related departments, and, more tellingly, the growth of joint courses which required negotiations between departments and the development of Combined courses with an independent power base. Perhaps more important was the modification of the internal departmental structure, when the headship, formerly in the hands of a senior professor for life, became short term and to a limited extent elective. The advantages of the removal of tyrannical heads and the notional participation of all departmental staff - coinciding as the latter did with the end of a period of university expansion which meant that junior staff no longer so frequently sought good-conduct references from their seniors in order to seek promotion elsewhere - were to some extent balanced out by the disadvantages. Internal departmental consultation and discussion multiplied excessively and here-today-and-gone-tomorrow heads could no longer press the individual departmental case within the Faculty as consistently and effectively as before, while awkward junior staff members had to be cajoled rather than instructed to undertake unpopular but necessary departmental administrative duties. Inasmuch as this change strengthened the Faculty over against the department, in some instances weakening departmental fossilization and allowing for overall changes, including the weeding out of weak departments, it was perhaps not entirely retrograde.

Nevertheless, the Faculty is, at base, the sum of its departments. That sum was altered for the Arts Faculty when half of its departments seceded in 1971. Elsewhere in this volume, I am told, the controversy over this change is re-enacted. With fewer departments being represented in Faculty affairs, heads and other senior academic staff found themselves more engaged, for instance, in Faculty committees; but at the same time the expansion of the Faculty Board, which notionally laid down Faculty policy, by the admission of virtually all less senior staff, altered its nature. For ordinary members of staff, the monthly meetings (within term) of the Faculty Board provided the only occasion for recognition of Faculty confraternity and for listening to those views of senior staff not expressed within departments - and generally for a fun occasion. While protests could be uttered and on odd items the floor could block or alter policy decided by committees and the officers, the Faculty Board was always as much for communication as for decision and action. Nevertheless, as with the Senate, the effect of wider participation drew out its discussions and diluted its capacity for swift and occasionally effective decision-making, except on red-hot issues, and in general led to a steady transference of power from the floor to the table, that is, to the 'centre', to the full-time managers and their short-term academic 'advisers'. It must be added, however, that this centralization was also the product of external forces, especially those relating to financial resources.

If during the period the strength of departments vis-à-vis the Faculty was weakened, that of the University admininistration vis-à-vis the Faculty was increased, which makes it even more difficult to ascribe changes in the Faculty power structure merely to internal causes. At the centre of Faculty decision-making were the committees and the officers. A Dean was appointed for a three-year term. He (or once, she) was always a senior and long-serving academic, normally a professor, selected less for decisive action on behalf of the Faculty, although that was indeed a consideration, than for fairmindedness among the departmental constituency, that is, he would not unduly favour his own department or group of departments. Thus the Faculty was less a confraternity than a web of competing interests. Notionally the Dean set the agenda of committees and signed Faculty papers. He answered questions in Faculty Board. But like the new departmental heads, his power depended largely on personality, and it was most in operation, not within the Faculty, but when he confronted University administration. This might be personal, chatting to the Registrar or even the Vice-Chancellor on urgent or vital matters, but more regularly was exercised in upper-level committees. These might be a range of Senate committees, such as the Library Committee where the views of the Arts Faculty, a major consumer, might prevail, or the Research Committee, where the views of the Arts Faculty, a non-laboratory-based Faculty (after the Great Divide) and therefore a miniscule receiver of outside funding, would be entirely ignored. With the coming of the 'democratic' Faculty Board, however, such committee duties were at times passed over to 'elected' representatives other than the Dean, no doubt to his relief.

In general, it was up to the Dean to obtain for the Faculty a fair slice of whatever University funding was available - although increasingly the main source of funds, the State, earmarked them in such a way that 'fair' took on a meaning unfavourable to the Arts Faculty. This was often done in informal back-stairs committees, especially a meeting of all Faculty deans, so that the share-out was agreed before the formal finance committees met. (During the period the actual structure of Senate committees was persistently under review and changing, but this need not be detailed here and the references above are general.) Thus a strong Dean who, on the one hand, made departmental heads cringe to his whims, might yet retain support (and there are no precedents or machinery for removal during the period of office) if he was thought to be be unduly successful, by hard means or soft talk, in manipulating the upper echelons of university power to the advantage of the

Faculty. The Dean reported back to the Faculty Board, but on such matters as major finance the decision was a fait accompli and those who didn't like it could only accept it as a Fact of Life and grumble pointlessly. Whereas departments and Faculty acquired a façade of all-staff participation, and even a gesture of student participation, the Arts Dean was selected, perhaps wisely, by a secret caucus of immediately previous deans, and a modicum of consultation with departmental heads.

The Dean had the prerogative of selecting a member of the Faculty academic staff, senior but non-professorial, as annual Chairman of the Faculty Board. The Dean's job took up much time and was allowed for within departments (which created a problem in the several tiny departments within the Arts Faculty). The chairman's job took up less time but was fairly exacting and therefore only for one year. Its main advantage to the individual was his (only latterly her) admission into the internal secrets, sometimes necessary secrets, of the Faculty and his observation of the distribution of power. A chairman had some say on the day in control of discussion in the Faculty Board: an over-obliging chairman once failed to stop a 20-minute speech. The chairman chaired a series of Faculty committees, in the dominating presence of the Dean and Sub-Dean, some of which were of considerable meaning because they involved, not so much policy as individals.

A Policy committee met several times a term to receive and normally confirm reports from subsidiary committees and subject boards, and thrash out policy items especially in relation to the subsequent Faculty Board discussion. The Library Committee involved settling claims for funds between rival departments, but increasingly spent time in negotiations with the library officers over declining facilities. An annual committee dealt with student admissions, at first mainly registering departmental scores but later haggling over allocated and on-going numbers, since Faculty resisted the student market and endeavoured to keep unpopular disciplines afloat by limiting the admission numbers of popular departments and shutting its eyes to the apparently low intellectual intake of the unpopular (a manoeuvre long notoriously practiced by the University in relation to less successful-at-recruiting Faculties such as * * *). Staff appointment committees were still frequent, and the majority of members being the representatives of the relevant department were generally allowed their pick, the chairman merely seeing to fair play between departmental rivals such as competing professors. Perhaps the hardest part of the chairman's job was to seek out and inform the unsuccessful candidates while assuring each untruthfully that it had been a near thing. An annual Staffing Committee dealt with staff promotions, a very delicate matter, with the non-professorial chairman having to cope with an emotional professoriate, certain members of whom lost all sense of proportion in putting forward or otherwise torpedoing the claims of individuals seeking higher status and more money. But on the whole being fair all round was an impossible task, carried out as justly as possible to the credit of all concerned. It was then up to the Dean to carry the recommendations upstairs to a Senate committee and fight for the Faculty's candidates - the Dean who failed was protected from Faculty wrath by the secrecy of the operation, only successes being announced, although of course leaks occurred.

A brief committee held after annual examination results noted State awards and decided a due share of university awards for second-degree research studies. Apart from annual registration of courses, done in a separate section of the Faculty office with the clerks there, students did not normally come into face-to-face contact with the Faculty machinery. The exception to normality was when naughty students were called before the Progress Committee, so called, *lucus a non lucendo*, because it dealt with non-progress, that is, with students who had failed exams or gone missing without good cause (pregnancy was allowed for by an automatic procedure) or otherwise misbehaved or fallen by the wayside. On the whole, it was a very tolerant and compassionate committee, even when listening to the most outrageous excuses; and unlike the other Faculty committees, to impress the customers with the solemnity of their summons and appearance, the Dean took the chair. This committee was assisted by a staff member who served for a term of years as Sub-Dean (Academic), a part-time post which mainly involved what would now be called 'counselling', talking to students who were tending towards the thralls of Progress Committee and advising them how to sort themselves out, usually in vain.

Finally, the only full-time managerial appointment in the Faculty was that of the Sub-Dean. The Sub-Dean held the records and prepared the minutes (as well as supervising the office clerks), and many tasks were routine and non-controversial. However, a 'briefing' before Faculty Board between the Dean, Sub-Dean and Chairman, notionally in preparation of an agenda, went a long way towards deciding Faculty matters, since individual issues could be conveniently prioritized in the agenda or quietly dropped (issues at the end of a long agenda could fall back to the Dean or a committee for decision if, by then, those on the floor actively interested had become sufficiently bored to pack it in and go home). While there were various ways in which other staff could influence the Dean, particularly by professors or heads of department dropping into his office and taking up his time till he agreed with them (or occasionally shaking their fists), the working together of the Dean and Sub-Dean was the most decisive factor in Faculty administration. Given that Deans came and went more frequently than Sub-Deans, a Sub-Dean had the tiresome task of establishing personal relations and a *modus vivendi* with new arrivals - and training them, as was at times necessary, in elementary administration - and then accepting some of the blame if the Dean slipped up along the way. Personality on the two sides counted, and on occasion it was hard for a Sub-Dean to resist a leap out of administrative neutrality into declaring and pushing a personal view on academic policy. Fortunately, Sub-Deans have tended to be already on appointment, or at least to become, sympathisers with the Faculty's academic causes, so in the end, 'all is for the best even in the worst of all possible worlds'.

THE HUMANITIES IN A TECHNOLOGICAL AGE:
a 1950s dialogue

Kenneth Muir[1]

When I was Dean I was instructed to write to all the Heads of Department in the Arts Faculty to ask how they would justify their existence in an age of technology. At the time the Faculty included subjects which afterwards set up a separate faculty of Social and Environmental Studies - Architecture, Psychology, Geography, Politics, etc - all of which were welcoming to the age of technology. I was much more worried by some of the arguments used by other respondents, who spoke condescendingly of science, although it shared many of the values the Arts men took for granted. I myself had been offered a free medical education by a London hospital on the strength of my examination results at the age of sixteen; I came from four generations of doctors and derived my love of Shakespeare and the King James version of the Bible from my father. I could not, therefore, believe that medicals and other scientists were Barbarians and Philistines (to use Matthew Arnold's labels).

I determined to set the record straight by writing a pamphlet - A Courteous Caveat, or A Short View of the Faculty of Arts in a Technological Age, by Jeremy Longstaffe, Gent *- intended to be published while I was still Dean. It contained numerous misleading clues in order to throw readers off the scent. There were two main reasons why I withdrew the pamphlet: its authorship was suspected by a member of the Press committee, and several colleagues to whom I showed the typescript, including Thomas Kelly, were convinced that my views and those of Longstaffe were identical. The pamphlet consisted of the views expressed to me by the departmental heads, together with some criticisms of their attitudes, and it ended with a 'Dialogue on Reform'. As I quoted from my (unpublished) Inaugural, from a published article in the* Universities Quarterly *and even from a sarcastic letter I had sent to* The Times Literary Supplement, *it would not have taken much research to establish the authorship of the pamphlet.*

Here, then, is the imaginary conversation that forms the last chapter of the pamphlet. I have made a few editorial changes, and made some cuts, but I have not attempted to revise the views expressed to make them tally with the orthodox wisdom of today.

A DIALOGUE ON REFORM

To advocate reform is such a dangerous occupation in academic circles that a man like myself who is not yet at the top of the grade may well hesitate before speaking out. In any case, I regard myself as a good middle-of-the-road man, too conscious of the good points in the present system to kick up a fuss about the few points which might be improved, too cautious to be a revolutionary, and too receptive to new ideas to be a reactionary, though 'reactionary', I confess, is the very term which has been applied to me by my friend, Vane, who belongs to the reforming party.

I have therefore decided that the best way of representing the varied views which are held about the future of the Faculty is to reproduce, in a condensed form, a conversation which was held a few months ago. There were present, besides myself and the reforming VANE, a former chairman of Faculty (whom I shall call DENBIGH) and a visiting scholar from one of the Middle West universities, over on a Fulbright, whom I shall call FRANKLIN. The conversation was reproduced on a tape recorder but I have taken the liberty of eliminating repetitions and of completing sentences which were left unfinished. The slight pomposity which is apparent at times may be due to the fact that we all knew that the conversation was being recorded.

LO. Go ahead.

FRA. You make no mention of the fine arts. Is there no department of music? Or of art?

LO. My list of departments was not exhaustive. There is a department of music, though students cannot take a degree in music alone. The other fine arts are not represented.

DEN. *(hurriedly)* Not at present. But you ought to tell Professor Franklin that if we get enough money in the next quinquennium we intend to enlarge the music department, and to appoint at least one lecturer in the history of art, attached probably to the School of Architecture.

VA. Don't let them kid you, Professor Franklin. Those projects have been in existence for as long as I can remember, but when it comes to the point the money is always needed for something nasty and useful. We have a few concerts, a few endowed lectures on the arts, and until recently we had another series on the art of the theatre - that is all that is done here about the fine arts. I have never seen a good poet or novelist in the university, except when one lectured to the Classical Association. We never even offer them honorary degrees. We invite a good many scholars to give lectures for a small honorarium but we have no fund to pay for the visit of a creative writer. Why haven't we got a resident poet, like some of your universities? Or even a poetry fellow, as Leeds used to have? Individually, Professor Franklin, we are tolerably cultured, but collectively we are complete Philistines. We buy electronic computers to make concordances of dead poets but we won't pay the train fare of a living poet.

DEN. Vane, as usual, is exaggerating. But it is true that we need more money for such pleasant luxuries.

VA. Luxuries! Beware lest the daughters of the Philistines rejoice!

FRA. You mentioned creative writing, Mr Vane. Do you have a course in creative writing?

VA. No - I gather the English Department regards creative writing as 'an American activity'. As you can see from Longstaffe's charitable manuscript they think their job is to turn out critics and scholars, rather than poets or playwrights.

DEN. And isn't it? You can't teach people to be poets or novelists. But they are more likely to develop into poets and novelists later on if they spend their time at the university in studying great literature than if they try writing television scripts and short stories before they have had any experience of life. But I wouldn't like you to think, Franklin, that we don't value creative writing. There is a prize for poetry. In the classics departments students are encouraged to write Greek and Latin verse ...

VA. In which any original phrase or sentiment would be penalised!

LO. People are not encouraged to write Latin verses for their value as literature, but because it enables them to think as a Roman, and so appreciate Horace more.

VA. But surely, Longstaffe, as Latin is a dead language, the study of the literature and the ability to translate it is infinitely more important than the ability to write Latin verse. In the seventeenth century Latin was a living language, and therefore English poets could write good Latin poems. I just don't believe that writing verse in a language not one's own helps one to appreciate it. Would anyone ask English students to write Anglo-Saxon verse to help them to appreciate *The Seafarer*? The only reason why students are made to write Latin verses is tradition. A much better test would be to insist that alphas should be reserved for those who translated their verse unseens into English verse.

DEN. There may not be so much wrong with the tradition. Surely classical scholars wouldn't continue with it if it had not proved its value - which is more than can be said for some of the things you do in your department.

VA. I don't deny it is a perfectly harmless occupation but it takes up time which could more profitably be spent on other things. Collingwood, in the book from which Longstaffe quoted, complains, if I remember rightly, of the anthology habit which had infected Classical Moderations. He himself had to read the whole of Homer, Virgil, and Demosthenes, not to mention Lucretius and Theocritus. I look at the Latin prospectus and I find that candidates have to read only two books of the *Aeneid*. How on earth can anyone understand two books if they don't read the other ten? No one would set six chapters of *Madame Bovary* or two books of *Paradise Lost*.

LO. Two books are set for special study but students are expected to read the remaining ten.

VA. Merely because a subject has been studied for hundreds of years, it doesn't follow that the traditional methods are necessarily the best in the present age. I studied classićs at school, not at the university, and I remember how irritated I was to read Canon Leeson's nostalgic account of a famous headmaster of a Public School who began the study of the *Iliad* in the Lower Sixth with a learned and elaborate introduction to the question of the authorship of the Homeric poems, he then 'discussed Homeric grammar, he then proceeded to the text and took it almost word by word, with philological and archaeological disquisitions where required, and a most careful discussion of disputed passages, with a tabulation of alternative views and a reasoned conclusion', so that by the end of the term they had covered little more than a hundred lines of the poem. Canon Leeson applauded what he called 'a wonderful example of accurate learning, thoroughness and expository power'. In my opinion this Headmaster deserved a horrible fate. He was guilty of a shameful betrayal of his trust. He was using great poetry as a means to an end, and all the perfumes of Arabia will not sweeten his chalk-covered hand. What, I ask you, should we think of a schoolmaster who taught *Hamlet* in such a perverted way? Would anyone begin a study of *Hamlet* with a discussion of the Baconian theory or of Kyd's *Hamlet*, and a formulation of Elizabethan grammar and punctuation? Would he then go on to discuss the text, word by word, with philological disquisitions, so that by the end of the term the wretched schoolboys had covered the first two scenes of the play? Should we not feel that those who so callously and deliberately arouse a lasting hatred of great literature should have millstones tied round their necks and be thrown into the sea? Even today, in some universities - though not here, I admit - there is a sinister mistrust of those who regard literature as anything but the raw material of scholarship. I was told by one of Housman's pupils that he used to give a series of lectures on Horace in which he confined himself entirely to textual matters. But at the end of his last lecture he read his own translation of one of the loveliest of the Odes - *Diffuere nives, redeunt iam aramina campis* - burst into tears, and rushed out of the lecture-room. He did not regard it as his job as a Professor of Latin to discuss literary questions. He chose to edit one of the feeblest of Latin poets. There was a complete divorce in him between scholarship and the literature which alone redeems it from sterility. Housman's morbid reticence on literary values has been followed by others who refrain altogether from declarations of love, and make it difficult to tell whether in fact they have anything to declare.

FRA. I must say, Mr Vane, that it's clear to me from Mr Longstaffe's account of Latin at your university that there's no danger of that sort of divorce here. But may I ask another question? I see from the Prospectus that in many departments your undergraduates have to write dissertations. Even though your first degrees are rather more advanced than ours, I should have thought it was a bit too much to expect.

DEN. Yes, it's in the prospectus but in many departments the dissertation is optional. The students enjoy getting down to a solid piece of work and ...

VA. I think they should be scrapped. What's the point of writing a dissertation which no one, except the supervisor and the examiner, will read, which is intended as a training in research, though not more than one in ten will proceed to further research, and which takes up a large part of the student's time in his final year? The list of titles of theses makes very dismal reading, though I admit that the reports which issue from the Dean's office run them close.

LO. But isn't it a good thing for a student of modern languages to write a long piece of prose? And isn't it necessary that a history student should have some practical training in historical method?

VA. There are other means of achieving that. The point is that it reduces the time which they spend in acquiring basic knowledge. Take French, for example. Students spend their last year in France but the only papers they have to write on their return are an essay and a paper on Modern French language. Wouldn't they be better employed, during their months in France, in reading some of the literature they've not had time to read before? They've been required to read two plays each by Corneille, Racine and Molière. Is it possible to understand two of Racine's plays without reading the rest of his masterpieces? Can one get an adequate idea of Flaubert from reading only *Trois Contes*? Can one understand the French novel without reading any of Balzac's works? Can one be regarded as competent to teach French literature in a school if one has not studied Rabelais, Montaigne, Hugo, or Valéry?

LO. There are several literature courses in which other writers are discussed. A set book does not circumscribe what is required, it is merely the centre of a much wider knowledge.

FRA. I appreciate that, but I notice that in both English and other modern languages the student devotes a good deal of his time to the study of old and medieval literature and to philology. Doesn't this mean that later and greater literature is crowded out of the curriculum?

DEN. You surely wouldn't suggest, Professor Franklin, a literature course with little or no philology?

FRA. Well, with Italian literature one must go back to Dante at least. But I guess that an educated man could remain ignorant of French literature before Villon, except the *Chanson de Roland*. Most great German literature and all great Russian literature was written during the past two hundred years. Can any of you mention the name of a single Russian author before the eighteenth century?

VA. Quite. If we considered the real needs of the students - and the needs of society which I know Denbigh despises - we should require them to study more great literature and less primitive literature, more modern language, and less historical grammar.

LO. But the particular discipline involved in philological study cannot be obtained in any other way.

VA. Agreed. But, valuable as it may be, it is bound to crowd out of the curriculum other things which are still more valuable for most students. If I were appointing a French mistress, or a German mistress, I should prefer a graduate who had studied the literature of the past 350 years to one who had a more cursory knowledge of the literature of the past 900 years. Wouldn't you, Longstaffe?

LO. No, I wouldn't. I should prefer a teacher with scholarly interests and scholarly training to one who had merely read enjoyable literature.

VA. That is because you are a puritan reactionary. You distrust pleasure and you don't believe that the study of literature demands the exercise of great intelligence. I suppose you would also prefer the student who had done *Beowulf* to the one who had studied Henry James or Melville?

LO. Certainly. He can read James after he leaves the university, but he is unlikely to read Anglo-Saxon if he is not compelled to do so by degree requirements.

VA. But if he spends half his time on linguistics he will necessarily receive an inferior training in literary criticism. It seems to me quite deplorable that students have to choose (as they do) between the novel and the drama. They ought to do both. The reason why they can't do both is that there is no time. I am not opposed to philological study. It is a perfectly legitimate study and I should fight to the death for it to be retained in the Faculty. But why should literature departments be overweighted in this way, merely because of the vested interests involved?

DEN. Really, Vane, you are being unreasonable, as well as offensive. You know perfectly well how impossible it is to separate language and literature. A student cannot read Villon or Chaucer merely by the light of nature and a good teacher of 'language' needs critical power as much as a good teacher of 'literature' needs a considerable linguistic equipment. They are not in opposite camps, but allies.

VA. You don't solve problems by pretending they don't exist.

FRA. I guess that I've stumbled on a subject which is liable to be controversial but it struck me in reading through your prospectus that the student who wished to avoid old and medieval literature could easily do so by taking what you call 'Combined Honours' - French and German, French and Hispanic Studies, German and Russian, English and Italian, English and Philosophy.

VA. It's not as simple as that. Most of these combinations demand the old texts of both languages, so that the student is faced with a double dose of philology.

FRA. But they can take 'Honours in General studies', which appears to be a three-year course, and in which they might study two languages for three years.

LO. Yes, they might do that but, on the whole, students, and the outside world, regard honours in general studies as inferior to a special studies degree - even though they are more difficult to obtain. Also, one must admit that French, Spanish and German demand even for general students the study of Old French, Old Spanish and Old German.

VA. You see, sir, how conservative most of us are. To suggest that we ought to move with the times would be regarded by most of our colleagues as treason of the clerks.

FRA. I suppose, then, it would be indiscreet to ask if you've been influenced at all by what's going on at Keele, where I've just been visiting the University College of North Staffordshire?

DEN. At one time nearly all our students, as at Keele, took a general course before they transferred to special studies at the end of their first year. But parents and Local Education Authorities complained that elsewhere a student could obtain an honours degree in three years, so we had to fall into line. More recently we have attempted to broaden students' interests by insisting that in their first year they should study a subject apart from those in which each was being examined. This proved to be a failure because some of our colleagues insisted that the extra subject should be closely linked to their main course of study, and because students did not work seriously if the results were not tested. Next we arranged a series of so-called 'Monday lectures' arranged by an inter-faculty committee, but most students attended only lectures of their own faculty.

VA. I understand that there were sometimes heated disputes in the committee. At one meeting "The peaceful uses of Nuclear Energy" was suggested as a suitable topic. 'No, no', said the Professor of Medicine, 'we can't have that ... it's political'. The chairman said the matter was surely a moral question. 'It is not our business', said the Professor, 'to discuss moral questions.' 'Are you not bound to give ethical guidance to your students?' 'No', said the Professor, 'that is the business of the churches and if they don't belong to a church, they can pick up enough from newspapers or the radio'. This seems to me to be an idiotic - dare I say, an immoral? - attitude for any teacher to take.

LO. In spite of criticisms which might be made, the lectures have introduced scientific, medical, legal and other topics to a large number of Arts students. I think we can say that the experiment has been encouraging.

DEN. The most recent experiment has only been running for a short time. It was recently decided to make all first-year General Degree (that is, Pass) students take an introductory course in some subject not related to the three with which they were mainly concerned. These courses are taught mainly in tutorial classes, and students are examined at the end of the session. A large number of these courses have already been arranged and next session other faculties have promised to arrange similar courses for Arts students. As far as can be seen at this early stage, the scheme seems to be having the desired effect of broadening the interests of the students.

FRA. I gather that your Honours students don't take these courses.

DEN. No, most of our colleagues think that special studies are the best means of broadening a student's interests.

VA. You broaden people by narrowing them! 'This was sometime a paradox, but now the time gives it proof.'

DEN. In spite of Vane's facetiousness, it is not so absurd as it may sound. It depends on how a subject is taught. To study four separate subjects is like having four streams in a mountainous country, which flow directly into the sea they never meet, and their catchment area is small. The study of a single subject - if it is properly taught - is like a broad river in a flat country, into which countless tributaries flow, and of which the catchment area is immense. So from the study of a single poem or a single historical incident the student is driven out into ever wider circles, literary, theological, philosophical, political, social and economic.

VA. When a man begins to argue by analogy ...

FRA. *(hastily)* There are several other questions I want to ask. I've been reading a book by Bruce Truscot, entitled *Redbrick University*. He complains that many of his colleagues are lazy, and that they publish hardly anything. Would you say that his complaints were applicable to your university?

LO. As a matter of fact 'Bruce Truscot' was a Professor here, as we found out from his obituary notices.[2] He himself wrote dozens of books and hundreds of articles, besides editing a more or less learned journal. He tended to judge others by his own standards of productivity, and good as his best work was it might have been even better if he had written half as much. I doubt whether his complaints were justifiable then and they would certainly not be justifiable now. During the past seven years members of the Faculty published about 75 books, over 1,000 articles, and a large number of reviews. I think myself that far too much stress is laid on publication. Some invaluable teachers are kept stationary at a salary of £1,350 because they have not published enough to satisfy the committee. Promotion now depends mainly on research. A bad teacher who produces his quota of articles gets promoted and a good teacher who publishes little is passed over. There is far too much pressure on young lecturers to publish at a time when they should be filling in the gaps in their knowledge and learning their job as teachers. He takes his first degree at the age of 21, he may spend three or four years on specialised research, and at the age of twenty-five he is appointed as assistant lecturer. His research for his doctorate may be on a subject on which he will never have to lecture, so that his basic knowledge may be little more than what he had when he wrote his Finals papers. He needs to spend four or five years in wide reading and this he will not have time to do if he is expected to publish at once. A major work of scholarship may take ten or twenty years to complete so the young lecturer, thinking of his wife and children, is tempted to shun the long and laborious task. He chooses instead to write a few articles which will be a better guarantee for his promotion.

VA. I agree with Longstaffe - for once. If Bruce Truscot were alive today he might complain that many of the notes and short articles which get written are merely designed to comply with the requirements of the grading scheme. The primary duty of a university lecturer is to teach, and most lecturers in our faculty realise this. But I understand from my colleagues in the science faculty that many young lecturers dislike teaching and resent what they call contact-hours. They regard themselves as research workers and they drag themselves reluctantly from the laboratory to the lecture-room, to give perfunctory and ill-delivered lectures. Why, they ask, bother with elementary instruction to undergraduates, when our promotion depends on our researches? Nearly all our colleagues, even those who are not very good at it, enjoy teaching, and even if they had the chance they would not devote all their time to research. But I would like to see it laid down that a young lecturer was not expected to publish anything until he had been at least five years in the university and it should be made clear that long-term research was regarded as more valuable than minor articles.

DEN. Perhaps we should explain to Professor Franklin that although we don't literally weigh books, as some American universities are said to do, we do occasionally accelerate promotion when a lecturer publishes a major work.

FRA. I've been thinking over those figures of yours - 75 books and 1,000 articles. For a small faculty like yours, that strikes me as a pretty impressive record. How does it compare with Oxford or Cambridge?

LO. Since the war most of the dons at Oxford and Cambridge have been shockingly overworked. Although their terms are much shorter than ours, the dons there have probably twice as many hours of teaching as we do. Unless something is done about it we shall find in a generation or so that the more productive minds will gravitate to the newer universities. Oxford and Cambridge will have the best students and the most sterile lecturers.

DEN. Nonsense, Longstaffe. Oxford and Cambridge have so many advantages that they will never have any difficulty in attracting good people. In any case, in the minds of many dons a stigma attaches to publication. They would rather point out the deficiencies of their colleagues' books than commit themselves to print.

FRA. Do you have any difficulty in finding a publisher for your work?

DEN. There is no difficulty at all in getting articles accepted for publication. We are lucky, too, in having a Research Committee which makes generous grants in aid of publication and still luckier in having a Press of our own, which publishes an increasing number of books every year. I'm not on the Press Committee but I gather that the committee is compelled to reject many good books every year because the authors, particularly those in less generous universities, are unable to obtain subventions. It is impossible for a married man, trying to live on £1,000 a year, to spare £300 to subsidise his own book, however much he believes in it. I know of one man who borrowed the necessary money and it turned out to be a profitable investment because he was appointed to a Chair as soon as his book appeared.

FRA. I suppose we are lucky in the States. Our scholars are able to publish huge volumes which no commercial publisher could touch.

VA. Yes, English scholars daren't embark on twenty volume editions because they know they will never find a publisher. Not only that. Your scholars not merely receive generous subsidies for the publication of their work, they obtain travel grants, leave of absence, research assistants, and various other advantages. When I first began teaching before the war I was told of the existence of sabbatical years. Every seven years, I was told, I could expect a year's leave of absence on full pay. But I have yet to meet an English scholar who has been granted a year's leave of absence - except to teach overseas - and I have never yet met an American scholar over forty years of age who has not had at least one year's leave of absence. How many have you had, Professor Franklin?

FRA. This is my third. I guess we are lucky in many ways but our teaching schedules are still much heavier than yours. And when Mr Longstaffe was complaining of the pressure on young lecturers to publish prematurely, I couldn't help feeling that you in Britain were much luckier than you realise. Your lecturers have security of tenure. The ratio between your lowest salary and your highest is one to three. Our ratio is nearer one to ten. You don't suffer from the same economic pressure to achieve promotion at almost any cost that our lecturers do. Hence the unreadable books which so many of our scholars produce. But when a scholar does get to the top in the States, he is given everything he needs.

VA. Some of our faculties do have research assistants and there is no reason why we shouldn't have them in the Faculty of Arts. Every large department ought to have them and I'm sure they could be provided at a comparatively small cost. Many post-graduate students, after they have taken their second degree, would be delighted to stay on for a year or two for a salary only a little higher than their previous studentship or fellowship.

LO. You can always use your post-graduate students or fellows as research assistants.

VA. No, we can't. They are allowed to do only three hours a week, and we need them to spend those hours in taking tutorial classes. Research assistants are regarded as luxuries and the Treasury cannot spare any money for luxuries.

FRA. I have one last question. How far do you think the Faculty of Arts answers the real needs of society in a scientific or technological age?

VA. Not as much as it ought. The faculties are drifting further and further apart. In the eighteenth century Newton read the classics and studied theology, and every educated man could read Newton. Even at the beginning of this century Ross and Sherrington both wrote verse. It wasn't very good verse, but it was at least an acknowledgement of the existence of other disciplines than their own. I can't imagine Professor Slingsby writing verse - I can't even imagine him reading a work of literature. Instead he makes speeches at school prize-givings in which he claims that the truly cultured man of today is the scientist and that the arts man ought to regard himself as illiterate because he has no understanding of the world in which he lives. Slingsby is partly right, of course. The arts man who takes no interest in science is a miserable creature. I would like every student in the faculty to take a course in his first year either on the history of science or on scientific method. The advantage of the former is that it could be demanded of all students, whatever their faculty and the students of different faculties would acquire a new respect for each other.

LO. They are more likely to become more conscious of the gulf which separates them. To a scientist the history of science is a record of the advancement of learning by the jettisoning of disproved hypotheses. To an Arts man the discarded hypothesis is interesting both for its own sake and for the light it throws on the past. No, Vane, I don't believe we should regard it as part of our duty to see that our students dabble in science. Many of them - the best of them, probably - will pick up a reasonable amount of scientific information in the course of their reading. And as for scientific method, what people don't seem to realise is that every subject taught in the university involves the use of scientific method. With some subjects this is obvious - Social Science, Psychology, Geography and Economics, for example. But Philology is also a science with its hypotheses and its laws. An historian collects facts, produces an hypothesis to explain the facts, and then tests the hypothesis. We don't need to go to another faculty to be taught scientific method.

DEN. As you will have noticed, Professor Franklin, our faculty is conservative. I don't mean politically, of course. Whereas the staff of the medical faculty would vote Tory almost to a man, we have all sorts, from Liberals, like myself, to floating voters, like Longstaffe, and from rightwing Tories to Marxists without a party. But in academic matters, apart from a few eccentrics like Vane, we are really very conservative indeed. The Dean recently quoted a remark to the effect that we were radical in theory but conservative in practice. It's not true. We are conservative both in theory and practice. We spent two years in discussing the reform of the General Degree, but most of us were secretly anxious to preserve the *status quo* and though we tried to appease Vane and his friends by introducing a whole set of new ordinances and regulations for the ostensible purpose of enabling more General Degree students to obtain Honours, the result - as the Dean in a moment of candour was forced to admit - is that not more than two or three additional students each year are likely to achieve Honours. So many of the subjects taught in the Faculty have traditions going back for hundreds of years - to a time when science was quackery - that it is natural that the Faculty as a whole should cling fast to tradition. There are obvious dangers, of course but, on the whole, I think our instincts are sound. In a world of change we have to bear witness to the unchanging values of western civilisation; in a world of materialism we continue to proclaim that man cannot live by bread alone; in a world of power we insist on the advancement of disinterested learning and strive for the ennoblement of life.

VA. Rhetoric is all very fine, but it doesn't begin to solve any of our real problems. I am quite willing to admit that most members of Faculty would agree with you but owing to the hierarchical system of university government, one becomes a member of the Faculty only when one has become thoroughly respectable and safe. If half the places on Faculty were filled by election, instead of by the method of self-perpetuation, you would find that the younger members of the teaching staff are less traditional in their views than the ageing caucus whose spokesman you are. They believe, as I believe, that the nature of a university is determined ultimately not by the wishes of its members but by the largely unconscious purpose of the society in which it functions. Whether you like it or not, the Faculty of Arts will have to change to meet the changing needs of the age and I believe that if we reform ourselves from within we are less likely to become harmless and ineffectual, diminishing in size and influence.

LO. What you don't seem to realise, Vane, is that although universities may change from generation to generation in order to satisfy the changing needs of society, the ideals and aims of society are influenced by the universities, through the work they do, through the books they write, through the teachers they train. By urging that the universities should fit in with the purposes of society you are doing your best to ensure that those purposes will be uninfluenced by the wisdom of ages - of which we are the unworthy repositories.

NOTES

1. [Editor] Kenneth A. Muir (1907-1996), FBA, King Alfred Professor of English Literature 1951-1974 and Dean of Arts 1958-1961, died as this volume was going to press.

2. [Editor] 'Bruce Truscot' was E. Allison Peers, Professor of Spanish 1922-1952. His *Redbrick University*, published 1943, with a follow-up in 1945, a lively discussion of the problems of provincial universities, by its vituperative condemnation of fellow professors who published too little no doubt helped to reduce the prestige of universities in the public mind.

OTIA MERSEIANA

THE PUBLICATION OF THE ARTS FACULTY OF UNIVERSITY COLLEGE LIVERPOOL

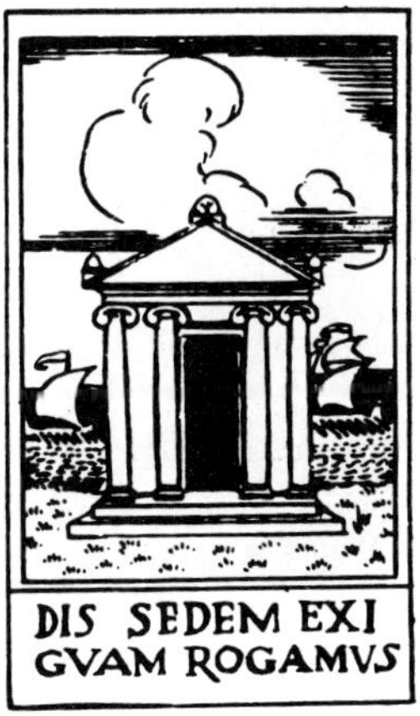

VOLUME ONE

1899

PARIS
C. KLINCKSIECK
11 RUE DE LILLE

LONDON
TH. WOHLLEBEN
45 GREAT RUSSELL STREET

NEW YORK
G. E. STECHERT
9 EAST 16TH STREET

Published in four volumes 1899-1903

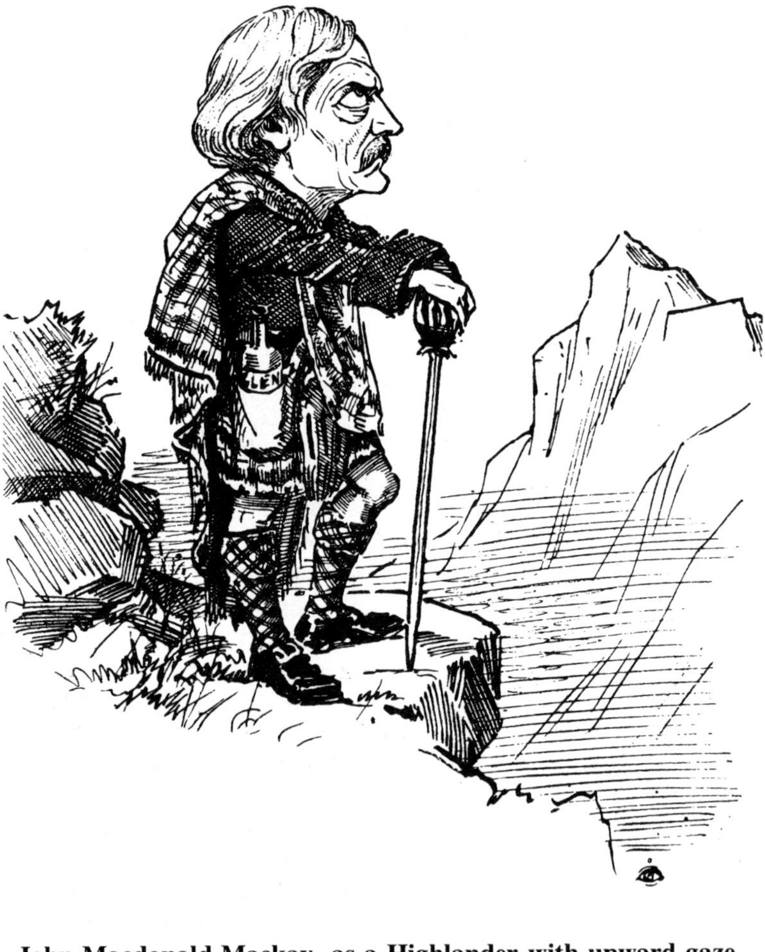

John Macdonald Mackay, as a Highlander with upward gaze
Cartoon from *The Sphinx* of 1901

THE REAL MACKAY

P.E.H. Hair

The tribute volume dedicated to John Macdonald Mackay in July 1914, and published later that year, is an extraordinary work now to tiptoe through.[1] First, because of its revelation of printing costs at the time. Strewed through the English are pages in Greek, German, French, Spanish, Irish, Welsh and Romany, all of course hand-typeset. Half of its 400 pages contain contributions that make no mention of Mackay but are merely chips from the workbench contributed by friendly scholars. One or two are pieces for the occasion, often frothy rhetoric, but most are genuine notes on recondite topics, probably lost to the relevant discipline's fraternity by appearing in such a place.[2] A section contains verse, including a long address to Mackay in Lallans. But a dozen prose contributions glorify Mackay in specific terms. A letter of glowing tribute at the front is signed by 140 individuals, the majority colleagues at Liverpool University. And these include a number who had already achieved, or were eventually to achieve, at Liverpool or elsewhere, great distinction, in a variety of disciplines.[3] The second extraordinary feature is this: given the over-the-top nature of the tribute, who or what was Mackay?

Mackay, Rathbone Professor of History 1884-1914, was the first Honorary Dean of the Faculty of Arts, and his 58-page address in this capacity, 'To Senate and Faculty', published in 1897 (but presumably not actually spoken at this length), is given in an appendix to the volume.[4] Mackay's pupil, assistant, and eventually rival professor and contestant for student lecture fees, was J. Ramsay Bryce Muir - despite his name a less genuine Scotsman - who became Dean of Arts in 1905 and described himself as the 'first Dean of Arts'.[5] An autobiographical account written by Ramsay Muir in 1940 and published posthumously in 1943 excoriates Mackay, as a teacher and researcher, and represents him broadly as a humbug.[6] Muir was certainly himself a researcher, for a time at least, and throughout his life a steady author of publications. But it is ironic that, having allowed Mackay a measure of status only as prophet and preacher, Muir in turn drifted from academic labours into this alluring vocation.

Muir's case against Mackay is that as an historian he was ill-informed and lazy. This seems true. He published - it seems - nothing. In 1889 a textbook on the Tudors was advertised as in preparation, and in 1894 several scholars testifying to Mackay's capacity had been shown some proofs, but the work was never completed.[7] And I can trace no learned articles by Mackay. He is alleged to have said - 'It is a good thing to write but an indifferent thing to print'.[8] Mackay's non-performance as a publishing historian was apparently recognised at Liverpool - most likely it was in the mind of Bruce Truscot, alias Professor E. Allison Peers of Liverpool, when a generation later he denounced non-researching professors[9] - since the letter of tribute tactfully noted that 'the gifts that might have made your name in other fields, you have devoted largely to affairs and to the fulfilment of dreams'4.

At the university's centenary exhibition in 1981, Mackay's teaching was represented by a notebook open at a page on which the professor of history had written, in a large hand, no doubt as a guide to a lecture, solely these words - 'The Tudors, a despotic dynasty'. Political correctness has, of course, always been with us, and pre-1914 British historians were expected to extol the nation's linear progress to parliamentary liberalism. The display was, however, somewhat unfair. Inspection of the whole notebook and of Mackay's unfinished textbook proves that he had a more nuanced view of Tudor history. The weakness of his teaching appear to have lain, not so much in his lecture notes, as in his ignoring of his lecture notes - although a few students preferred to consider this a gain rather than a loss. Apart from the Tudors, Mackay's forte was Ancient History as then defined, that is, Graeco-Roman history.[10] This is what one might expect from an 1870s graduate, at Scottish universities, in Classics and Philosophy, even one with a later first-class degree in what Oxford then termed 'Modern History'.[11] Yet, in his first decade at Liverpool, Mackay singlehandedly taught 'Greek and Roman history, medieval and modern history, and the History of England with Scottish and Irish relations'.[12] At this period, much of the Arts teaching was in evening classes and at sub-degree levels.[13] It is perhaps not surprising that his degree teaching was ill-prepared and lacking in sound factual content. So at least claimed his severest critic.[14]

One is not reassured about Mackay's teaching by the tribute volume's only anecdote about this aspect of his career. The opening contribution, a wholesale tribute by Walter Raleigh, the English literature guru, contains the following.

> I once heard a description of a passage in one of his lectures on early Roman history. He had been telling how Rome absorbed or destroyed

> the neighbouring civilisations, and he came to the Etruscans. His sentences were punctuated by long pauses for thought; he walked up and down the wooden dais; he gazed out of the window. "What did the Etruscans think?" he said. "You don't know what the Etruscans thought." "I don't know what the Etruscans thought." "Nobody knows what the Etruscans thought." The audience made no entry in their note-books, and waited for something more tangible. Probably no single one of them understood that passion of thought.[15]

No, indeed. The present writer is something of an historical sceptic, even agnostic, but it is all too easy for doubt to slip into vapidity.

Muir found Mackay's lectures -

> ... boring and incoherent. But every now and then he would put on the prophet's mantle, and in these moods he was very impressive. Gazing through the window at the horizon, while his strong left hand made mystical gestures, he suggested unutterable things. We could not recall or reproduce what he said: I doubt if he ever coined a memorable phrase. But we felt we had been somehow lifted us out of the workaday world and made to feel the majesty and mystery of history.

Again, Muir describes an 1890 tutorial.

> Mackay sat on the hearthrug in his private room, idly poking the fire, and told us he was going to discuss the constitution of Lycurgus. That was the last we heard of Lycurgus, except that his name meant light-bringer. Then followed a rambling discourse upon light, including a reference to Goethe, which passed into a rhapsody upon the limitations of human life, and finished up with a quotation of "We are such stuff as dreams are made on", just as the bell rang. Some students were mightily impressed by this sort of meandering rhapsody: I, for one, thought it rather wonderful. But it was not history.[16]

Muir's wonder persisted. In 1894 Mackay unsuccessfully applied for the Chair of History at Edinburgh. Among the sheaf of printed testimonials to Mackay's capacity was a glowing one from five former pupils, two women and three men, all by now at Oxford, all of whom 'missed his marked power of inspiration', and one of the signatories was J. Ramsay Bryce Muir. Liverpool colleagues and Balliol tutors said nice things about Mackay, but perhaps the most telling was the statement of an Oxford examiner that he remembered Mackay for a 'really brilliant *viva voce* - the best I have heard'.[17]

Muir's diatribe can in part be put down to a generation gap and professional rivalry.[18] One name is patently missing from the list of 140 signatories in the tribute volume, that of Muir.[19] If academics are not quite as loathsome, malicious and lubricious as represented on current televison, nor are they pure saints. Two later professors of history, working in the same building, communicated for years only in writing or through a secretarial intermediary. Nevertheless, Muir does seem to have had good grounds for thinking that he was shabbily treated by Mackay. Although it is curious that those signing the letter of tribute included some former pupils who later achieved considerable standing in historical studies, even at London or Oxbridge, it is hard to rebut Muir's judgement that Mackay as an historian was a nonentity and that his apparent refusal to recognise Muir's greater talents held back the discipline at Liverpool. It is even worth considering whether the spat between them had something to do with the fact that each was a lifelong bachelor and therefore concentrated his emotions on his vocation.

Yet Mackay had, rightly or wrongly, by 1914 earned enormous esteem, at least in some quarters. Before considering his other credentials, there is one more point to make about the tribute volume. It exudes an air of pre-1914 optimism and energy. Things at Liverpool, and by implication in the world at large, had gone latterly from better to better. It was a good time to be alive, and with a little effort and prophetic forethought, even better would inevitably be achieved. Of course it would be too much to expect the band of colleagues and chums who extolled Mackay to have precise foresight - and not even the Highlander, Mackay himself. But within twelve months of the publication, fifty thousand young British men, non-graduates and graduates, proletariat and gentry, were being slaughtered in Flanders and at Gallipoli; and the vogue of unquestioning rational optimism was at an end. One signatory, a professorial colleague and a member of Mackay's clique, having in 1911 retired to Germany (presumably together with housekeeping sister, a contributor), by late 1914 was giving 'comfort to the enemy' by supporting Irish rebels. We do not know what Mackay, in retirement until his death in 1931, thought of the Great War and the changing 'passion of thought'.[20] In cutting Victorians down to size it is not fair to go as far as Lytton Strachey - momentarily a student of the Liverpool School of History[21] - but Mackay retired just before Armageddon.

What did Mackay do in the university? John Garstang, the Egyptologist, assured readers of the tribute volume that 'Mackay had opened out before me the full width and depth of the field of study which remains the chief interest of my life'. Garstang had referred a point to Mackay. 'He grasped the point at once; and after an interval during which his eyes roamed in characteristic fashion among things unseen, he unfolded to us the idea which had leapt to his mind, that possibly the Asian element in Etruscan culture might be explained by a Hittite influence on the Lydian coast of Asia Minor'. Thus Mackay's mind-leap revolutionised Etruscan, Hittite and Egyptian studies, perhaps.[22] As for the study of Russian at Liverpool, according to Bernard Pares, 'no move in the shaping of the School of Russian Studies was taken without his advice, and most of our steps were the direct result of conference with him'. Furthermore, according to C.H. Reilly, 'that architecture is a full subject in the academic curriculum of the University of Liverpool, with a chair devoted to it, is largely due to Professor Mackay'. And indeed Appendix II presents an 1892 talk in which Mackay explains how he set about to encourage the teaching of architecture, although he hoped to see it become the nucleus of a School of Fine Art (an entity which never came about, despite regular campaigns, the last in the early 1980s). Another contributor, applauding the 'study of German in an English university', wrote - 'Dear Mackay, ... I know that you have the cause of German very much at heart'.

Nor was Mackay's concern limited to those disciplines in 1996 still housed within the Arts Faculty. 'Associated from the very first with all great educational movements',[23] he supported those 'striving towards higher education for Commerce', his object being 'the establishment of a school of higher studies in Economics, History, Science and Languages, applied to industry, trade and finance'. Perhaps modern 'Business Studies'. The contributor on 'Chemical Research in a modern English University' forgot to actually mention Mackay.[24] But the contributor who argued that Mathematics was as much an Arts subject as a Science one, proclaimed, albeit somewhat tortuously, that the 'institution of a Chair of Mathematics associated with the Faculty of Arts - I refer of course to the Chair of the History and Philosophy of Mathematics which I have the honour to hold - ... a momentous step, it seems to me, not only in the history of the University, but also in that of Learning in England, has been, I believe I am right in stating, largely due to the initiative of J.M. Mackay, the Professor of History'. C.S. Sherrington, the neurophysiologist of future fame, provided a sonnet which is about Liverpool rather than about Mackay, but Oliver Elton broke into eighteen verses on the sage, of which the twelfth advances the argument (and is reasonably comprehensible to Sassenachs). 'For ye'd the prophet's distant gaze / On towers unseen ye help'd to raise; / Ye let wiseacres tak the praise; / But painter GUS / has fix'd, for a' succeedin' days, / Your saul for us.'[25] The portrait of Mackay, as horizon-seeking Prophet, by the young Augustus John, then in tenuous association with the university, I return to.[26]

Ramsay Muir made a great thing of his travels in India and general interest in the British Empire. For some decades his scholarly pot-boilers on the history of the Empire were standard texts in schools and universities. He genuinely took a wider view of the global past than did Mackay, who was stuck on the Etruscans.[27] The present writer, an overseas historian, was responsible for having the second chair of modern history labelled the Ramsay Muir chair; and it was symbolic that when the first occupant retired and the Ramsay Muir chair was 'frozen', this coincided with a distinct retreat from overseas history in the department. Yet Appendix V gives a 1909 letter in which Mackay advised on a national college of agriculture in South Africa - 'a rapid summary on the main heads where my experience and opinion may be of use'. The last paragraph provides examples of his writing style. 'Open the Empire and its resources to the South African. Let the trek expand again inland, henceforth on scientific knowledge, over British Africa. As the Dutch and British have through the ages turned their native silt or gravel into gardens of civilisation, let the two races cooperate in the face of immense natural obstacles to do the like for Imperial Africa.'[28] One contribution to the tribute volume discussed the evolution of a Canadian university. Although the differences between the Canadian and British experience were underlined and Mackay was not cited as a trans-Atlantic influence, the piece came 'from one who has had the good fortune to study under him in the University whose form and spirit he has done so much to create and foster'. Nearer home, Mackay advised on the constitution of the University of Birmingham, and a contributor from that place noted that 'the debt of Birmingham to Mackay can never be repaid'. Similarly a contributor from Sheffield University asserted that 'we are heavily indebted to Mackay'.[29]

Ramsay Muir claimed that he established links between Town and Gown previously disregarded by Mackay. Muir wrote on the history of Liverpool and did important research in that field, and he played a decisive role in the development of 'extra-mural' studies. Had he lived in the 1990s he would undoubtedly have received brownie points for his 'community involvement'. But his local advantage over Mackay was a half truth. Mackay had local connections, and made good use of them, but the connections were chummy ones with the Merseyside rich. Liverpool in Mackay's early days was stocked with millionaires - as well as with the unwashed at the other end of the social scale. Mackay and others in the university were good at relieving local businessmen of large sums, in return for which the university's new chairs and other awards received the benefactor's name. Local beneficence, even when it made a very limited dent in the benefactor's resources, set Liverpool University on its feet. By Ramsay Muir's day there were fewer opportunities for named chairs and perhaps fewer benevolent millionaires. Where Mackay linked up with the well-to-do, Muir went for the *hoi polloi*.[30]

Mackay was made Professor of History at the age of 28, on what a century later would be considered a weak track record - a Scottish M.A., an Oxford degree ('four years at Balliol'), and teaching as 'Senior English master at the High School of Edinburgh' for 'over one year'.[31] But his subsequent thirty years at Liverpool coincided with the explosive growth of the university, and as a Grand Old Man he could be credited with much of what had been achieved. The extent of his influence in the setting up of new disciplines via new chairs is now difficult to assess,[32] but there is no reason to doubt that in 1914 a number of perfectly sensible academics were sincere in believing that his was probably the greatest individual influence on the development of the university to date. Even looking back in 1938, C.H. Reilly swore that, between his own arrival in 1904 to Mackay's retirement in 1914, 'he was, by force of character, the undoubted head of the university'.[33] Whatever Mackay's failings in the School of History, he deserves treatment - and more detailed assessment than can be presented in an essay based on limited research - for his wider activities in the university, not least since these related fundamentally to the development of the Faculty of Arts.

It is unclear whether Mackay wrote and circulated many memoranda but certain that he mainly worked by talking. No doubt he talked in committees and Senate, but he particularly talked in club armchairs, or around the table at dinner parties, to select individuals. If we are to believe the lively memoirs of the roguish Reilly, pre-1914 professorial life at Liverpool was one long round of dinner parties (and flirting with the wives while the carriages were kept waiting). Mackay's writings on university matters indicate that he was invariably carried away by the exuberance of his own verbosity. But in man-to-man chats - we have no idea what women thought of him, and Reilly, who knew a thing or two about the University wives, hints that he never bothered to allow them into the presence of his monologues - his charismatic blether overcame most weaker souls.[34]

The tribute volume contains one account of a visitor from London who having found his way to Mackay's lodgings was kept up all night while Mackay smoked his pipe at him and talked incessantly. In prose nearly as exaltedly flowery as that of the master, the Secretary of the University Extension Society described the subject matter. 'The business of a University in a great city had been unfolded - how it stands for the spirit in a world of getting and spending ... How unite humane learning with an appreciation of Art and with that frank acceptance of the world of sense which is the mind of Science? ... To urge the significance of the theory of knowing on those who profess to know, and the value of knowledge upon those who undertake to do. To unify the whole with the practice of the presence of God!' High thoughts indeed. But Wyld added another half page of topics. 'Such was the citadel of his thought; but he rambled by innumerable byeways, through the surrounding fields.'

Byways rambled through included the following: academic prerogative; the English delight in compromise; respect of liberty and property; our compact of inevitable convictions; desirable university schools of classics ... language ... social science ... medicine ... commerce; education dependent on psychology; the application of pure science; research, training for the professions, [and] the diffusion of knowledge, as the co-efficients of a living unity; the visible and the invisible Universe in fee. And finally, a shade bathetically, 'the Club, the Monastery of our time, the preserver and begetter of this ideal'.[35]

After Mackay's death, Bernard Pares - an admirer who described Mackay rather oddly as 'a Russian without knowing it' - referred to the rambling. 'He could ramble indefinitely, but from time to time, sometimes on a subject of which one would have expected him to be quite ignorant, came a flash that ignited up in clear outline the whole point of the matter in question'.[36] An anonymous obituary in the *Liverpool Post*, obviously by a former colleague, was less complimentary. 'He talked, as some Highlanders do, with a suggestion of what the Welsh call a *hwyl*, and he made you feel, even when he was uttering commonplaces, as he often did, that he was making you a confidant in some rather awful secret'.[37]

Mystical waffler though he may have been, Mackay was also, Scotsmanlike, a canny operator. 'No man held more tenaciously to his ideals or seemed to see more clearly each step that must be taken to attain them. It was always a surprise and delight to notice the way in which each small and often innocent looking proposal at Faculty or Senate meeting would be tested by him by first principles. Was it for the real spiritual good of the University or the Faculty as a whole or merely for the glorification of one section of it? If we agreed to such and such a step now, would it tie our hands later on in some more useful action? Any question might give occasion for a speech of a mounting, rather broken, eloquence, which seemed as one listened, to be for ever taking one to higher and higher planes of thought, to be continually breaking as it were into a new and finer sky.'[38]

It seems that the Highlander (many accounts underline Mackay's ethnic origin, so perhaps it was his accent that helped) mesmerised those around him. Decades later Collinson wrote that Mackay's portrait in the 'New Testament' group study was outstandingly successful, 'for the artist has caught his chief personal characteristics: his stature and broad frame, his prophetic posture, his slightly unkempt appearance, his homespun clothes and above all the look - attributed to the Highlanders - of "feyness" and "second sight"'.[39] Mackay's line was Higher Things, and it is likely that, in his period at Liverpool, the late-Victorian agenda and its continuing shadow made even intelligent individuals pay unsuspicious deference to those who invariably dwelt on the high moral ground and then talked down to them. Mackay's Higher Things were Universities and Learning. There is no reason to doubt that he believed in them sincerely, and therefore convinced others that certain courses of action were necessary in the light of those ideals, even although later generations - and surely a few at the time - found difficulty in knowing exactly what he meant by the ideals and were sceptical about the idealness of all that eventuated. By 1914 some younger colleagues spoke irreverently of 'the old windbag'.[40] Yet Bernard Pares, looking back twenty and more years, still spoke of Mackay in hushed tones. 'The central source of all our ideals and efforts [at Liverpool] was John Macdonald Mackay, to whom I owe anything that I know of university construction. He had a second sight. For him the streets of the great city of learning which we wished to build lay all clearly laid out before his mind.'[41] Patently Mackay's language of allegory and metaphor was catching.

The tribute volume, and some earlier and later commentators, credited Mackay with two achievements in particular. The first was the establishment of an independent University of Liverpool, by the separation in 1903 of University College from the previous federal Victoria University. Little need be said on this subject here. Undoubtedly Mackay had campaigned for separation.[42] So, in his turn, did Ramsay Muir, who probably did more to win local middle-class backing. However, to some extent the 'struggle', of which much is made in the official history, was pushing against a door destined to open. Looking back over six centuries in which England had possessed for most of the period only two universities, the educational reformers of the late nineteenth century understandably felt that they had to struggle to set up half a dozen new ones. But looking back in 1996, when every town of any size now possesses or demands a 'university', it seems inconceivable that the great late-Victorian industrial cities could have been long denied a separate university each, given the strength of municipal feeling and the power in the nation of the local wealth. The fulfilment of a Mackay dream, the independent Liverpool University was thus also, as was said at the time, the result of 'the patriotic thoughts and aspirations of Liverpool men'.[43]

Mackay's second achievement, and the one very relevant for this essay, was the establishment within the university of a system of Faculties. In 1895 Mackay persuaded Senate to appoint a commitee, with himself as convenor, 'to consider and report upon the advisability of forming committees of Faculties, defining their constitution and functions'. The Senate committee recommended Faculties of Arts and Science (there already existed, although in rather a different form, a Faculty of Medicine). Only the Arts Faculty was at the time established, and this only with very limited functions, yet allowing a first meeting to be held in December 1896.[44] In 1897 Mackay, as

Honorary Dean, wrote what he termed 'the First Report on the Faculty of Arts'.[45] This contained limited information about the current state of the Faculty.[46] Instead it presented a potted history of university events up to 1895; and then many pages setting out why Mackay thought that a Faculty was a Good Thing. The official history refers sniffily to Mackay's 'high-sounding but not particularly illuminating references to the role of university faculties in medieval Europe and Scotland, and in contemporary France'. On France, Mackay inserted, in translation, enormous quotations from French educationalists, 20 pages out of the 58. Since this 1897 piece was truly Mackay's magnum opus, it seemed to the present writer only fair to seek a second opinion on its quality of argument, and this opinion is now presented.

Commenting more extensively on medieval universities in an earlier 1888 paper, Mackay had made blunders about their history and expressed views so general as to be scarcely significant as historical argument.[47] However, his 1897 paper is somewhat better informed, probably because he had read a seminal work (Rashdall) that had appeared two years earlier, although the medieval references are in fact slight. His observations on Scottish universities and nineteenth-century French ones tend to the general but appear to be reasonably sound, probably because he is often quoting authorities. He seldom analyses to any significant extent and his flowery language becomes irritating to the modern reader. His half-truths and errors are not impressive. Nevertheless, what he deduced from the historical examples he supplies - for instance, he dimly glimpses that university autonomy remained an important aspirational goal in the medieval period, and he commends all representational procedures in the past - was relevant to university development in his day, and perhaps is equally so today. Summing up - 'In all the waffle, there is something of embryonic value.'[48]

To Mackay, the Faculty represented the embodiment of his high ideals. While this is clear, it is far less clear why, at the practical level, he thought this. If the Faculty was a defensive position, against whom was it set up? It is conventionally held that Mackay was aiming to fight off, as the official history puts it, 'lay government in university affairs'. This is a popular cause among academics, and at a later date Reilly supplied suitably hair-raising examples where laymen on the university Council attempted to influence appointments, academic salaries, or tenure.[49] It is understandable that this interpretation has been put on Mackay's agenda since, at more or less the only point where in his address he broke free from woolly historicising and moralising, he attacked the American university. 'I desire to see the European University rise in England and not the repellent American type'.

It may be doubted whether Mackay really knew much about American universities and his European universities tended to be only the French - he had visited France but never America.[50] (A decade later, Muir actually visited some universities in the United States - probably to Mackay's annoyance - and on return made a more sympathetic assessment of higher education Over There.[51]) What exactly Mackay thought was wrong with American universities has to be interpreted from verbiage. 'The defect in the American type, without disparagement to its virtue, is not that it has through ignorance and isolation, through modern specialism and overpowering commercial habit, broken with a very ancient nobility of the human spirit, dissolving needlessly a classic and symmetric structure into a *débris* of classes and lectures and petty inconsequential committees, but that the University across that continent is not, as once in feudal and now in democratic Europe, a hearth and a home of autonomy on every range, a training ground consecrate to self-government.' Like all Mackay's pronouncements, the multiplication of clauses provides fodder for any number of reader's hobbyhorses. But the nub seems to be that, in the United States, commerce, fronted as vulgar fund-raising, manages academic affairs. So Mackay invents, or re-invents, Faculties, to be the second barrier, after the first, the Senate, against commercial and lay interference. Many present-day academics will approve.

But there is a second, alternative explanation of Mackay's strategy. In 1896 John Sampson, the University College and University Librarian, a friend and supporter of Mackay, wrote a little skit in Liverpool-Irish dialect entitled 'Mr Dooley on "How me Frind Mackay come to shtart a Faculthy av Arts"'. Here Mackay - described as a 'Celtic ganius, that's all poethry an' imagination an' goes about raisin' Cain' - is given another, very plausible reason for creating a Faculty of Arts: to strengthen the hands of the Arts professors against their colleagues in Science, who were so much more successful in securing grants from College funds.[52]

Finally, the present writer thinks that a third Mackay motive can be detected. Particularly via the French examples, he appears to be suggesting that the creation of Faculties, and especially an Arts Faculty, will further the cause of an independent university - somehow.

* * *

Mackay, who did no observable primary research himself, was an enthusiast for research by others. If he inspired some pupils, his concern for students in general seems to have been negligible.[53] It may be correct that his lifework was to make Liverpool University what it became. But in 1894, before much had happened, he was attempting to desert the ship. His decrial of American universities was unprophetic, in that North America soon outreached Europe in academic research, at least in many fields. No doubt it was achieved partly by superior funding, that is, the vulgar fund-raising that Mackay deplored. Yet Mackay had done more than his share of fund-raising for Liverpool University, and it might be argued that in the long run it would have been better if he had he left fund-raising to others and concentrated on research and publication.

Mackay is usually said to have fought for 'academic freedom' against 'lay pressure'. But no freedom is absolute, and academic freedom is another name for academics' privileges. Certainly Liverpool academics enjoyed a range of privileges for a long time after Mackay, and the university's centenary volume, written by an academic for academics, was duly grateful, for instance, by lauding the Faculty system. But in realising an ideal Mackay was ignoring reality. He was happy to receive lay money but not to accept lay direction. Yet he who pays the piper eventually calls the tune.[54] Happily, the Liverpool millionaires may have been otherwise engaged.[55] But over the decades the financing of universities became more and more dependent on State funding, and in the end the debts were called in.[56]

The supplementary volume of the university's history, published in 1994 and covering the period from 1981, sings a very different tune, a somewhat gloomy one. Very little here is said about Liverpool's contribution to knowledge - Mackay's vaunted 'Learning' - and research is justified mainly in terms of funds received and collectivities invented. The leading characters in this institutional history are administrators: the managers in Senate House who respond, by enthusiastic collaboration or occasional sullen resistance, to orders from a reactionary government which holds the purse and demands 'public accountancy'. Academic staff, apart from those hijacked to support committees in Senate House, appear principally as a chorus of victims. Mackay is mentioned once. 'Could it be only four years since the then Vice-Chancellor quoted with approbation Professor Mackay's wish that the University should be based on "brotherhood among friends and comrades" rather than to have a style of government borrowed from the business world?'[57]

In the recollection of the present writer one long groan was not the entire story of the 1980s: distinguished research was done and published, certainly in the Arts Faculty, and in this Faculty mainly with funding from the researcher's own purse, not the public one. And meanwhile large numbers of students were nourished and sent out into the world intellectually equipped in socially appropriate measure. Yet the picture of a university with its traditional reflexes challenged all along the line is largely a true one. The Faculty system had always had a downside. Like the departmental system it was basically a system for administrative convenience, disguised as one for perpetuating high ideals. The universality of knowledge implied in the term 'university' was too high-minded ever to exist in modern times. Faculties sanctioned and positively encouraged, by toffee-nosed disinterest and boastful ignorance, barriers between areas of knowledge. Thus, between Medicine, Science, and the laboratory-based disciplines in general on the one hand, and the Humanities on the other, there was little or no intellectual contact, and by the 1980s a great deal of cut-throat competition for funds. In this the Arts Faculty found that the rules of the game openly and aggressively disfavoured it. All the while, however, Mackay's system allowed fearful Faculties to summon up the troops to defend ossified traditions and beat off the challenge of change. When external pressures finally broke through, the claim that the existence of a Faculty system safeguarded the freedom of academics to teach and research exactly what they liked, and precisely how they chose to do it, proved a dream - one of Mackay's dreams. Yet it was a very nice dream, while it lasted.

And even a small measure of Mackay's 'brotherhood' (albeit terminologically sexist) is worth having, and deserves applause. The scope for intellectual brotherhood in a university is distinctly limited. Indeed, brotherhood may be merely a defensive reflex rather than a positive agenda. All sorts of self-interest daily militate against what the chapel prayer of the present writer's student college called 'love of the brethren', with the result that, if not actual hate, at least mild contempt of the brethren (and sistren) is more common. Yet personal experience in the Arts Faculty over a couple of recent decades generates the reflection that there were odd acts - and rare moments - and occasional encounters - when it was easy to believe that Mackay was on to something constructive, organic, and essential when he invoked a common and shared pursuit of knowledge. His final publication, *A New University*, was dedicated 'To the Fellowship of the New University 1894-1914'. His high talk certainly heart-warmed, for a time at least, a number of his colleagues; and it may well still serve, a little, in today's millenial times.

Every clerisy deplores the laity, wrongly when it is a career gambit, rightly when intellectual leadership is challenged by forces of vulgar opportunism. It is possible to believe that there was far too little public accountancy in past years and yet hold that the academic freedom postulated by Mackay and subsequently enjoyed by generations of Liverpool academics was not without some virtue. Indeed, it might be argued that in the end the State and the populace do themselves better if they tolerate the eccentricities and non-accountable strokes of research genius inherent in an untidy body of academics. Be that as it may, not even Mackay's prophetic instinct could reasonably be expected to see a century ahead.

The portrait of Mackay by Augustus John, which hung at first in the University Club, by the 1970s had found its way into the Common Room of the School of History - before it was 'borrowed' for an exhibition and subsequently enshrined in the University Art Gallery. According to Reilly, it failed to receive the Gold Medal for painting at an 1904 international exhibition only because the Royal Academicians on the jury withdrew the whole English entry in order to spite the painter. Someone at the time saw in the portrait 'a knight of the Holy Ghost'.[58] Muir saw in it 'the grim strength of his jaw, [and] the coldness and even cruelty of his stone-grey eyes'.[59] At departmental meetings held in the Common Room I tried not to sit opposite the portrait's dourness. I complained about the portrait's borrowing but was somewhat relieved.

* * *

In 1931, the year that Mackay died, his former colleague, Oliver Elton, presented Liverpool University Library with a book, a very thin volume of 'Verse', so merely entitled. The author was one J.M.M. Each of the thirteen poems is of passionate, seemingly unrequited or at least unfulfilled heterosexual love. '*We two who should in love be one / By bar of fortune are undone, / Who are never woo'd, and never won.*' Each poem is brief, the language is fairly simple, the sentiments not without some dignity. '*In the dawn a pair of young lovers, / Midsummer's epiphany.*'[60] If the sentiment is autobiographical, and it is difficult to believe otherwise, there are no clues as to the circumstances. It is not patent that the verbal content bears any relationship to Mackay's overheated prose. Nevertheless Mackay it is. In a private letter Elton wrote: 'The whole thing is very moving - and surprising - and few of us, I imagine, divined this Mackay.'[61] Elton's surprise covered both the fact that Mackay had left instructions and money for the publication, and his earlier knowledge of Mackay as Poet.[62] In 1914, in secrecy, Mackay had shown Elton, and another close colleague and friend, a collection of verse, unpublished but set up in print, and in 1927 had discussed it again. The friends had apparently not been very encouraging, and in 1931 Elton was very doubtful whether any of the verse should appear, lest it damage Mackay's reputation. However, Elton opined that Mackay 'had the poet's soul and passion, and I am sure nursed for years the idea that he would win the poet's glory'. With misgivings, Elton selected thirteen poems from the collection, had them published by the Oxford University Press as a private edition (although this is not stated on the book), slightly concealed the author's name by using only initials on the title-page, and slightly apologised by adding on the title-page 'These poems were not finally revised by the author before his death in 1931', a statement which pointed to Mackay. This in-and-out play by Elton reminds one of the conspiratorial semi-secrecy beloved by the New Testament caucus.

Probably the selected poems were among those Mackay showed in 1914, although it is possible that some were composed later. Whether the loss of love was long before 1914, or more recent, is not clear. There are perhaps echoes of *fin-de-siècle* self-pitying verse. If these were the writings of Mackay's younger years, why was he so keen to have them published when he was in his later decades, and even posthumously? Elton's unkind explanation that he sought poetic glory may not be the whole story. Reilly expressed surprise at Mackay's decision to retire from Liverpool when only aged sixty (it was actually fifty-eight), and put it down to greed for a handsome pension.[63] Could it possibly be that instead some Liverpool circumstance, something in relation to a once hoped-for attachment, precipitated retirement? It would be nice to think that the posthumous publication of the verses was intended by Mackay as a last message to someone still alive. One thing is certain. This final appearance on the stage of John Macdonald Mackay does not fit his earlier public roles, being startlingly at odds. It is therefore to an historian convincing, since this is how things often really are.

* * *

Mackay was a figure destined for caricature, and if the present essay is thought to incline to caricature the writer can only plead his tonsure against his guilt.[64] Genuine puzzlement has been the lot of those contemplating Mackay. In 1914 Oliver Elton versified in Lallans on Mackay. In 1938, seven years after Mackay's death, he versified again, this time in plain English, generally on those of the New Testament group who appeared in the group painting, but at greatest length on Mackay, as follows.[65]

> He in the centre was MACKAY,
> A man, they say, much loved, much hated,
> Part crazed, and more than half inspired.
> And with a holy passion fired,
> Too easily by 'joltheads' baited;
> Historian, who never wrote;
> The theme of many an anecdote, -
>
> Of how in Council he exploded,
> In Faculties and Senates; how
> O.T.s[66] with contumely he loaded.
> His simple creed he would avow,
> 'Whate'er they do, is *Wrong*!' He meant it,
> And let them curse him, and resent it.
> And some goodnaturedly forgave
> The Highlander and 'let him rave';

While other, sourer spirits hoarded
Their animosities, their fume,
And let it smoke beyond the tomb.[67]
Historic truth must be recorded, -
Our dear MACKAY, 'less strong was he
In tactics than in strategy'.[68]

He loved his friends, and yet would choose them
Chiefly as God's own instruments
Entrusted to MACKAY, to use them;
And seldom counted their expense,
But in the sacred war enlisted
Them all, - and few of them resisted.
And for long years he waged it well,
And bade his foes go to hell;
And so, by dogged resolution
And genius, though often scarred
And often tripped when off his guard,
Achieved a decent Constitution,
And fought, with changeable success,
For Learning - he did not profess.

His talk at times was Ossianic,
And swathed in mist from some far hill;
At time fuliginous,[69] volcanic;
Then, on a sudden, he would thrill
Our ears with some strange divination
Of mother-wit - not calculation;
From sources far within it welled,
And fears of wavering souls dispelled.
Of contradictions he was fashioned:
We all *supposed* we knew MACKAY;[70]
And yet he baffled us - and why?
Because the fellow so impassioned,
Was of simplicity immense -
- was one of God's own innocents.[71]

NOTES

1. [Oliver Elton and W. Garmon Jones], ed., *A Miscellany presented to John Macdonald Mackay, LL.D. July, 1914*, University Press, Liverpool/Constable, London, 1914. The present essay is based mainly on this work and on the following accounts: Thomas Kelly, *For advancement of learning: the University of Liverpool 1881-1981*, Liverpool, 1981; Stuart Hodgson, ed., *Ramsay Muir. An Autobiography and some Essays*, London, 1943; C.H. Reilly, *Scaffolding in the Sky: a semi-architectural autobiography*, London, 1938; W.E. Collinson, 'Portraits from the Past' [c. 1965], typescript, University Archives D. 5/3. These works are hereafter referenced as *Miscellany*, Kelly, Muir, Reilly, Collinson. In addition, limited but significant material on Mackay in the University Archives, at D.105/1-4, has been consulted.

2. But in this respect the tribute volume continued the tradition of an earlier project. Between 1899 and 1904 the Arts Faculty published an annual volume called, rather coyly, *Otia Merseiana*, each volume containing about a dozen learned research articles, in any of the humanities disciplines, contributed by staff of the Faculty (for the editors, see Kelly, p. 115). A student reviewer found the first volume overwhelmingly erudite but 'stodgy' (*The Sphinx*, 7, 1899, p. 16). Significantly, it was Mackay who wrote a one-page introduction to the series, which, in his usual style, commended universities and learning; equally significantly, he made no further contribution to the series.

3. Those of the signatories who can be identified included the Vice-Chancellor and Pro-Vice-Chancellor, almost every dean and every other professor in the university, and many surviving predecessors, also a sprinkling of less exalted staff, such as all the staff of the History Department (except G.S. Veitch, later Professor of Modern History, who in the 1940s wrote a warm account of Ramsay Muir which was cool about Mackay: Muir, p. 167). The lay officers of the university were not signatories, but a number of local lay benefactors, or their widows and children, signed. Other females (20 women signed) were either wives of professors or - certainly in some instances, almost certainly in others - former pupils of Mackay, as no doubt were some of the unidentified males. Two long-serving Arts professors, Campagnac and Gonner, did not sign. According to Collinson, Campagnac was opposed to Mackay's 'New Testament' caucus (and he and Ramsay Muir were friends), and Reilly, who was a member of the group, does not mention Campagnac in his autobiography. Gonner was the first Arts professor to desert the Clubland area around the university handy for professorial plotting, by going to live at Hoylake in the Wirral, and he 'belonged to the wrong party in university politics' (Collinson; Muir, p.71; Reilly, p. 75). Another conspicuous absentee was Herdman, Professor of Natural History, described by Reilly as an 'Old Testament colleague' (Reilly, p. 139), that is, an opponent of Mackay; but in general the other Faculties were as well represented among the signatories as was the Arts Faculty. At least a dozen of the signatories were to make the *Dictionary of National Biography*, although not Mackay himself. However, tributes on retirement may come not only from those who feel regret but from those who feel relief. Mackay was awarded an LL.D. by his final undergraduate Scottish university, St Andrews, but received no academic honour from Liverpool.

4. As reprinted in *Miscellany*, Appendix III, pp. 363-88, only the above short title is given. The 1897 title-page reads as follows. VICTORIA UNIVERSITY / UNIVERSITY COLLEGE OF LIVERPOOL / FACULTY OF ARTS / THE RELATIONS AND FUNCTIONS AND WORK / OF SENATE AND FACULTY OF THE MODERN / UNIVERSITY IN FRANCE AND ENGLAND TOGETHER WITH AN ACCOUNT OF THE FACULTY OF ARTS / IN LIVERPOOL / J.M. MACKAY, M.A. / HONORARY DEAN OF THE FACULTY / AND RATHBONE PROFESSOR OF HISTORY / *Atque hac re nequeunt ex omnibus omnia gigui / Quod certis in rebus inest secreta Facultas* / Lucretius I. 173 / PUBLISHED BY COUNCIL / D. MARPLES & COMP. / LIVERPOOL / 1897 (The Latin quote might be translated - 'Thus all from all cannot be; each has its progenitive faculty'. Apart from the play on the word 'faculty', the relevance of the quote to Mackay's argument seems limited.) In 1917, all the appendices in the *Miscellany* were reprinted in a slim volume entitled *The Making of a University. Academic Addresses by J.M. Mackay, M.A., LL.D., Emeritus Professor and Sometime Professor of History, University of Liverpool.* A Preface was added by Mackay's protégé, Garmon Jones, now Dean of the Arts Faculty, who gave as the reason for the publication 'the desirability of familiarizing Welsh public opinion with the ideas of University contained therein', as put forward by 'Dr Mackay'.

5. In his 1897 address and 1897-1898 annual report Mackay described himself as 'Honorary Dean', while in his autobiography Muir described himself as 'the first Dean' - this was apparently in 1905 (*Miscellany*, p. 367; Muir, p. 50). The official history simply lists Deans of the Faculty of Arts from Mackay on, with two names between Mackay and Muir, and the text is very unclear about when the Faculty of Arts, instituted in 1896, and given extended powers in 1902, acquired a formal dean (Kelly, pp. 125-6, 521). It is perhaps significant that the student magazine which had from its start regularly reported on 'Arts students', only got round to noting the 'Faculty of Arts' in 1900, and it then described Mackay as 'the first Dean of the Arts Faculty' (*The Sphinx*, 7, 1900, pp. 186-7).

6. Muir, pp. 25-7, 41, 43, 46, 50-51, 63-8, 82-5.

7. Muir, p. 26; 'Chair of History, Edinburgh. Letter and Testimonials of J.M. Mackay M.A. [1894]', printed sheets, two copies, Liverpool University Library and University Archives (D. 105/3). Galley proofs of one section of Mackay's Tudor text representing probably some twenty pages of a book are in the University Archives (D. 105/3). It seems likely that this was the only section that went into print, and perhaps the only section written. The text, though without references, is not contemptible. Making allowance for the date of production, it shows that Mackay had read up his subject. Unlike his florid prose style elsewhere, sentences are short and pithy. There is a touch of ODTAA, but occasional striking descriptions and quotes from contemporaries lighten things up; and the range of interests covered is impressive. Judgements are reasonable. The unfinished work does not rule out the possibility that Mackay could have become a historian of some standing. The general work was a *History of England for the use of middle forms of schools*, 3 vols., London, whose general editor was F. York Powell, author of the first volume, 'from earliest times to the death of Henry VII', published in 1885. The second volume, advertised as to be produced by Mackay, was eventually produced by an historian who was to become very distinguished, T.F. Tout of Lampeter and then Manchester, the volume appearing in 1898. Tout was author of the third volume, already published in 1890, this being Tout's first book and one of the potboilers of his early career (*The Collected Papers of Thomas Frederick Tout*, 3 vols., Manchester, 1932-1934, I, p. 5). Since York Powell gave Mackay a warm testimonial in 1894, it seems that the latter procrastinated after using the proofs of the incomplete work for his 1894 application. His delay in completing the volume may account for the change of author, which must have happened in 1895 or 1896; or it may have been that York Powell considered that the sample text was insufficiently simplistic for middle school.

8. *The Sphinx*, 3, 1896, in J.A. Twemlow's 'portrait' of Mackay. But if Mackay said this, perhaps he did so only after his textbook venture collapsed.

9. Bruce Truscot, *Redbrick University*, paperback reprint of 1943 work and 1945 addition, Harmondsworth, 1951, especially the chapter 'The Leisured Professor at Bay', which specifically indicts 'Faculties of Arts'. For Truscot/Peers' contempt for non-researchers specifically at Liverpool, and especially for most of Mackay's surviving chums (quite unfairly), see E. Allison Peers, *Redbrick University Revisited: the autobiography of 'Bruce Truscot'*, ed. Ann L. Mackenzie and Adrian R. Allan, Liverpool, 1996, chapter 5.

10. When Mackay retired his chair became a chair of Ancient History alone.

11. But Mackay only transferred to History, allegedly on the advice of Jowett of Balliol, in his third year, after obtaining a third class in Classical Mods. (*The Sphinx*, 3, 1896, pp. 159-60). Muir got an Oxford 'Double First'.

12. The details are from Mackay's application as a candidate in 1894 for the chair of History at Edinburgh (see note 7 above). As an undergraduate, Mackay had attended Aberdeen, Edinburgh and St Andrews universities (surely an odd procedure which requires some explanation). 'Medieval and modern history' apparently means European history, as distinct from British history.

13. It can be argued that Kelly does not point up sufficiently the low level of much teaching in the early period, possibly because of his own interest in extra-mural studies. Even by 1896 only half of all the students in the university were working for university examinations, and in 1902 a government report still noted, at provincial universities, 'the multiplied classes of elementary students'. At Liverpool in 1885, it was stated that 'the quality of Male Day Students, particularly upon the Arts side, leaves much to be desired' (Kelly, pp. 57, 89, 91). Mackay's 1897 report on the Arts Faculty supplies figures. There were 681 'students in the Faculty', of which 361 were evening students. 'Students attending university classes and Faculty courses' numbered only 320, and of these only 113 were 'proceeding to degrees', the remainder being teacher training students and some of the Architecture and Applied Art students. Latin and Greek classes had 203 and 113 students respectively, History followed with 110; other subjects had under 100, down to 14 in Italian (Mackay, pp. 48-9).

14. Muir, pp. 26-7.

15. *Miscellany*, p. 5.

16. Muir, pp. 26-7. For another view of Mackay's teaching, see note 18 below.

17. See note 6 above. C.H. Reilly, a delightfully unreliable source, reported a further tribute to Mackay's inspirational teaching. Garmon Jones, a Welshman, later an Associate Professor of History, allegedly converted his undergraduate studies from engineering to history because 'passing one day under the windows of the Victoria Building he heard someone [i.e. Mackay] lecturing on Greek history and its implications for today' (Reilly, p.170).

18. A sympathetic and thoughtful account of Mackay's teaching and role in the School of History was given by his pupil and successor in medieval history, G.W. Coopland, in a long and very able tribute on Mackay's death in 1931 (*The University of Liverpool Society Chronicle*, 1/1, 1931). Yet even Coopland wrote as follows. 'Mackay was always an offence to those poor souls who kept an anxious eye on the syllabus. It must be said that he never gave a lecture in his life in the ordinary acceptance of the word lecture, but there were always others who kept the balance at the reasonable level in this respect. [Editor: this cannot have been true for the period when Mackay taught single-handed.] What he impressed was the sense of the enormous momentousness of human thought and action. ... He was not learned as we use the word nowadays, he knew no modern language well, he did no research, though he made many others do research ... He wrote but little and the sentences of what he wrote often contained more packed thought than they could well carry.' About Mackay's lectures much the same was said in a detailed and extraordinarily frank 'portrait' published by J.A. Twemlow, Mackay's pupil and later assistant, in the student magazine in 1896, to the effect that students who wanted knowledge were baffled and frustrated, while other students were enthralled and inspired (*The Sphinx*, 3/27, 1896).

19. The other former students of Mackay who signed the testimonial in 1894 also were signatories in the tribute volume twenty years later. One of them, however, was J.A. Twemlow, who had drafted the 1894 testimonial and who later took up a post under Mackay.

20. Born in Caithness (on 4.4.1856), he died at Inverness, where he had been living with his sister. On retirement he left Liverpool, but during the war spent some time in London organising an Anglo-Spanish society (he had had a brother in Spain and had spent holidays with him). The ostensible aims of the society were academic, but it may have had a hidden agenda, combating German influence in Spain, and this may have led to the statement in an obituary that Mackay was 'associated with [British] intelligence in relation to Spain', an unlikely state of affairs. Peers claimed to have known him in London, and said - with deliberate malice - that 'about his work in that capacity, the less said the better: he was an elderly man and must have lost his grip' (Peers, *Redbrick University Revisited*, p. 142, and note 8). In 1920, when Peers applied for the chair of Spanish, Mackay wrote from London in support of a rival candidate (Adrian Allan and Ann L. Mackenzie, *Redbrick Revisited: The University of Liverpool 1920-1952* [an exhibition brochure, 1994], p. 27). For the re-publication of Mackay's addresses in 1917, see note 4 above.

21. Strachey's view of Mackay, expressed in letters and diaries, tends to the Stracheyan. 'Professor Mackay is very weird and somewhat casual. The first difficulty is to hear what he's saying as he speaks in a most extraordinary sing-song. When that has been mastered, the connexion between the lecture and Roman History. Lastly, but most important, to prevent and curb shrieks of laughter.' And again - 'Mackay's lecture on Greek History, this was dull today. M is rather inclined to think himself funny and laugh at his own jokes. He *will* look at me when he means to be witty, which is most inconvenient as I feel that I must smile and yet do not like pandering.' The explanation of the last remark is that Mackay gave special attention to Strachey, he being the nephew of Mackay's colleague Walter Raleigh, and Mackay having been at Balliol with Strachey's cousin (Michael Holroyd, *Lytton Strachey: a critical biography*, 2 vols., London, 1967, I, p. 82).

22. The Hittites had been the subject of a 1903 letter in *The Times* from Garstang and Mackay.

23. As regards Mackay's support for developments in Education, especially the university's role in teacher training and extension courses, see his 1888 address, 'The New University and Primary Teachers' (*Miscellany*, Appendix I, pp. 341-54). This 1888 address seems to the present writer more to the point than the 1897 address, being less florid, and containing a number of admirable points, well-expressed. 'It was John Mackay ... who in May 1887 first directed the attention of Senate to the possibility of direct participation in teacher training' (Kelly, p. 77).

24. An anonymous piece on the opening of the Thompson-Yates laboratories in 1898 (*The Sphinx*, 6/1, 1898), with inter alia much commendation of science, has been attributed to Mackay, but was in fact by Sherrington.

25. *Miscellany*, pp. 83, 48, 9, 355-62, 56, 42, 32, 336.

26. The photograph of an elderly Mackay in the tribute volume reflects the image of the prophet. Only the side of his head and one hand show up: he stares, neck forward and muscle-tight, out beyond the frame, his features hidden, and the clenched hand raised across the chest is ready to thump.

27. In fairness, Mackay's school text on the early Tudors did mention the 'Discoveries'. It did not advance chronologically far enough to discuss late-Tudor overseas expansion, but his lecture notes contain a section on the topic.

28. *Miscellany*, Appendix V, pp. 393-7.

29. Ibid., pp. 76, 79, 30-31.

30. Or at least the literate *hoi polloi*, viz, the lower middle classes. But Muir did not spurn the wealthy, and he described how he went fund-hunting among the rich with Rankin, the ship-owner, as well as how he enjoyed the social invitations of the local elite (Muir, pp. 49-50, 74).

31. See note 7 above. Even at the time this was an unusual appointment. Kelly misleads by describing Mackay as 'of Balliol College' (Kelly, p.63). But other Liverpool appointees similarly described, e.g. 'of Trinity College, Cambridge', were apparently Fellows of the colleges, not merely ex-students. Kelly states that 20 out of 30 non-medical professors appointed 1892-1903 were from Oxbridge, certainly directly from there, and therefore presumably holding appointments there, as Kelly specifies in many instances (ibid., p. 92). Earlier, in the mid 1880s, when Mackay was appointed, of the half dozen professors in the Arts Faculty all the others had been Oxbridge Fellows, except perhaps Strong of Latin, a graduate of Glasgow, but he had previously held a chair at Melbourne (ibid., p. 63). Yet in 1882, apparently as soon as he finished his studies at Oxford, Mackay had applied for a chair of English Literature and History at an unstated university (according to an 1882 reference which Mackay re-used in 1894).

32. 'Reading between the lines, it seems likely that many of these new ventures were due in large measure to Mackay and his New Testament group, which was still active as a caucus and policy-making body within the Faculty of Arts' (Kelly, p. 151).

33. Reilly, p. 170. It must be questioned, however, whether this degree of adulation extended outside the Arts Faculty. Peers considered those who adulated Mackay as fellow conspirators of the New Testament clique, anxious to elevate their leader as justification for their secret activity (Peers, *Redbrick University Revisited*, chaper 5). But 'Peers' acid comments on some Arts Faculty professors probably reflect the bitter quarrels at the time of his appointment' (Kelly, p. 221) - the appointment having been at first blocked, apparently by the surviving New Testament caucus. For Mackay's contribution to the opposition, see note 20 above.

34. Apart from one occasion when his long-windedness put one elderly prospective benefactor almost to sleep (according to Reilly, p. 105).

35. *Miscellany*, pp. 80-2. Mackay was the first Chairman and President of the University Club, located within walking distance of the university site (Kelly, p. 127). In 1903 Oliver Elton wrote that 'the University Club was founded for the establishment and increase of a Liverpool University' (*The Making of the University*, Liverpool, 1903, p. 71). Even Muir thought that the University Club was 'a very human and delightful place'. On one occasion, 'a member got himself up in women's evening dress and a huge picture hat, was introduced as Marie Corelli, and made furious love to Mackay, to his blended delight and embarrassment' (Muir, p. 49). Mackay did not spend all his time talking: he had no hobbies but walked alone for two hours daily, no doubt ruminating (*The Sphinx*, 3/27, 1896, p. 160).

36. Bernard Pares, *My Russian Memoirs*, London, 1931, p. 53. Pares discussed his Russian problems with Mackay and says that on one occasion, to sort out an issue, Mackay dictated to him a telegram to be sent to the Russian government (p. 248).

37. *Liverpool Post*, 13 March 1931. *hwyl*, 'emotional quality inspiring impassioned eloquence' OED.

38. Reilly, pp. 169-70.

39. Collinson. Given that Mackay was something of a religious mystic, it still might be thought unseemly that he allowed his coterie to be known as the 'New Testament' group, since this could be interpreted as referring to a set of disciples surrounding a Messiah.

40. Ibid. This same source makes a perceptive point. 'Mackay's well-known allusion to Elton's "sickening rectitude" is a revelation of Mackay himself, somewhat like the cheap gibe at "do-gooders" today'.

41. Pares, *My Russian Memoirs*, p. 53.

42. 'It was, we can almost certainly say, Mackay who set in train the movement which led to the break-up of the Victoria University' (Kelly, p. 127). In 1903 Oliver Elton wrote - 'To say that for years the voice of Professor Mackay was that of one crying in the wilderness will be counted no wrong to the indispensable gifts and services of his associates' (*The Making of a University*, p. 71). Perhaps this indicates a slight feeling that the underway canonisation of Mackay as the sole progenitor of the independent university was going rather too far.

43. J. MacCunn in *The Making of the University*, p. 33.

44. For the received view of the event and Mackay's influence, see Kelly, pp. 124-6.

45. See note 4 above.

46. The 1914 version to some extent misleads in this respect, however, since it abbreviates the original 1897 version slightly, by omitting a table of the numbers of students in various Faculty courses and 'classes' (pp. 48-9), and two paragraphs, one listing named holders of scholarships and the other mentioning a handful of staff publications (pp. 54-5). Mackay as Honorary Dean produced two later publications: the Arts Faculty's *Annual Report for 1897-8* and *An Address to the Faculty of Arts* (1899). The former approximates to a modern annual report, being largely factual and informative, while even the latter is much less rhetorical than the 1897 address. (A 1900 Report was summarised in *The Sphinx*, 7, 1900, pp. 186-7). Thus the tribute volume's re-publication of the 1897 address was unfair to Mackay, inasmuch as it under-represented his capacity as Dean to handle and write factual information. However, in 1914 Mackay published a revised version of a talk he had first given in 1900, under the title *A New University*, and this is wildly rhetorical, ranging through every conceivable topic in time and space, with the prose even more purple than that of the 1897 address.

47. See Appendix I in *Miscellany*, pp.341-54.

48. This paragraph summarises comment on Mackay's two pieces kindly supplied by Dr A.B. Cobban of the Department of History, a graduate of a Scottish university and an authority on the history of medieval universities.

49. Reilly, pp. 64, 165, 167. But Reilly's account of a clash between a lay-dominated Council and an academic Senate over a professorial appointment is substantially modified when reference is made to the records (Kelly, pp. 199-200). The appointment threatened by lay interference was that of G.S. Veitch to the chair of Modern History and in the light of Veitch's later career it is not transparent that he was the better candidate.

50. Curiously, his only reference in his writings to a specific American university was a complimentary one, praising the facilities for the humanities at the University of Baltimore (see his 1899 *Address to the Faculty of Arts*).

51. Muir, p. 57 ('at least a respect for knowledge, and an understanding of where it could be obtained when it was needed, were being diffused').

52. Kelly, op. cit., pp. 125-6 (which disagrees with Sampson's explanation).

53. As far as can be judged from flipping through the hundreds of pages of the student magazine, *The Sphinx*, between 1893 and 1914, Mackay had played little or no part in students' collective activities - whereas Muir had revelled in them. Since a final sixth issue of 1913-1914 either did not appear or is missing, it is not known whether the magazine noted or commented on Mackay's retirement, as it normally did on other retirements. But in June 1913, after several issues containing encomia of Muir, it printed a mercilessly cruel account of a supposed interview (by 'Junius') with the ageing Mackay (*The Sphinx*, 20, June 1913, pp. 184-5). An extract reads as follows.

'I had handed over a box of matches. It is worth the price of a box to see how he carefully strikes match after match, and forgetting its existence, allows it to burn down to his fingers, while he discourses learnedly on bygone ages. It occurred to me that he might give me a few thoughts for the 'Sphinx'. I mentioned such to the Professor. 'A - ah, yes, quite so. The very name 'Sphinx' - it calls one's mind back - to - the - la - and of Egypt. Ah! That land of the Pha - aroahs. It had a glorious civilization of its own - quite so, quite so. Its power was great, its power - ah! - was great. And then it fell in - to - the power of the Persians who were - ah! - in course of time overthrown by Al - ex - ander. And then we get the culture of the Ptolemies, who came to an end with Cle - o - pa -tra. Then it became the granary of the world. But she has fallen. Ah! That is what becomes of all nations. Isn't that so? D'ye see? However - by the way, what did you say was the name of your paper?' During his oration the Professor had been gazing longingly at the workhouse chimney-pots, now crouching as he uttered his sayings in a melodious and rapid whisper, now drawing himself up to his full height as he rolled out fine sounding words with magnificent diapason. The last sentence, however, was uttered as he fixed on me a steely eye that seemed to read my inmost thought. I carefully refrained from a smile, because I had a mental vision of a wrathful figure wielding the shillelagh that stood in a corner.'

There is a certain resemblance between Mackay's vocal mannerism and that of a fellow-Highlander and near contemporary, Ramsay Macdonald (1866-1937), at least when each was in decline. Is it the influence of the Gaelic?

54. This was not unappreciated at the time. Lay individuals issued warnings. When 'Professor Mackay, so brilliant, so effervescing with ideas, but sometimes so difficult ... [wanted] power vested in the Academic Staff, and not merely power over academic questions', this was resisted by the laity. And one of them in 1901 told the University Club that - 'You may depend upon it, that in order to give confidence to men of business it will be necessary to give power to those who hold the purse'

(Kelly, p. 130).

55. But not entirely. For instance, the notorious ban on theological studies within the university, laid down in 1903 (Kelly, p. 130), was clearly due to the influence of two wealthy Unitarian benefactors.

56. Curiously, the percipient Bruce Truscot, writing in the 1940s, still feared the intervention of local laity but was blithely optimistic about the likelihood of extended State intervention (Truscot, *Red Brick University*, pp. 303-4).

57. Sylvia Harrop, *Decade of Change: The University of Liverpool 1981-1991*, Liverpool University Press, 1994, p. 34. The index is revealing. Of the university staff listed, a good half were administrators, while the references to the members of the academic staff, when inspected, turn out to relate almost exclusively to administrative duties. Individual research has no place, thus no scholarly publication and no scientific or medical advance is noted. It is historically significant that, as regards students and staff, ethnic and gender discrimination is given more weight than any positive achievement.

58. Reilly, p. 88

59. Muir, p. 26

60. Perhaps in conclusion - '*Accept the lonely way instead, / And cease from dreams of home and wife.*'

61. Elton to Garmon Jones, 2 August 1931, Special Collections, Liverpool University Library, MS. 5.26, item 31.5.

62. In 1901, the student magazine printed a semi-comic poem by J.M.M. (*The Sphinx*, 9, 1901, p. 198). If J.M.M. was Mackay - and he was reported to have a sense of humour - this seems to have been his only contribution to the magazine, ever.

63. Reilly, p. 171. There are probably better explanations of the retirement. Muir asserts that, when he and Mackay clashed in 1913, friends of Mackay hinted that he would soon reach the age of retirement. But as Muir pointed out, when Mackay was appointed there was no age of retirement, and 'Mackay himself said that he wanted to retire, but would not do so until the year after I did' (Muir, p. 83). In the event Mackay did just that, but not necessarily for merely the spiteful reason suggested by Muir. Yet, for a man who lived till he was almost 75, retirement at 58 does seem curious. Wilberforce of Physics, appointed in 1900, retired only when 75. A recent publication suggests that in 1911 there was a 'tremendous crisis' in the university: Kuno Meyer resigned his chairs and Mackay took a year's leave of absence, being, according to Meyer, 'no longer of any account in the university' (Peers, *Redbrick University Revisited*, p. 142, note 8). However, this view of Mackay's impotence is difficult to reconcile with Muir's claim that in 1913 Mackay manipulated the reorganization of the History Department to his own advantage. Perhaps it was the immediate consequence of this reorganization, Muir's abrupt departure, which the *Liverpool Post* obituary was alluding to when it claimed that Mackay was 'the cause, in later years, whether conscious or not, of a fierce and passionate academic controversy'. Possibly Mackay did realise that his influence was waning, and a decisive event may have been a 1913 inquiry into research across the university which resulted in the appearance in 1914, for the first time, of a list of staff publications in all Faculties, a list from which Mackay's name must have been absent.

64. The cartoon of Mackay contemplating his Highlands appeared in *The Sphinx*, 8, 1901. Captionless, it was listed as of Mackay in the Index, and was passed to the magazine by Sampson (p. 186).

65. Some verses in Allan and Mackenzie, *Redbrick Revisited* [brochure, 1994], p. 14; all the verses in Mackenzie and Allan, *Redbrick University Revisited*, 1996, pp. 460-1.

66. Old Testaments, i.e. opponents of the 'progressive' New Testament clique.

67. This cannot be a jibe at Ramsay Muir's 'Memoirs' which had not yet appeared.

68. Said reputedly by Walter Raleigh, professor of Modern Literature and English Language 1890-1900.

69. Sooty, dusky, obscure.

70. Probably a reference to the verse, since a surprised Elton had seen it through the press.

71. A nice sentiment, from Elton, a professed agnostic.

THE ONCE AND FUTURE FACULTY

Stephen R.L. Clark

The University had three Faculties in the beginning: Arts, Science and Medicine. Over the years we acquired yet more: Law, Engineering, Veterinary Science, Social and Environmental Studies, and Education. Education has shrunk again to a Department, and joined Social and Environmental Studies. There is talk of merging Engineering with the Physical Sciences, and letting the Life Sciences loose. Sometimes it seems that Arts must be a poor relation, or a gaggle of departments left behind as others seek their own way in the world. After the Faculty was divided, back in 1971, 'the rump Arts' were left to call themselves the Faculty, because anything that could be settled by numerical or experimental means had been hived off to SES (whence, in its turn, Psychology seceded into Science). Are we merely what's left, as wiser people manage to find ways of settling things for real (or at least to the satisfaction of established thinkers)? Might Archaeology join Earth Sciences; Music join Engineering; Languages and Linguistics join Education or Psychology; Philosophy be torn apart to join Computer Science, Physics, Psychology, Political Theory; History (Ancient, Medieval and Modern) turn wholly Economic? At the end the 'rump Arts' might be only literary: an excuse for reading entertaining fiction, and adorning it with critical gloss and reminiscence that no-one ever will prove 'wrong'. Maybe a few musicians and musicologists, and even some art critics, could join that rump: their brief, to entertain and train new entertainers - till that task too is taken over by technologists. Maybe the rest of us will somehow survive to teach 'Contemporary Studies' for journalists and business people: nothing written before five years or so ago will have much importance. Each narrowly defined department might pursue its own perceived advantage, and Faculty Offices be nothing more than unimportant, arbitrary aids. In nationalistic wars a given village might lie on this or that side of the border, and never owe more than notional allegiance to the nation's laws. Might our departments seek their own convenient place, feeling no sense of solidarity or intellectual sympathy with others notionally within a single administrative unity? *My argument is otherwise.*

Once upon a time, Education, Geography, Architecture, Politics were all part of our single Faculty, alongside Languages, Literature, History, Philosophy, Music and Archaeology. Once upon a yet more distant time, what we call 'Science' was a part of Humane Letters, distinguished from Revealed and Churchly Knowledge. Perhaps there are good reasons to distinguish 'Arts' and 'Science', and even to divide 'Social and Environmental Studies' from 'Arts and Humanities' (as is recounted elsewhere in this volume). But perhaps those reasons are not quite what people think, and do not have the implications they desire or fear.

There are of course plenty of undergraduate courses straddling Faculty divisions, plenty of research groups quite as much at home in Science or SES as Arts. Even if, as I shall argue, there is a real and important unity in 'Arts', it does not follow that the whole Academy, the University, is not also whole. On the contrary, it will be my claim that 'the Arts and Humanities' are what guarantee that wholeness.

There are still those who disagree. Some would repeat that 'the Arts at Liverpool' are only those departments that did not depart: 'the rump'. Others suspect or say that 'the rump' is merely superstitious. In the wider world, at this tail-end of twentieth century progress, a host of ideological perils wait. The more evangelically-inclined of scientific materialists assert that nothing written about the human condition before 1859 (when Darwin's *Origin of Species* appeared) can be worth studying. 'Sociobiology', they claim, (which is the 'scientific' study of *human* beings on the same terms as others) is due to absorb the Humanities.[1] Computerised translation will eliminate the need for linguists. History should not have happened anyway: let's start afresh. Some such evangelists believe that Truth (which is scientific truth) does matter of itself. Others wish only to sustain 'the industrial base' (by financing good - which is useful - scientific research). Even those who spot the ideological foundations of such rhetoric may not be, quite, our friends: for alongside scientific materialists who claim that only 'science' tells us truths, and only industry makes profits, are those who, weirdly, say that nothing tells us truths, and that 'profit' is only what 'we' want to happen. History, they say, is no more than the story that 'we' tell. No literary text has one 'real' meaning, nor is there any 'really right' way of reading it. If either materialists (truth- or profit-loving) or 'anti-realists' are right, it seems that 'the Humanities' have no other status than astrology, soap-opera or crossword puzzles. The scholarly community is only, so it seems, an excuse for gossip, a haven for 'young, mad lecturers' or 'ageing, crabby professors'.

Why should the public purse be picked to sustain the Humanities? Why even should private benefactors be asked to help? Such pursuits are amusing enough for the young[2] (and keep them off the streets), but why should grown-ups (or those who won't grow up) be kept to become 'Characters' for later reminiscence? Perhaps - till the computers work - we need trained linguists, with some understanding of the superstitions and ancestral anecdotes that influence our business rivals. Perhaps there is some small function for those who recount what *was* the case (to remind us how much better things are now)? Maybe some scholars could retrain as business management consultants, advertising copy writers, advisers to the tourist board, or computer programmers. Arts Departments are expected to defend themselves by pointing to the number of their graduates who have got good jobs in business by virtue of 'transferable skills' acquired - almost by accident - while they were reading Classics, History, Philosophy. Most often those skills are really those of Rhetoric: to write a report or speech with aplomb but insufficient knowledge, and easily evade the question. Maybe - as one of the Founders of the Academy argued[3] - 'real knowledge' and 'rhetoric' (a knack with words) are far apart. If only we knew what really influenced people, we could abandon the Humanities for good. Until we do, perhaps it is best to offer what our masters want: 'contemporary studies', rapid language courses, contacts in big business or the media. And the more we move in that direction, the more depressed we get.

For although we might agree - and many reminiscences confirm - that, after all, Arts and Humanities do offer skills, and even substance, that assist our pupils in the Big World Over There, the chief assistance always is that Something matters more to us (and them) even than national or commercial profit. Mad young lecturers and crabby old professors stand as images for something that matters more to us (and them). In listing the achievements of the Faculty in the last one hundred years, or at least of those departments and research groups that still belong to us, what we identify are contributions to our understanding of ourselves. Recent Research Assessment Exercises conducted under national rules have acknowledged national and international excellence in Ancient History and Archaeology (including Egyptology), Classics, Oriental Studies, English Language and Literature, Modern European Languages and Literature, History, Music and Philosophy. Before the days of National Assessments the whole scholarly community acknowledged excellence in many individuals: Fellows of the British

Academy, Honorary Graduands of other Universities, synthesisers and creators whose work is still remembered (some of whom are listed elsewhere in this volume).

But what can be said, in general, about those 'excellences', those contributions to self-understanding? Why are they to be valued, and how maintained into another century? It has been part of our tradition at least since Plato to interrogate such claims, and part of our tradition to insist that everyone before us got it wrong. Are we immune to drastic refutation? Scholars not trained in the Humanities can frequently be found extolling the outsiders' contributions: non-academic philosophers, amateur psychohistorians, and popular writers sure that (for example) 'Arts Archaeologists' can't recognize the engines or impedimenta they dig up for what they are. Typically, the popular press derides 'Professors': what can an Arts Professor do but merely repeat what textbooks say, without the 'scientific' expertise to imagine otherwise? 'Scholars' are deemed to be 'scholastic', and their 'scholarship' no more than memory.

Our pupils, of course, to judge from kindly reminiscence, might not care. Most of them will remember us by what we happened to say that stuck with them, in lecture or tutorial or tea-party chat. Maybe what they recall is not even what we thought we said or did, or what we thought important: the professor who could vamp a lecture at a moment's notice, or the tutor who demanded to know what a student *herself* thought (never mind the competent portrayal of the textbook answer), or those (long, long ago) who entertained the young with tea and cakes, or sherry. We exercise, by that account, a mildly civilizing or inspiring craft. We should be glad to think that someone somewhere is exchanging anecdotes about us (and sorry to discover, after all, that no-one is).

But of course that afterlife in anecdote is not confined to Arts. Little in those reminiscences depends on the Professor being an Arts Professor, whether in the older wider sense or in the accidentally narrow one defined by our surviving Schools. Most probably all institutions breed their Characters, and certainly all universities. What is that Arts Professors, Lecturers, Tutors 'teach' that's their excuse for being? Most of us, of course, don't quite like thinking that we 'teach' at all. Textbooks and Instruction Manuals have their place, but what we do in lectures or in seminars is not the same. A student who repeats the information he/she thinks has been conveyed is likely enough to get the quoted response, 'That's all very well and competent, but what do *you* think?'. Is that because there is no real answer? Or because we think they *might* think something new? Many a pupil comes away convinced either that we are holding out on them, withholding some strange truth, or that we're lazy sceptics, indolently undermining anything they think they know. Many decide to play the game, by saying something startling or outrageous: not what they think themselves (who knows what any of us *think*) but what they think might get attention. Just a few, occasionally, maybe see what scholars see: the elusive possibility of understanding, which is not to be equated with repeating what the Textbook (or the Professor) says, nor yet with saying something Quite Outrageous, for the sake of it.

Once again: we seek the possibility of understanding. How? The mathematician with a Great Idea can check the calculations. The scientist can try to devise experimental tests, to support or to confute the new hypothesis. Medics and engineers can hope to cure or build. Lawyers can at least outline the likeliest decisions, under the law, the courts can come to. Is that the defining character of Arts, that there is no settling our disputes by any agreed procedure? Is our task simply to go on being difficult?

Maybe it is: that is what the post-Platonic Academy was known for, after all, that its professors argued against themselves. Carneades impressed the Roman Senate by his arguments for Universal Justice - till (next day) he argued against those arguments with equal verve and skill.[1] Do we do it for the argument's own sake, or do we (after all) believe that there's an answer which will not be answered? Often enough, the latter. But we (most of us) resist the idea that every answer might be incorporated in a fully 'scientific' theory, one that assigned numerical values to human imponderables and could conduct control experiments on different social theories. Why do we distrust the easy answers of the textbooks or our students' essays (or our own)? One answer - the merely cynical - is that we know there *are* no answers (or we haven't got them): one augur meeting another in the streets of Rome could not resist a grin. Another, that it is not the *answer* that we mind about, but the getting-there. The answer which I shall develop here is that the question changes. For as long as we are human there will be need of the Humanities, and for just so long there can be no last answer.

Suppose there were a purely Anthropic Science, enacted by non-humans, which examined human behaviour as we might examine ants.

Suppose its authors are utterly non-human, that their modes of argument and reasoning are alien to us forever (as are ours to ants). Such a science might be more or less productive: our own analogue of this investigation, sociobiology, has identified some useful algorithms for predicting social change, and thereby changed our own perception of such change, and even engineered it. But Anthropic Science cannot replace History (or Philosophy or Literary Inquiry) for just those reasons. On the one hand, we accept and argue for new theories because they offer 'reasonable' ways of seeing things: we cannot at the same time think that we accept and press them simply (for example) as the securest way of multiplying our own chance of procreation. Once seriously think that we are advancing Theory X because that gives us our best chance of having children, neither we nor anyone else can give much credence to that Theory: it may indeed be true, but that is not why we have favoured it. Acceptance of a purely Anthropic Science would devastate the Sciences quite as much as the Humanities. It follows at once that there are rules of argument and evidence that must transcend the biological (even if, as seems quite likely, they take their growth from there). Theories are propounded and accepted as being 'reasoned and reasonable responses to the evidence': and neither discovery nor demonstration can be wholly algorithmic. There are laws of logic, certainly (though it is not as obvious as some think just what they are), and even of statistical evidence, but not of inductive inference. There are ways of forming new hypotheses, but no laws to dictate whhich hypotheses worth trying out are formed. Discovery in every field is, genuinely, an Art and not a Science: Science itself is an Art - which is to say, a discipline conducted without any way of predicting what its results will be, or seeing that there could have been only one result.

On the other hand, every question answered about what we do and think creates a question, since it changes us. Each generation is dissatisfied with an earlier age's answers: often enough, this is because those answers were inadequate before (and criticised with good reason), but it is also because the questions have now changed, and changed because we had those earlier answers. There is no final answer to the question, who we are, because successive answers change us, and suggest new aspects even of that question. The tutor who demands, 'And what do *you* think?', presses the pupil to incorporate the textbook answer, and now see beyond it. Not that it was wrong, nor that the pupil is to drag some answer up from her untutored past, but that she should now see another question that the earlier answer missed. Sometimes it might be wiser not to ask that question if we wish the earlier answer to be given in full: a moral that applies to more than the Academy! 'History does not consist of completed and crumbling ruins. ... It consists of half-built villas abandoned by a bankrupt builder'[5] - or villas whose builder suddenly decided on another model. On the other hand, some models are deservedly abandoned, having served their purpose.

The Humanities, as long as we are human, will be with us. And as long as we are human, we will have scope to ask new questions of the evidence. 'The whole object of history', so said Chesterton, 'is to make us realize that humanity can be great and glorious, under conditions quite different and even contrary to our own.'[6] Realizing that, we grow. Realizing how others write and dream and reason we become aware of our own possibilities, and the questions we have not yet asked.

What follows for the Humanities here-now? One error that we have lived with is the supposition that 'the Sciences' have another province, that 'mere Humanists' must put up with what is left: a Faculty, as it were, of the Gaps, a 'rump'. But if I am right, the truth is otherwise. Nothing that Human Beings do is alien to the Humanities. There is a History and Philosophy of Engineering, as well as of political change. There is scope for the study of medical rhetoric as well as of Elizabethan poetry. If, as some have said, Science (in all its subdivisions) is a human triumph to equal or surpass medieval cathedrals or scholastic logic or Roman Law or Shakespeare, it can and should be studied humanistically. We have changed ourselves, and the questions, by new understanding of our past, and new techniques for altering our futures. We need not fear, as Humanists, that attending to the development of Scientific Theory, or Engineering Practice, or Medicine, we shall find ourselves 'doing science, engineering or medicine' instead. Numeracy is not a sin, but neither is it all that matters. In an age when popular science books reach best-seller status far ahead of modern novels it is folly to ignore them. The arrival in the University of the Science Fiction Foundation Library, and the growth of Science Fiction Studies, is one small cloud, about the size of a man's hand: the storm of Science Studies will be coming soon, affecting every area of the Faculty, and of the University.

What other feature of our age has seemed a threat? The Canon of Western Literature and Thought has been defended (as the foundations of our thinking) and attacked (as offering a prejudiced and parochial vision). But the value of that Canon does not depend on denigrating or ignoring other Canons. We here-now are heirs of many nations, many civilizations. At our beginning back in 1896 it was not unreasonable to begin with Europe (and at once - like James G. Frazer - reach beyond it). In the coming century, to survive as a nation and a University, we shall be dealing globally: migrations, economic ties, the Internet decree that we must draw upon the histories and cultures of other continents - as we have, in fact, already done. We stand at the confluence of cultures - but so has Europe since it first began, and so has Liverpool. Even the local students who dominated our first intake were of many origins and heritages: that was one reason why we were to be entirely 'non-sectarian'. Liverpool has been at once an English, Irish, Welsh, Italian, Greek, Caribbean, Chinese city. Our academic departments have always contained scholars with such distant, non-European links, by which Europe and European Civilization have been defined. In grappling with our need to expand our expertise, to offer fresh understanding of people and places no longer quite so distant, we will be doing what we were before.

Departments are defined by the courses they offer undergraduates. Those courses will change as students find new questions, incorporating (let us guess) study of the fraught relationship between Islam and Old Europe, of the Pacific Rim, of languages so far too unfamiliar in our schools (or to Examination Boards). In an earlier round of cuts we were so ill-advised as to allow Russian and Italian to run down. Our future may lie in resurrecting them, and finding others. Even the notion of 'transferable skills' may not be as destructive as some fear: perhaps it is our business, as a Faculty, to offer something like the medieval *trivium*, of grammar, logic and rhetoric - the applied study of the laws of speech and thought (for rhetoric is more than cheating speech). Maybe we need to provide our pupils with at least one other language than their own. Maybe we need to learn, as well as teach, the perils and advantages of Computer Talk. Maybe we need to give them some real sense of Europe's history, and the human world's, whatever else they do. Maybe, in short, we need to return to our own earlier model, when we saw our duty was to educate, to guide our young. Maybe these are gifts for us to give to students of all faculties, not only ours.

Departments exist, and struggle to survive, around their Single Honours courses, and sometimes neglect those interdisciplinary, 'transferable', 'foundational' skills, in favour of inspiring interest in their own special disciplines. But Departments also house individual scholars with overlapping, interrelated interests, and it is from these that future subjects grow. Interdisciplinary, interdepartmental research groupings are responses, once again, to ever-changing questions. I can single out for mention Late Antique and Medieval Studies, the Enlightenment and the Nineteenth Century (comprising centuries that defined Modernity). Amongst the presently most successful groups (successful in attracting funds and students alike) are two concerned with English Language and with Popular Music (both eminently appropriate to Liverpool). Both matter to us because they have mattered from the start, and build their questions upon earlier answers.

The study of English leads naturally to the study of Language: how languages are structured, how they are learnt, how they affect our thought. As we need greater linguistic excellences even to survive into the 21st century, so we will need to understand the importance of the many tongues there are. The Enlightenment dream of one perfect language is a form of the search for one final answer, and as futile. For even if there were one language - in a particular generation - we can guarantee that succeeding generations would deform and divide it into many (as English itself already branches into pidgins, dialects and styles). That will not be an error: on the contrary, to keep one language only is the final error, since it would lose us the experience of finding things are otherwise than we supposed. This may serve as a metaphor for the Humanities themselves, and for their value: unless we preserve and build upon our pasts we run the risk of thinking there is one way only.

The study of Popular Music, here in Merseyside, inevitably runs into a concern for local life and culture. Liverpool itself is another metaphor, and another field for the Humanities here-now. Our city is at the confluence of cultures, and the port from which the ancestors of many round the world once sailed. In understanding and retelling the stories of immigration and emigration, riot or convergence, we are telling the story of our age (and every age). Local History relies on and informs a Global History. In this enterprise the many disciplines of the Humanities (Language, Literature, History, Archaeology, Music, Philosophy) unite. From meetings, new life grows.

'Arts and Humanities' are at the centre of anything to be called a

University: the constant effort to understand, as human beings, what human beings do, and help them do it better. Doctors, Engineers and Chemists, Veterinary Scientists and Physicists, Geographers and Social Workers: all act and argue and achieve (or miss) their goals. All, to be understood, engage in acts of meaning: write, gesture, build. Everything they do embodies meaning, and it is that meaning which the Humanities most cherish. If we have failed at all it is because we thought they weren't our business. Our future lies in knowing that they are.

We have no need to lose our confidence, imagining a swift decline into 'service teaching', Business Management Studies, Media Studies and Sociobiology. What we will do, no doubt, is something utterly different from anything I guess: the game of Cheat the Prophet is the oldest game of all (and 'for a race of simple tastes, great fun'[7]). I remain convinced that the study of our humanity, in texts and tunes and artefacts and arguments, is of far more than entertainment value. Whatever human beings do with their humanity is our affair. Perhaps, after all, it is our business, as scholars, to remember: to house whatever human beings do and have done within the Palaces of Memory to be recalled at will. The particular feature of those palaces, devised as *aide-mémoires* by ancient and medieval rhetoricians, was that they enabled new connections to be made between the remembered anecdotes and theories.[8] Those who remember their past do not repeat it (or not quite). Those who forget where they have been do not know where they're going. Those who have read this volume, and refreshed their sense of who and where they are, may be moved to ask new questions of the past, and move, with confidence, into another future.

NOTES

1. See (for example) E.O. Wilson, *Sociobiology*, Cambridge, Mass., 1975. There are similar attempts to eliminate what is called 'folk psychology' by philosophers and psychologists convinced that human thought and action are to be 'explained' neurologically, without reference to such superstitious relics as 'intentions', 'thoughts' and 'meanings'. See, for example, Daniel Dennett, *Consciousness Explained*, London, 1991; and my discussion of that work - 'Minds, Memes and Rhetoric', *Inquiry*, 36, 1993, pp. 3-16.

2. As Callicles said of philosophy in general, adding that those who kept it up when older needed a good thrashing: Plato, *Gorgias*, 485d.

3. Namely, Plato, founder of the (Platonic) Academy: see - amongst other dialogues, *Gorgias*, *Ion* and *Phaedrus*.

4. Cicero, *De Re Publica*, 3.9 (as preserved by Lactantius, *Institutiones*, 5.14, 3-5): see A.A. Long [formerly of this faculty], *Hellenistic Philosophy*, London, 1974, p. 104.

5. G.K. Chesterton, *What's Wrong with the World*, London, 1910, p. 47; and see A.S. Dale, *The Outline of Sanity*, Grand Rapids, 1982, p. 144. The aphorism, some might say, applies with especial force to schemes for reorganizing universities.

6. G.K. Chesterton, *Fancies versus Fads*, London, 1923, p. 176. My larger discussion of Chesterton's view of history was first read to the Centre for Medieval Studies here at Liverpool, and is to be published as 'How Chesterton Read History', in *Inquiry*, 1997.

7. G.K. Chesterton, *The Napoleon of Notting Hill* [1904], Penguin edition, Harmondsworth, 1946, p. 9.

8. See F.A. Yates, *The Art of Memory*, London, 1996; John Crowley, *Aegypt*, London, 1987, offers a fictional evocation of what the Art might mean (and what the study of History involves).

APPENDIX

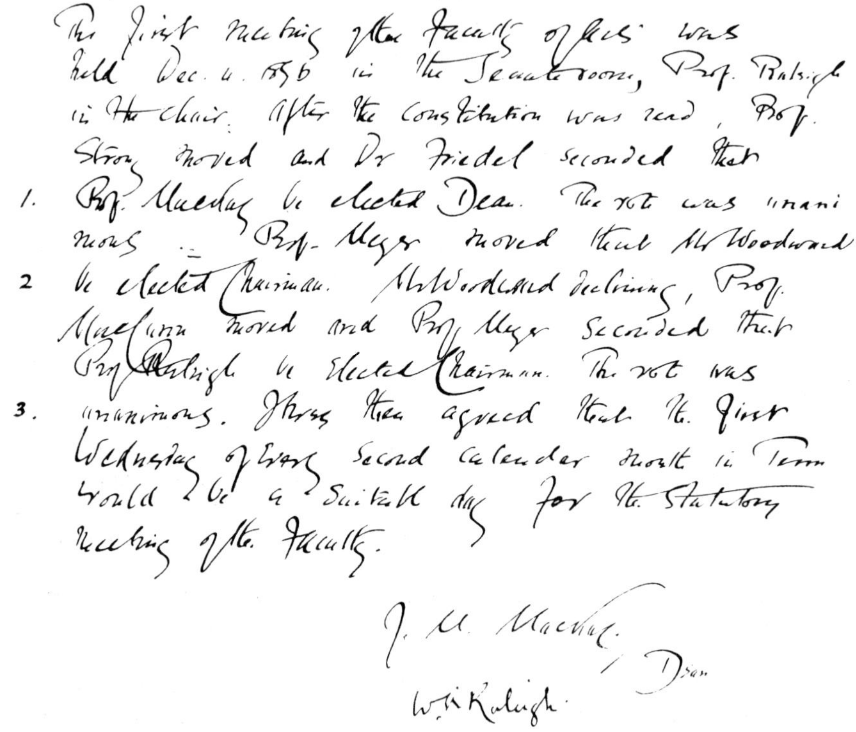

The first meeting of the Faculty of Arts was
held Dec. 4. 1896 in the Senate room, Prof. Raleigh
in the chair. After the constitution was read, Prof.
Strong moved and Dr Friedel seconded that
1. Prof. Mackay be elected Dean. The vote was unani
mous. Prof. Meyer moved that Mr Woodward
2 be elected Chairman. Mr Woodward declining, Prof.
MacCunn moved and Prof. Meyer seconded that
Prof. Raleigh be elected Chairman. The vote was
3. unanimous. It was then agreed that the first
Wednesday of every second calendar month in Term
would be a suitable day for the Statutory
meeting of the Faculty.

J. M. Mackay. Dean

W. A. Raleigh.

Minutes of the first meeting of the Arts Faculty in December 1896

SELECT CHRONOLOGY OF THE FACULTY OF ARTS 1896 - 1996

The information is mainly drawn from the Faculty's Annual Reports.

Key * = establishment (of chairs, departments, etc)

> = relocation (of departments, etc)

1896 The first meeting of the Faculty of Arts was held on 4 December in the Senate Room in the Victoria Building.

> Professor John Macdonald Mackay, Rathbone Professor of History, was elected Dean and Professor Walter A. Raleigh, King Alfred Professor of Modern Literature and English Language, Chairman. It was agreed that the first Wednesday of every second calendar month in term would be a suitable day for the statutory meeting of the Faculty.

(At its meeting on 3 June 1896 the Senate of University College, Liverpool, agreed to the appointment of a Faculty of Arts. On the motion of Professor Mackay, the Senate had, in November 1895, appointed a Committee 'to consider and report on the advisability of forming Committees of Faculties'. The Constitution of the Faculty provided that it should consist of the Principal of the College, the Professors of Greek, Latin, History, Modern Literature, Teutonic Languages, Philosophy, and Economic Science, and of the Lecturers in French, Italian, English, and Education, and such other Professors, Lecturers, Assistant Lecturers, and Readers as were from time to time added by the Senate. The Faculty was, inter alia, empowered to make suggestions to the Senate for the improvement and regulation of Arts studies.)

1897 The special inspectors commissioned by the Chancellor of the Exchequer to inquire into the work done at University Colleges reported in 1897 upon the visit which they made to University College Liverpool in the Summer Term 1896.

> 'The Classical Languages, English, French, and German, are represented and taught by men of first-rate ability, who unite in a high degree learning and scientific scholarship with the sympathy and stimulus necessary for the teacher; and the same may be said of Philosophy, History, and Political Science ... In French and German especially ... the teaching at Liverpool is of the highest order, while the command of the language acquired by a number of lady students in Italian is very remarkable.'

The Day Training College integrated into University College

1898 * School of Commerce

1899 * University Press
* City of Liverpool Chair of Education
* Secondary Education Department
* Society for University Extension in Liverpool and District
* Arts Students Association

Annual Report of University College, Liverpool, includes first report on the Faculty of Arts

1900 * Class or Departmental Libraries
* Honours School of Architecture

Women admitted to the Primary Department of the Day Training College

1902 Treasury inspectors report that the Arts side at Liverpool was relatively stronger than at any of the other colleges visited by them, with one exception

Faculty constitution empowers it to 'supervise and control the studies of the Faculty', defined as 'Languages, Literature, History, Economics, Philosophy, Education, Art (Architecture)'

1904 * Baines Chair of English Language and Philology
* University Institute of Archaeology
* University School for Training in Social Work

St Aidan's College, Birkenhead and Edge Hill Training College affiliated

Publications of Arts staff listed in the University's annual report

1905 * James Barrow Chair of French
* Lectureship in Archaeology
* Boards of Studies (in Languages; Classics; Modern Languages and Literature; History, Economics, Geography and English Literature; Philosophy and Education)

University Club's new premises at 2 Mount Pleasant, the 'New Testament' meeting-place

School of Architecture ceases to teach applied arts

Mount Pleasant Training College affiliated

1906 * Bachelor of Architecture (B.Arch.), replacing B.A. Honours Architecture.
* Andrew Geddes and John Rankin Chair of Modern History
* Chair of Classical Archaeology
* Readership in Modern Russian History

Faculty annual report claims that, in its Honours Schools, independent work, as shown by dissertations, now played a more important part than in the degree schemes of any British or American university

1907 * John Rankin Chair in Methods and Practice of Archaeology
* Brunner Chair of Egyptology
* Honorary Chair of Social Anthropology.

Assistant to the University Librarian appointed to supervise Faculty of Arts class libraries

1908 * Bowes Chair of Russian History, Language and Literature
* Gilmour Chair of Spanish
* Honorary Chair of Celtic
* Honorary Chair of Mediaeval Archaeology
* Lectureship in Palaeography and Diplomatic
* Lectureship in Welsh Language and Literature
* Bachelor of Commercial Sciences (B.Com.Sc.)

> Department of Classical Archaeology to No. 38 Bedford Street

M.A. henceforth not automatically awarded after a time to Honours graduates but only after examination

1909 * Department of Civic Design
* Diploma and Certificate in Town Planning
* Lectureship in Regional Geography

> School of Architecture and Department of Civic Design to the former Bluecoat School

1910 * Certificate in Commercial Knowledge

1911 * Lectureship in the Methods and Practice of Social Work

1912 * Lever Chair of Civic Design

University Training College course extended from three to four years

1913 * Honorary Chair of the Philosophy and History of Mathematics (in the Faculty of Arts)
* William Noble Fellowship in English Literature

1914 Reorganisation of the School of History into Departments of Modern, Medieval and Ancient History
* Chair of Modern History
* Chair of Ancient History
* Lectureship in Mediaeval History

> School of Social Science and of Training for Social Work to 56 Bedford Street
> New building for the Faculty of Arts in Ashton Street opened

1916 * Honours School in Geography

Wartime timetable revised and lectures confined to the morning and early afternoon

1917 * John Rankin Chair of Geography

School of Social Science, previously affiliated, fully integrated

M.A. to take at least two years

Second Class in the Honours Schools to be arranged in two divisions

1918 * Degree of Doctor in Philosophy (Ph.D.) and Diploma in Social Science

> School of Architecture and the Department of Civic Design to 'temporary premises' in Ashton Street ('Reilly's Cowshed')

1919 *Andrew Cecil Bradley Chair of English Literature
* Lectureship in Music (in the Department of Education)

1920 * Chaddock Chair of Commerce
* Diploma in Social Studies
* Certificate and Diploma in Archaeology
* Honours School in Italian

> Department of Geography to 10 Abercromby Square
>Institute of Archaeology to 11 Abercromby Square

* School of History

Final-year French Honours permitted to reside at a French university

Bachelor of Architecture course extended to five years

1921 * Shute Lectureship in the Art of the Theatre
* Diploma in Commerce
* Honours School in Spanish
* Education Library

> Department of Education to 20-22 Abercromby Square (Abercromby House)

Chester Training College affiliated

1922 * Degrees of Master of Architecture (M.Arch.) and Master of Commerce (M.Comm.)

Session's work to be taken into account in first-year results

1923 * Charles Booth Chair of Social Science.
* Diploma and Certificate in Archaeology, Architecture, Civic Design, Education, and Social Studies

1924 * Alsop Lectureship in Music

1925 > School of Social Studies to 26 Abercromby Square

1926 * School of Social Sciences and Administration

1927 > Department of Civic Design to 176 Brownlow Hill.

1928 * Special Forwood Lectureship in Non-Sectarian Divinity.
* Board for the Examination of Students in Training Colleges

1929 * Lectureship in Hebrew and the Semitic Languages and Literature

1930 * Special Lectureship in Esperanto
* Lectureship and Diploma in Public Administration

1931 > School of Social Sciences and Administration (Departments of Economics, Commerce, and Social Science) to 'Bishop's Palace', 19 Abercromby Square

1932 Chester Training College first-year students taught entirely away from the University

1933 > School of Architecture and the Department of Civic Design to 24-27 Abercromby Square (Leverhulme Building)

1934 Department of Spanish becomes Department of Hispanic Studies

1935 * School of Oriental Studies
* Special Lectureship in Art

1936 > Department of Geography to 12 Abercromby Square

Three Registration Advisers appointed to guide students entering the Faculty

1937 Series of Public Lectures given by members of the Faculty on important topics of current interest

1938 * Lectureship in Psychology

Most Class Libraries centralised in the New Arts Building or Harold Cohen Library

1939 Part of Faculty evacuated to Coleg Harlech, a working-men's residential college at Harlech

1941 Department of Education to Coleg Harlech

1942 * Polish School of Architecture (at the School of Architecture)

'The Faculty's work suffered no interruption ... compared with the previous Session, strain caused by air-raids has been negligible.'

1943 * Short University Course for Naval Cadets

1945 First member of Senate to be appointed Vice-Chancellor, James F. Mountford, Professor of Latin and Dean of the Faculty of Arts

1946 * Honours School of History

1947 * Diploma in the Study of Records and the Administration of Archives
* James W. Alsop Chair of Music
* Chair of Psychology

Appointment of two staff members as part-time Sub-Deans

1948 Institute of Archaeology merged in the School of Archaeology and Oriental Studies

1950 * Master of Civic Design (M.C.D.)

1951 > Department of Civic Design to new building in Abercromby Square

Latin or Greek in School Certificate no longer required for admission to Economics, Social Science, Psychology, or Geography, instead Mathematics

1953 > Departments of Egyptology, Hebrew and Ancient Semitic Languages, Prehistoric Archaeology, and Classical Archaeology to 16 Abercromby Square

A language course no longer required for B.A. Honours in certain subjects

1954 * University Institute of Education
* William Roscoe Chair of Education

1955 Weekly lunchtime lectures on general topics for students in all faculties

1956 * Chair of Political Theory and Institutions

University's first woman professor appointed to Chair of Russian

1963 * School of Business Management

Arts Reading Room (Rendall Building) opened

1964 * Bachelor in Philosophy

1965 * Eleanor Rathbone Chair of Social Science
Tutorial scheme extended to include 'academic' as well as 'moral' tutoring

> Modern Languages Building and the Social Studies Building (Roxby Building) rehouses thirteen Arts departments.
> Faculty Office and School of Classics to 12-13 Abercromby Square

Department of Education placed within School of Education and Board of Studies in Education, thus removed from Arts Faculty.

1966 * Chair of Applied Economics
* Chair of Transport Studies
* Centre for Latin-American Studies

> Departments of Prehistoric Archaeology, Egyptology, Hebrew and Ancient Semitic Languages, and the Classical Archaeology section of the Department of Ancient History and Classical Archaeology to the building previously occupied by the Faculty of Law in Abercromby Square

Full-time Sub-Dean appointed

1967 * Chair of Business Studies

1969 * B.A. in Architecture

1970 * Department of Economic History
* Chair of Latin-American Studies

1971* Research Lectureship in Local History

> Latin-American Centre to 86 and 88 Bedford Street South

Faculty of Arts divided. New Faculty of Social and Environmental Studies comprises Departments of Architecture, Civic Design, Economics, Economic History, Commerce, Geography, Political Theory and Institutions, Psychology and Sociology, and also the School of Business Studies and the School of Social Studies

1973 * Lectureship in Linguistics

Faculty Board henceforth to include all members of the full-time staff holding permanent appointments

1974 * Second Chair of French.

> Department of German to 7 Abercromby Square

Chair of Fine Art and second Chair of Modern History deferred

1975 * B.A. (Colleges)
* Board of College Studies

1976 Communication Studies becomes three-year subject within the School of Combined Honours

Sydney Jones Library opened

1977 Department of Celtic Studies closed

1978 B.Phil. to become M.A. and the M.A. (Research) to become M.Phil.

1979 * Second (later Ramsay Muir) Chair of Modern History
* Department of Linguistics
* M.Mus. replaces B.Mus.

1980 * B.A. (General) with Honours

First Lady Chairman of the Faculty

1981 * Master of Archive Administration (M.Ar.Ad.) replaces Diploma in Archive Administration
* Joint Honours degrees, in Prehistoric Archaeology and Geography, French and History, and French and Mathematics

1982 Faculty of Arts restructured into two small departments (Music and Philosophy), two large departments (fusing English Language and English Literature, and Mediaeval History and Modern History), and two schools, the School of Antiquity and Archaeology (grouping the departments of Ancient History and Classical Archaeology, Greek, Latin, Oriental Studies, and Prehistoric Archaeology) and the School of Modern Languages (the four Departments of French, German, Hispanic Studies, and Russian, with the staff of the former Departments of Italian and Linguistics).

Single Honours degree in Italian to be phased out

1985 * Centre for Applied German Studies
* Centre for the History of Social Policies

1986 Several Joint Honours Schools to be subsumed within the School of Combined Honours

M.A. courses in Victorian Literature, Spanish Literature, and Spanish and Portuguese Literature, to have part-time versions

1987 * Inter-faculty B.Sc. in Early Hominid Studies and Archaeological Sciences, and in English Literature and Communication Studies

Department of Classics and Archaeology replaces Departments of Ancient History and Classical Archaeology, Greek, and Latin

1988 * Institute of Popular Music
* Institute of Irish Studies and Board of Irish Studies

Department of Russian closed

1989 ERASMUS staff and student exchanges with European universities commences

1990 * Chair of Archaeology
* School of Archaeology, Classics, and Oriental Studies
* School of Modern Languages
* M.A. in Popular Music Studies
* Languages Centre

1992 * Centre for Manx Studies

Department of English Language and Literature and the English Language Unit to merge

1993 * M.A. in Contemporary Irish Studies
* M.A. in Women's History

1994 * Humanities Graduates School
* new M.A. courses include Science Fiction Studies

> Languages Centre to converted chapel on Chatham Street

1995 Forwood Lectures in the History and Philosophy of Religion given by Professor Robert Markus, a former member of staff

1996 Centenary Celebration

Compiled by A.R.A.

STATISTICS FROM SELECT ANNUAL REPORTS

1899 The number of students proceeding to Ordinary degrees in Arts was 65, the number reading for Classical Honours 5, and for the M.A. degree 4; in addition, there were 7 students attending full courses, and 56 taking occasional courses, principally English Literature, while 8 students were taking full courses for London degrees.

1914 During the Session 1913-14, the Faculty had 276 full-time and 107 part-time students. After the Faculty of Medicine (including Dental and Veterinary students), which had 419 full- and part-time students, the Arts Faculty had the largest number of students.

1915 Save in the case of students taking professional courses, the preponderence of women students in the Faculty had, by Session 1914-15, so far prevented any excessive decline in student numbers in consequence of the war. Of the total of 357, 257 (79 men and 178 women) were students reading for degrees.

1920 During the Session 1919-20, the number of students in the Faculty swelled to 878 (635 full-time and 243 part-time), rendering it the largest Faculty in terms of student registrations.

1925 The Faculty of Arts, alone among the Faculties, showed a considerable increase in the number of students in Session 1924-25 as compared with the previous Session. The Vice-Chancellor noted that this increase was in women students and was to be correlated to a remarkable increase in the number of students who were taking the Diploma in Education course. 'Obviously the decisions of the Burnham Committee and the improved stipends of women teachers have ... made teaching a desirable profession for women'.

1947 The Faculty reported a large increase in the number of students in Session 1946-47, to 1247. Priority had been granted to ex-service men and women in the case of new admissions, a policy whch necessitated a large increase in the total number of admissions to the First Year, if those leaving school were not to suffer unduly.

1958 The Faculty referred to the basic problems of admission which have been aggravated by the very small grant that has been made available to the Faculty for the present Quinquennium. In each of the last five years the number of applicants for admission has increased, the number of offers of a place has been reduced, and the percentage and number of students accepting a place has steadily increased. At the same time there has been a profound change in the nature of our intake, for in the present Session 71% of the new first year registrations for B.A. and B.Com. were from outside Merseyside, as against about 40% five years ago.

1962 The number of full-time students in the Faculty of Arts rose from 1,450 to 1,588. The number of applications increased from 2,039 to 2,539 and the number of acceptances from 277 to 291 for the B.A. course and from 21 to 39 for the B.Com. course.

1967 The number of students admitted to undergraduate courses in the Faculty of Arts was 557, compared with 534 in Session 1966-67, and the total number of students in the Faculty, including the School of Education, rose to 2,451.

1972 In Session 1971-72 there were 1,087 registered students in the Faculty of Arts, following the division of the Faculty. Of the 1,087, 1,008 (401 male and 607 female) were full-time students and 79 (54 male and 25 female) were part-time students.

1980 The total of undergraduates in the Faculty was 1,206, the highest ever reached. The average standard of attainment among the 401 new entrants at A-level (near to B/B/C) was a cause for congratulation.

1991 Admissions to the Faculty in 1990-91 reached an all-time high (519 undergraduates and 129 postgraduates) and were expected to increase even further in 1991-92 as the Faculty responded positively to the recruitment of fees-only students. This expansion did not involve any diminution in standards - for the major undergraduate courses B/B/B at A Level was the typical offer - but staff:student ratios were becoming uncomfortably high in a number of areas.

DEANS OF THE FACULTY OF ARTS

Titles assumed during the period of office shown in round brackets

1896-1899	Professor J.M. Mackay
1899-1902	Professor E.C.K. Gonner
1902-1905	Professor G.A. Davies
1905	Mr J.R.B. Muir
1905-1906	Professor G.A. Davies
1906-1907	(Professor) J.R.B. Muir
1908-1911	(Professor) Alexander Mair
1911-1913	Professor E.T. Campagnac
1913-1916	Associate Professor R.H. Case
1916-1920	Mr W. Garmon Jones
1920-1923	Professor A. Bruce Boswell
1923-1926	Mr G.C. Field
1926-1928	Associate Professor W. Garmon Jones
1928-1934	Professor A. Bruce Boswell
1934-1937	Professor L.C. Martin
1937-1941	Mr F.J. Routledge
1941-1945	Professor J.F. Mountford
1945-1949	Professor H.A. Ormerod
1949-1953	Professor F.E. Hyde
1953-1956	Professor Wilfred Smith
1956-1958	Professor H.W. Fairman
1958-1961	Professor K.A. Muir
1961-1962	Professor A.E. Sloman
1962-1965	Professor W.D. Williams
1965-1968	Professor R.W. Steel
1968-1971	Professor F.B.R. Smallman
1971-1974	Professor J.E. Cross
1974-1977	Professor F.W. Walbank
1977-1978	Professor G.W. Ribbans
1978-1980	Professor A.R. Myers
1980-1983	Mrs Irene Collins
1983-1986	Professor K.G. McWatters
1986-1992	(Professor) J.R. Fisher

1992-1995 Dr. R.E.A. Waller
1995- Professor S.R.L. Clark

Some distinguished scholars

Distinguished scholars who served long or short periods in the Arts Faculty have included the following. Deceased scholars (up to the 1980s) listed in the *Dictionary of National Biography* are marked DNB; deceased and living scholars elected Fellows of the British Academy are marked FBA. Unless otherwise stated, dates are of chairs held.

L.P. Abercrombie DNB (Civic Design 1915-1935)
G.E.H. Abraham FBA, DNB (Music 1947-1962)
S.D. Adshead DNB (Civic Design 1912-1914)
G.C. Allen FBA (Economic Science 1933-1947)
A.H. Armstrong FBA (Greek 1950-1972)
G. Barraclough DNB (Medieval History 1945-1956)
A.M. Blackman FBA (Egyptology 1934-1948)
R.C. Bosanquet DNB (Classical Archaeology 1906-1920)
C.O. Brink FBA (Latin 1951-1954)
C.N.L. Brooke FBA (Medieval History 1956-1967)
A.M. Carr-Saunders FBA (Social Science 1923-1937)
S.G. Checkland FBA (lecturer, etc, Economic Science 1946-1953)
H.C. Darby FBA (Geography 1945-1949)
J.K. Davies FBA (Ancient History and Classical Archaeology 1977-)
P.W. Edwards FBA (English Literature 1974-1990)
O. Elton FBA, DNB (English Literature 1901-1925)
G.C. Field FBA (lecturer, etc, Philosophy 1919-1926)
J. Fitzmaurice-Kelly FBA, DNB (Spanish 1909-1916)
J.G. Frazer DNB (Honorary Social Anthropology 1907-1922)
J. Garstang DNB (Methods and Practice of Archaeology 1907-1941)
W.G. Holford DNB (Civic Design 1936-1947)
R.W. Hunt FBA (lecturer Palaeography 1934-1945)
A.E. John DNB (tutor, Applied Art 1901-1902)
A.C. Lloyd FBA (Philosophy 1957-1983)

A.A. Long FBA (Greek 1973-1983)
R.A. Markus FBA (lecturer, etc, Medieval History 1959-1974)
A. Mawer FBA, DNB (English Language and Philology 1921-1929)
H.M.R.E. Mayr-Harting FBA (lecturer Medieval History 1960-1968)
J.R.B. Muir DNB (Modern History 1906-1913)
K.A. Muir FBA (English Literature 1951-1974)
J.L. Myres FBA, DNB (Greek 1907-1910)
P.E. Newberry DNB (Egyptology 1907-1919)
B. Pares DNB (Russian History, Language and Literature 1908-1917)
J.D.Y. Peel FBA (Sociology 1974-1989)
E.A. Peers DNB (Spanish 1922-1952)
T.E. Peet DNB (Egyptology 1920-1933)
J.P. Postgate FBA, DNB (Latin 1909-1920)
F.M. Powicke FBA, DNB (lecturer, History 1905-1906)
D.B. Quinn Hon. FBA (Modern History 1957-1976)
W.A. Raleigh DNB (Modern Literature and English Language 1890-1900)
C.H. Reilly DNB (Architecture 1904-1933)
J. Sampson DNB (University Librarian 1892-1928)
G.L.S. Shackle FBA (Economic Science 1951-1969)
D.A. Slater FBA (Latin 1920-1932)
M.O. Talbot FBA (Music 1986-)
F.W. Walbank FBA (Latin 1946-1951, Ancient History and Classical Archaeology 1951-1977)
C.K. Webster FBA, DNB (Modern History 1914-1922)
H.C.K. Wyld DNB (English Language and Philology 1904-1920)
W.H. Young DNB (Philosophy and History of Mathematics 1913-1919)

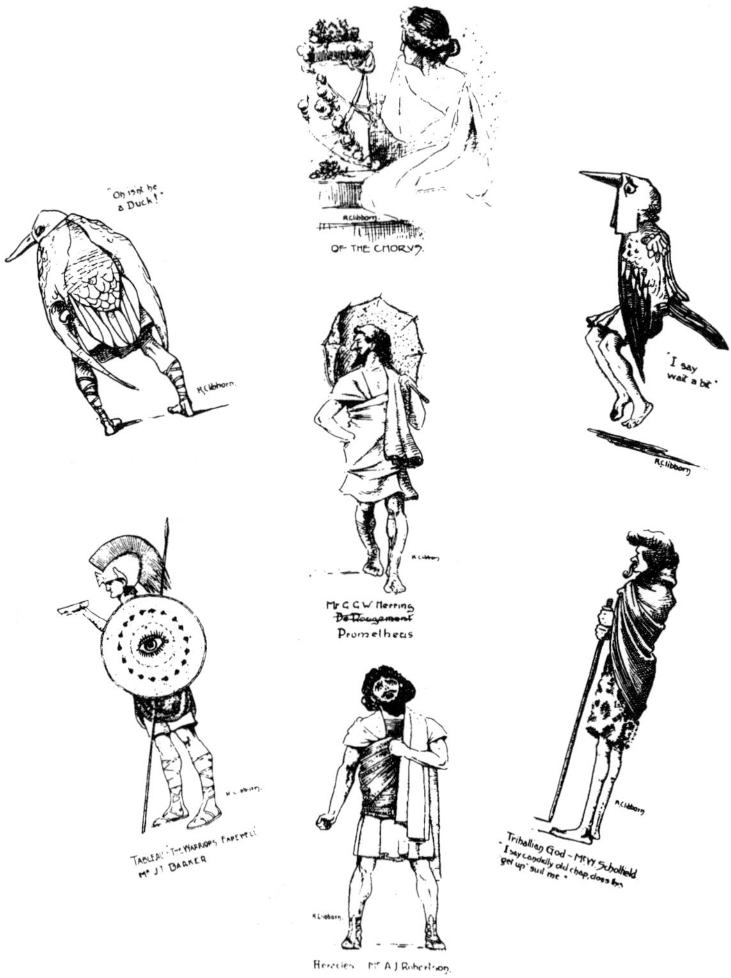

Greek plays in the Arts Theatre 1906
Drawing from *The Sphinx*

LIST OF ILLUSTRATIONS

The originals of the illustrations are owned by the University of Liverpool Archives, University of Liverpool Art Collection, or Liverpool University Press.

INDEX

THE UNIVERSITY OF LIVERPOOL

departments/faculties/disciplines

locations

members of staff

Names with forename initials are given in full in Kelly; other names are given as they appear in the present text.

former students contributing reminiscences

student activities

other university activities and functions

OUTSIDE THE UNIVERSITY

Liverpool locations

locations/peoples outside Liverpool

other persons